Collins
English for Business

Pre-Intermediate
BUSINESS GRAMMAR & PRACTICE
Nick Brieger & Simon Sweeney

D1322286

HarperCollins Publishers
77–85 Fulham Palace Road
Hammersmith
London W6 8JB

First edition 2011

Reprint 10 9 8 7 6 5 4 3 2 1 0

© HarperCollins Publishers 2011

ISBN 978-0-00-742058-2

Collins ® is a registered trademark
of HarperCollins Publishers Limited

www.collinslanguage.com

A catalogue record for this book is available
from the British Library

Typeset in India by Aptara

Printed in Italy by LEGO SpA, Lavis (Trento)

About the authors

Nick Brieger has worked around the globe in
the fields of language teaching, team building,
communication and intercultural training. He has
worked with a wide range of major international
organisations. He is also the author of more than
20 books in the areas of language, communication
and culture.

Simon Sweeney is a Lecturer in International
Business at The York Management School,
University of York. He has written numerous
textbooks for international English and business
communication skills and has worked in a variety
of teaching and training contexts with clients from
across Europe, Japan, and China.

Contents

Introduction

Targets and objectives

Business Grammar & Practice: Pre-Intermediate is for pre-intermediate to intermediate speakers of English who need to master the type of English used in professional situations. Whether you are studying to enter the workplace or already using English at work, accurate use of English grammar will make you a more effective communicator. If you feel you already know the core grammar for business English, the Intermediate book in this series will take you through more complex grammar.

To ensure that the language you learn is relevant for the workplace, the book uses example sentences from the Collins corpus. This is a constantly updated database of English language from a range of print and spoken sources. You can therefore be sure that any example used is an authentic use of English in a business context.

Business Grammar & Practice: Pre-Intermediate can be used together with any business English course book to provide more detailed explanations and supplementary exercises in the grammar of business English. It is suitable for both classroom and self-study use.

Organisation of material

There are 84 units and 6 Business Files.

Each unit consists of:
1. Language presentation through:
   - sample sentences to show the language forms in use;
   - an explanation of the language forms;
   - a description of the uses of these forms.

2. Practice through:
   - controlled exercises to develop recognition of the language forms (Exercise 1);
   - controlled exercises to practise combining language form and language use (Exercise 2);
   - controlled or guided exercises focusing on language form and meaning (Exercise 3);
   - transfer activities to practise transferring the language presented in the unit to the student's own personal and professional experience.

3. Answers to the controlled and guided exercises.

Using a unit

You should work through the presentation by:
- reading through the sample sentences and noting the use of the language forms (Section A);
- studying the language forms presented (Section B);
- studying the uses of these forms (Section C).

Next you should move on to the practice exercises. There are three types of exercises: controlled, guided and transfer.

Before you start an exercise:
- make sure you clearly understand the task;
- look at any examples that have been given;
- refer back to the language forms and uses, if necessary.

After you have finished a controlled or guided exercise, check your answer with the key at the back of the book.

Controlled exercises have only one possible solution; guided exercises have a model or suggested answer marked (**M**). If your answers to a controlled exercise are wrong, look again at sections B and C. If your answers to a guided exercise are different from those suggested, check if your answers are possible alternatives.

Finally, a few words about the transfer activities: the reason for including these is that they act as a bridge to your world by providing an opportunity to transfer to your own personal situation the language presented and practised in the previous exercises.

Key Grammatical Concepts

It is important to know the names of the main grammatical terms and forms in order to use this book. It is also important to think about the corresponding forms in your own language. In the following section, you can find out information about the grammatical terms you will need to know.

Grammatical Terms

Active (see also **Passive** and **Voice**)
A verb or verb phrase which has the person or thing doing the action as its subject, e.g. *The government increased taxes*.

Adjective
An adjective gives more information about a noun, e.g. *a successful company, huge profits*. An adjective can also be used after the verb *be*, e.g. *the company is successful, profits are huge*.

Adverb
An adverb gives more information about a verb, e.g. *The company grew quickly*.

Article
The words *the* or *a/an* which are used before a noun, e.g. *the manager, a desk*, or the **zero article** e.g. *subsidiaries*

Auxiliary verb
The verbs *be, have* and *do* when they are used with other verbs:
- continuous verbs (be), e.g. *Sales are increasing*.
- passive verbs (be), e.g. *The factory was sold last year*.
- the perfect (have and had), e.g. *We have already placed an order*.
- negative and interrogative verbs (do), e.g. *We don't agree with the plan. What do you think?*

Cardinal number (see also **Ordinal number**)
The numbers *1, 2, 3, 4, 5, 6*, etc.

Clause
A group of words containing a minimum of a subject and verb, e.g. *I wrote the report*.

Command
A command tells someone to do something, e.g. *Prepare the report. Call the supplier*.

Comparative (see **Comparison of adjectives**)

Comparison of adjectives
The three forms of an adjective, i.e. *high – higher* (comparative) *– highest* (superlative), or *expensive – more expensive – most expensive*

Conjunction
A word which links words, phrases or clauses, e.g. *but, and, because*.

Consonant
One of these letters: b, c, d, f, g, h, j, k, l, m, n, p, q, r, s, t, v, w, x, y, z.

Continuous (aspect)
A verb construction in the form *be + infinitive...ing*, e.g. *is working*.

Countable noun (see **Noun**)

Definite article (see **Article**)

Definite frequency
A phrase that tells us exactly how often something happens in a period of time, e.g. *every day, twice a year*.

Demonstrative
The words *this, that, these* and *those* when they are used in a noun phrase, e.g. *This email is from James*.

Determiner
A class of words which includes articles, possessive pronouns, demonstratives and quantifiers.

Doer
The person who does the action in a passive sentence. The doer has the word 'by' before it, e.g. *The mistake was discovered by the accountant*.

Expression (see also **Clause** and **Sentence**)
A group of words, e.g. *last week, in the company*.

Future
The time that happens after now or one of the grammar forms that expresses the time after now, e.g. *We are going to buy the company. I am leaving tomorrow morning. The meeting starts at 9 o'clock*.

Genitive
A noun written with an apostrophe which shows possession or a similar relationship, e.g. *the manager's decision, last year's results, the countries' economies*.

Grammar
Grammar describes the forms of words, e.g. *sell, sells*, or *selling*. It also determines the way words can be combined to make phrases, e.g. *is selling; must have sold; employment agency*, and the way words can be arranged into larger units of meaning, e.g. *The store has sold all its stock*.

Imperative
The verb form when you are telling someone to do something, e.g. *Prepare the report. Call the supplier*.

Indefinite article (see **Article**)

Indefinite frequency (see also **Definite frequency**)
An expression showing approximately how often something happens, e.g. *always, often, sometimes, rarely, never* etc.

Infinitive
The base form of a verb without 'to', e.g. *be, make, write*.

Infinitive + to
The base form of a verb with 'to', e.g. *to be, to make, to write*.

Intransitive verb (See also **Transitive verb**)
A verb which cannot take a direct object, e.g. *Costs rose by 5 per cent last year*.

Irregular verb
A verb that does not form the past tense and the past participle by adding *–ed*, e.g. *come – came – come, buy – bought – bought*.

Main clause (see also **Subordinate clause**)
A group of words with a subject and a verb which can be a sentence, e.g. *We sold the company*.

Main verb
A verb which is neither a modal nor an auxiliary verb. *Be, have* and *do* can be main verbs or auxiliary verbs depending on their use.

Modal verb
These verbs and their negative forms are modals: *will, can, shall, may, must, would, could, should, might*

Modals are followed by an infinitive, e.g. *You must attend the meeting.*
Needn't and *daren't* are also used in this way.

Noun
A word that names persons, places or things, e.g. *manager, factory, computer.*
A **countable noun** is a noun with a singular and plural form, e.g. *a machine, 20 machines.*
An **uncountable noun** is a noun that does not have a plural and you cannot put a or an before it, e.g. *information, equipment.*
A **noun compound** is a group of words with two or more nouns, e.g. *sales director.*
A **noun phrase** is phrase with a noun as the main word, e.g. *a very good* <u>manager</u>.

Object
A noun or noun phrase that is used after a transitive verb, e.g. *We played* <u>golf</u>.

Ordinal number
The numbers 1st, 2nd, 3rd, 4th, 5th, 6th etc.

Passive (see also **Active** and **Voice**)
A passive construction contains a verb or verb phrase in the form *be* + past participle, where the doer of the action is expressed as the agent rather than the subject, e.g. *Taxes were increased by the last government* (passive) versus *The last government increased taxes* (active).

Perfect (aspect)
A verb construction in the form *has/have* + past participle which puts the action or event in a different time from the time of speaking or writing. The present perfect shows that the action has been completed by the time of speaking or writing, e.g. *We have already seen the report.*
The past perfect shows that an action has been completed by an earlier point of time, e.g. *We had already seen the report.*

Phrasal verb
A verb phrase that consists of a verb + adverb, e.g. *to* <u>look up</u> *a word* (in a dictionary).

Phrase
A group of words, but less than a clause, i.e. not containing a subject and verb.

Plural (see also Singular)
A form of a noun, pronoun or verb which shows that there are more than one, e.g. *companies, they, profits are increasing.*

Preposition
A word that is used before a noun and shows us something about time, e.g. <u>in the morning</u>, <u>at</u> *7 o'clock*, place, e.g. <u>on</u> *the desk*, or manner, e.g. <u>by</u> *car.*

Pronoun
A word that takes the place of a noun or noun phrase, e.g. *she, my, this, who.*

Quantifier
A word which describes quantity, e.g. *all, many, some, few, no.*

Question tag
A short question which makes statement into a question, e.g. *We sent the goods last week,* <u>*didn't we?*</u>

Regular verb (see also **Irregular verb**)
A verb that forms the past tense and past participle by adding *–ed*, e.g. *start – started – started.*

Relative clause
A clause beginning with a **relative pronoun** such as *who, whose, which, that* or a relative adverb such as *when, where, why.*

Sentence
A group of words with a subject and a verb between two full stops, e.g. *My name is Paul. I come from London.*

Short form
A short form of a verb that is written with an apostrophe to show that some letters are missing, e.g. *it's, we're, can't.*

Simple
A verb construction in either the present simple or past simple tense.

Simple sentence
A sentence which is only one main clause, e.g. *Sales have increased.*

Singular (see also **Plural**)
A form of a noun, pronoun or verb which shows that there is only one, e.g. *company, I, she* <u>lives</u> *in York.*

Subordinate clause (see also **Main clause**)
A group of words with a subject and verb which is not a sentence because it needs a main clause to be complete, e.g. *He worked for ITCorp* <u>before he joined MegaTech</u>.

Subordinating conjunction
A word which introduces a subordinate clause, e.g. *because, although, if, who.*

Superlative (see **Comparison of adjectives**)

Tense
The grammatical form of a verb which shows the time of the action, e.g. present or past.

Time marker
A phrase which shows when something happens, e.g. *last year, at the moment, next week.*

Transitive verb (see also **Intransitive verb**)
A main verb which takes a direct object, e.g. *We* <u>played</u> *golf last week.*

Uncountable noun (see **Noun**)

Verb . . .ing
The verb form infinitive + *ing*, e.g. *helping.*

Voice
The grammatical category of either active or passive verb form.

Vowel
One of the letters *a, e, i, o, u.*

Wh-question
A question beginning with *who, what, why* etc or with *how.*

Yes/no question
A question to which the answer must be *yes* or *no*, e.g. *Is your name Mary?*

Zero article (see **Article**)

UNIT 1

Be (1)

See also
Unit 2   Be (2)

A Sample sentences

A: Where are you from?

B: I am from Asciano. And my colleagues are from Pisa.

A: I'm sorry. Where is Asciano?

B: It is in Tuscany. It's near Siena.

B Form

The present tense of **to be** has three forms:
the positive, the negative and the question.

Positive form		
Subject	Verb	Short form
I	am	I'm
you	are	you're
he/she/it	is	he's/she's/it's
the manager	is	the manager's
the company	is	the company's
we	are	we're
they	are	they're
the managers	are	the managers're
the companies	are	the companies're

Note

The first seven short forms are used in spoken or informal written English;
the last two (the managers're etc.) are used in spoken language only.

Negative form		
Subject	Verb	Not
I	am	not
you/we/they	are	not
he/she/it	is	not
the manager/the company	is	not
the managers/the companies	are	not

Question form	
Verb	Subject
am	I?
are	you/we/they?
is	he/she/it?
is	the manager/the company?
are	the managers/the companies?

The negative short forms are:
I'm not, you aren't, he isn't, she isn't, it isn't, we aren't, they aren't

C Uses

Look at these sentences with the verb **to be** in different forms:

Questions

A: Are you from New York?

A: Excuse me. Is your name Billy Ray?

A: Am I in the right place? Is this the room for the sales meeting?

A: Where are the main markets for your products?

Positive and negative forms

B: No, I'm from Boston.

B: No, it isn't. I'm Millie Ray.

B: Yes, it is.

B: They are in the US and Asia.

Exercise 1

In the dialogue below, Peter Hay is talking to Jane Field and Arnold Weiss at a trade fair. Put the verb forms in sentences 1–14 into the correct box. The first one is done for you.

Present positive	Present negative	Present question
1		

PH: Hello, I'm Peter Hay. [1] Where are you from? [2]
JF: We're from Seattle in the USA. [3]
PH: Oh, are you American? [4]
JF: I am. [5] But Arnold isn't. [6]
AW: I'm from Austria. [7] But we're from the same company, Inter Corp. [8]
PH: Oh, yes, Inter Corp. What are your names? [9]
JF: My name's Jane Field. [10] This is Arnold Weiss. [11]
PH: Pleased to meet you. Are you in banking? [12]
AW: No, we're not. [13] We're in insurance. [14]

Exercise 2

Complete the spaces. Use short forms where possible.

1. This is Dave King. ____**He's**____ an engineer.

2. My name's Pierre Lapin. _____ a Sales Manager.

3. Mary and Hans are from my department. _____ computer programmers.

4. This is Naomi Cox. _____ a research scientist.

5. Hello. My name _____ Franz Johann and this _____ Tomas Doll. _____ from Salzburg.

6. Ah, Franz and Tomas! _____ very welcome!

7. This is our office. It _____ very big.

Exercise 3

*Complete the following text about Axdal Electronics. Use a form of **be**.*

Axdal leads the way

Axdal Electronics ____**is**____ a world leader in control systems. We _____ suppliers to the car industry. Car manufacturers _____ our only customers. We _____ also suppliers to other industries. AE _____ an international company. Our customers _____ in the USA, Japan and Europe. Our Chief Executive _____ Paul Axdal. 'We _____ a family company and business _____ very good', says Paul.

Transfer

*Write short sentences about yourself and some friends. Use different present tense forms of **be**.*

3

UNIT 2

Be (2)

See also
Unit 1   Be (1)

A Sample sentences

A: **Hello Raj. Where were you yesterday?**
B: **I wasn't in my office. I was at a meeting.**

A: **I haven't seen you all week!**
B: **I know. I have been very busy.**

B Form

The verb **to be** has three main tenses: the present (see Unit 1), the past and the present perfect. Look at the positive forms in the past and the present perfect.

Past		Present perfect		
Subject	Verb	Subject	Verb	Short form
I	was	I	have been	I've been
you	were	you	have been	you've been
he/she/it	was	he/she/it	has been	he's been/she's been/it's been
the manager	was	the manager	has been	the manager's been
the company	was	the company	has been	the company's been
we	were	we	have been	we've been
they	were	they	have been	they've been
the managers	were	the managers	have been	the managers've been (spoken only)
the companies	were	the companies	have been	the companies've been (spoken only)

In the negative we use **not**:

Past
I was *not* in the office yesterday.
You were *not* with a customer yesterday.

Present perfect
They have *not* been here today.
I have*n't* been to Spain.

The negative short forms are:
I **wasn't**, you **weren't**, he/she/it **wasn't**, we **weren't**, they **weren't** I **haven't been**, you **haven't been**, he/she/it **hasn't been**, we **haven't been**, they **haven't been**

Now look at these question forms:

Past
Where were you yesterday?
Was Mr Brown with you?

Present perfect
Have you been to Switzerland?
Has he been with a client?

C Uses

Look at these sentences with the verb **to be** in different tenses and different forms:

A: **Where were you yesterday? You weren't in your office.** (past question and negative)
B: **I was in Bolton.** (past positive)
A: **Why were you in Bolton?** (past question)
B: **I was with a client.** (past positive)
C: **I'm sorry. Bolton? Where is Bolton?** (present positive and question)
A: **It is in the north of England, near Manchester. In the past it was a famous textile centre.** (present positive and past positive)
C: **I haven't been to Manchester. But I've been to Liverpool.** (present perfect negative and positive)
B: **I was in Liverpool last week. When were you there?** (past positive and question)
C: **I was there in January.** (past positive)

Exercise 1

In the dialogue below, Henry Leer and Joe Fisher are in a hotel bar in Amsterdam. Put the verb forms in sentences 1–10 into the correct box.

Past positive	Past negative	Past question
Present perfect positive	**Present perfect negative**	**Present perfect question**
		1

HL: Have you been to Amsterdam before? (1)

JF: Yes, I've been here on business. (2) I was at the Telecommunications Fair in June. (3) Were you here then? (4)

HL: No, I wasn't. (5) I haven't been here before. (6) We were on holiday in June. (7)

JF: Where?

HL: Mexico. Have you been there? (8)

JF: Yes, I've been to Mexico. (9) I was there in March. (10)

Exercise 2

Complete the letter below with words from the box.

| have not been   was(2) |
| were(3)   have been |

Delco Ltd.

16–20 East Mount Road, Lincoln LN3 5RT

6 November.....

Dear Mary,

Last week Tom and Paula _____ here for a meeting. It _____ very useful. They _____ here for two days. We _____ to Oslo in the last few days. We _____ there for a meeting with our Norwegian colleagues. Arne Sillessen _____ very interested in our ideas. Until now, I _____ happy with the project. Now I am very optimistic.

See you next week.

Best wishes

Sandy Peel

Sandy Peel

Exercise 3

Complete the spaces in the email below. Use short forms where possible.

From: ipcs3@cc.uat.es
Sent: Mon 28 November 15:40
Subject: Short Bros

Dear Frances,

I am sorry I _____ (not) at the meeting yesterday. I _____ (not) in the office this week. Tom and I _____ in London. We _____ at a Sales Conference. I _____ very busy recently. _____ Short Brothers happy with the contract? _____ they _____ in contact today?

Please contact me by email tomorrow.

Thanks

Juanito

Transfer

*Write a short paragraph about yourself and a local industry or institution. Use past tense and present perfect forms of **be**.*

UNIT 3   The Present Continuous Positive

See also	
Units 1, 2	**Be**
Unit 4	The present continuous negative
Unit 5	The present continuous question
Unit 9	The present continuous vs. the present simple

A Sample sentences

- **At the moment 70% of consumers are using the Internet to buy things.**
- **Prasad is currently preparing a business plan.**
- **At present I am eating my lunch.**

B Form

The present continuous positive has two parts:
the present tense of **to be** + infinitive . . . *ing*

Long form			Short form
Subject	to be	Infinitive . . . ing	Subject + to be
I	**am**	presenting	I**'m** presenting
you	**are**	making	you**'re** making
he/she/it	**is**	calling	he**'s**/she**'s**/it**'s** calling
the company/the department (= it)	**is**	preparing	the company**'s** preparing
the manager/the boss (= he/she)	**is**	reading	the manager**'s** reading
we	**are**	meeting	we**'re** meeting
you	**are**	looking	you**'re** looking
they	**are**	visiting	they**'re** visiting
the companies/the departments (= they)	**are**	doing	the companies**'re** doing (spoken only)
the managers/the workers (= they)	**are**	discussing	the managers**'re** discussing (spoken only)

We often use the short forms in spoken language; we sometimes use them in informal written language:
We're planning a new product for this year. (spoken and written)
At the moment the company's doing very well. (spoken)

C Uses

We use the present continuous to talk about:

1. activities at or around the time of speaking:
They are building two nuclear power stations.

2. temporary activities in the present:
Bella, what are you doing? I'm reading a report.

Note
With C1 and 2, we can use the following expressions:

at the/this moment	currently	at present	now

but not

actually

TASKS

Exercise 1

*Look at the email below. Underline **five** present continuous forms.*

Date:	12 march 20…
To:	all staff
From:	Jenny Palmer
Subject:	John Bramwell leaving

Dear All,

John Bramwell is leaving the company after 30 years. We are organising a collection to buy John a present. Please see Janet in Room 40. Janet is planning a leaving party for John. At present, John is recovering in hospital after an accident. He is hoping to return to work next month, but only until the summer.

Best regards
Jenny Palmer

Exercise 2

Here is part of a telephone conversation. Complete the spaces with the correct form of the word in brackets. Use short forms, where possible.

DL: Hello, Peter. Listen, I **'m reading** (read) your report. There's a problem on page 50.
PT: Okay, I _____ (look) at it right now. What's the problem?
DL: It says we _____ (invest) $250,000 in research. That's wrong. It's $25,000, not $250,000.
PT: Okay I'll change that.
DL: Right. Remember, you _____ (meet) Mr Lally and his colleagues today.
PT: Yes, I know. They _____ (come) here at 2.30.
DL: Fine. Good luck. See you tomorrow, then.

Exercise 3

Look at the graph below. It shows total company sales and sales for two products, A and B. Write four sentences. Use the prompts below.

1. Total sales (go up).

2. Product A (increase).

3. Product B (fall).

4. The company (stop) production of Product B.

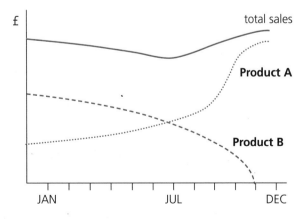

Transfer

Write four sentences about you, your friends or a local business or institution. Include phrases from the box.

now	at the moment	currently	at present

UNIT 4   The Present Continuous Negative

See also	
Units 1, 2	**Be**
Unit 3	The present continuous positive
Unit 5	The present continuous question
Unit 9	The present continuous vs. the present simple

A Sample sentences

- **I am not working at the moment; I am looking for a job.**
- **The company is not growing quickly enough.**
- **Managers are not dealing with the issue at the moment.**

B Form

The present continuous negative has three parts:
the present tense of **to be + not** + infinitive ...*ing*

Long form				Short form
Subject	to be	not	Infinitive ...ing	Subject + not + to be
I	am	not	presenting	I'**m not** presenting
you	are	not	making	you'**re not** or you **aren't** making
he/she/it	is	not	calling	he'**s not**/she'**s not**/it'**s not** calling or he **isn't**/she **isn't**/it **isn't** calling
the organisation (= it)	is	not	preparing	the organisation **isn't** preparing
the director (= he/she)	is	not	reading	the director **isn't** reading
we	are	not	meeting	we'**re not** or we **aren't** meeting
you	are	not	looking	you'**re not** or you **aren't** looking
they	are	not	visiting	they'**re not** or they **aren't** visiting
the teams (= they)	are	not	doing	the teams **aren't** doing
the employees (= they)	are	not	discussing	the employees **aren't** discussing

C Uses

We use the present continuous to talk about:

1. activities at or around the time of speaking:
The company is not/The company isn't investing enough to improve its network.

2. temporary activities in the present:
We are not starting/We aren't starting the meeting yet because John isn't here.

Exercise 1

*Look at the text below. Underline **four** present continuous negatives.*

> We are not increasing our prices this year. The market is not strong enough. We are
> launching new products for the domestic market. Most of our products are selling well at
> home. At present, we are not planning any new products for export. Sales are not
> increasing in our export markets. The company is not expecting improved sales this year.

Exercise 2

Write sentences with a present continuous negative. Use short forms, where possible.

1. I/not visit/a customer/in Rome
   I'm not visiting a customer in Rome.

2. We/not spend/much time/in Milan

3. The company/not look at/new markets in southern Europe

4. At the moment many companies/not invest/in new products

5. Our marketing experts/not change/our present sales strategy

6. You/not stay/in a hotel

Exercise 3

Make negative or positive sentences for pictures 1–4 below. Use the words in brackets.

1.

(this year/the company/do well in the USA)

3.

(at present/we/present a good image)

2.

(at the moment/we/build/new production plant)

4.

(Mr Jackson/work hard/these days)

Transfer

Write six sentences about your current activities. Use the present continuous tense, with some positive and some negative sentences.

UNIT 5

The Present Continuous Question

See also	
Units 1, 2	**Be**
Unit 3	The present continuous positive
Unit 4	The present continuous negative
Unit 9	The present continuous vs. the present simple
Units 53, 54, 55	Questions

A Sample sentences

Yoshie:	Henry, what are you doing?
Henry:	I'm checking the figures. There is a mistake here. What is Janet doing?
Yoshie:	She is calling a taxi for you. Are you leaving now?
Henry:	Yes, but Janet is staying.

B Form

The present continuous question has two parts:
  the present tense of **to be** + infinitive . . .*ing*

We put the subject between part 1 and part 2:

to be	Subject	Infinitive . . .ing
am	I	presenting?
are	you	making?
is	he/she/it	calling?
is	the computer (= it)	analysing?
is	the consultant (= he/she)	reading?
are	we	meeting?
are	you	looking?
are	they	visiting?
are	the specialists (= they)	doing?
are	the machines (= they)	preparing?

C Uses

We use the present continuous question to ask about:

1. activities at or around the time of speaking:
   A: Why is he leaving the building?
   B: Because he is going to a meeting.

2. temporary activities in the present:
   A: What are you working on?
   B: At the moment we are developing new processes to speed up production.

Exercise 1

Underline the mistakes in the following sentences. Then correct them.

1. <u>Is you</u> working very hard?   **Are you working very hard?**

2. At the moment they working with Poland?   _____

3. Is Leo and Sam planning the conference together?   _____

4. What you think about?   _____

5. Is raining in Bangkok?   _____

Exercise 2

Make questions to complete the dialogue below. Use the words in brackets.

1. **What's Mary doing**_____? She's telephoning Signor Fini.
    (What/Mary/do?)

2. _____? To invite him to the meeting on Friday.
    (Why/call/him?)

3. _____? To talk about the La Paz report.
    (Why/we/have a meeting?)

4. _____? Yes, I'm still working on it.
    (You/work on/the report now?)

5. _____? No, I'm doing it alone.
    (Anyone/help/you?)

6. _____? No, they aren't.
    (Kim and James/come/to the meeting?)

Exercise 3

Make questions for the pictures 1–4. Use the words in brackets.

1. (why/computer/not work)   **3.** (why/birds/die)

2. (why/fire alarm/ring)   **4.** (why/oil/leak)

Transfer

Write five questions about your colleagues using the present continuous form.

UNIT 6

The Present Simple Positive

See also	
Unit 7	The present simple negative
Unit 8	The present simple question
Unit 9	The present continuous vs. the present simple

A Sample sentences

- **We always investigate a job applicant's background.**
- **The manager normally has total responsibility for this process.**
- **Many people say they never eat breakfast.**
- **I often go to France.**

B Form

The present simple positive has one part:
  infinitive(s)

Subject	Infinitive(s)
I	make
you	present
he/she/it	call**s**
the company/the department (= it)	prepare**s**
the manager/the boss (= he/she)	read**s**
we	meet
you	look
they	visit
the companies/the departments (= they)	do
the managers/the workers (= they)	discuss

C Uses

We use the present simple to talk about:

1. a general or permanent activity:
   I work for a research company.
   The company makes frozen food for supermarkets.
   We finish work at 2pm.

2. how often an activity is done:
   We usually meet twice a year.
   I play golf every week.

TASKS

Exercise 1

Make sentences with the following words. See the example.
I live in a city.

I	work	new solutions.
You	live	a lot for work.
He/She	makes	foreign languages.
We/You/They	studies	for a multinational company.
The company	develops	better products.
Our Research Department	travel	in a city.

Exercise 2

Match the sentences below to the correct picture a–e.

1. In the evening I get the train home.

2. In the afternoon my PA gives me letters to sign.

3. At 8 o'clock I arrive at the office.

4. At 10 o'clock we have a meeting.

5. We usually have lunch with a customer.

Exercise 3

Complete the following text. Use the words in brackets. Put the verbs in the present simple.

Atsuko Kyoto _____ (live) in Tokyo. She _____ (be) a freelance journalist. She _____ (often/travel) to other countries. In London and Paris she _____ (like) to visit friends. She _____ (usually/write) for newspapers and magazines and she _____ (sometimes/make) television programmes. She _____ (usually/stay) in four star hotels and _____ (often/eat) in top class restaurants. She _____ (never/drink) wine, beer or any alcohol.

Transfer

Write a short paragraph like the one in Exercise 3 about someone you know. Include some of the following words.

| usually/often/sometimes/occasionally | live/work/travel/study/fly/write/read/sleep |

13

UNIT

7

The Present Simple Negative

See also	
Unit 6	The present simple positive
Unit 8	The present simple question
Unit 9	The present continuous vs. the present simple
Unit 31	**Do**

A Sample sentences

- **We don't use complicated equipment or technology; we use very simple processes.**
- **He doesn't work with me anymore; he works in Beijing now.**
- **The company provides nurses and healthcare staff, but it doesn't provide managers.**

B Form

The present simple negative has two parts:
  don't/doesn't + infinitive

Subject	don't/doesn't	Infinitive
I	**don't**	live
you	**don't**	work
he/she/it	**doesn't**	produce
the organisation (= it)	**doesn't**	employ
the director (= he/she)	**doesn't**	discuss
we	**don't**	meet
you	**don't**	know
they	**don't**	like
the teams (= they)	**don't**	prefer
the employees (= they)	**don't**	make

C Uses

We use the present simple to talk about:

1. a general or permanent activity:
  I don't smoke.
  He doesn't work for any of the big American companies.
  Small companies don't usually employ their own IT professionals.

2. how often an activity is done:
  The company doesn't buy new computers every year.
  I don't play every week.

TASKS

Exercise 1

Make negative sentences with the following words. See the example.
I don't work in the oil industry.

The management		like working	in research.
The company		understand	many people.
I	don't	want to invest	in a new factory.
They	doesn't	improve	for a drug company.
My friend		employ	in the oil industry.
You		work	what I am saying.

Exercise 2

Make negative sentences with the following prompts.

1. we/manufacture/finished products
   We don't manufacture finished products.

2. we/advertise/on television

3. the company/sponsor/sport

4. I/like/fish

5. Nakko S.A./process/written orders for goods

6. Cable PLC/despatch products/by train

7. we/deal with/Latin America

8. you/live/in an apartment

Exercise 3 .

A local newspaper attacked Teal Ltd for damaging the environment. The owner, Peter Teal, wrote a reply. Give the negative forms of the words in the brackets.

Dear Sir,
I want to tell your readers some facts about Teal
Ltd. The company (use) chemical dyes in its products
or bleach to make our materials white. The management
(encourage) the use of company cars. We (allow) staff
to park private cars on company premises. We (burn)
our rubbish and we (throw away) glass or paper.
Yours faithfully,
PJ Teal
PJ Teal
Managing Director (Teal Ltd)

Transfer

Write six present simple negative sentences about the place where you live and/or work.

UNIT

8

The Present Simple Question

See also	
Unit 6	The present simple positive
Unit 7	The present simple negative
Unit 9	The present continuous vs. the present simple
Unit 31	**Do**
Units 53–55	Questions

A Sample sentences

Eduardo: **What do you do?**
Yu Yin: **I work as a translator for a company in London.**
Eduardo: **And what does the company make?**
Yu Yin: **It doesn't make anything. It offers legal advice.**

B Form

The present simple question has two parts:
   do/does + infinitive

We put the subject between part 1 and part 2:

do/does	Subject	Infinitive
do	I	present?
do	you	make?
does	he/she/it	solve?
does	the computer (= it)	analyse?
does	the consultant (= he/she)	reach?
do	we	compete?
do	you	look?
do	they	visit?
do	the specialists (= they)	fix?
do	the machines (= they)	prepare?

C Uses

We use the present simple question to ask about:

1. a general or permanent activity:
   Who do you work for?
   Where do you live?
   How many people does the company employ?

2. how often an activity is done:
   How often do you eat in a restaurant?
   How often does she travel by plane?

Exercise 1

*Underline **do** or **does** and the main verb (infinitive) in the following questions. Then answer them.*

1. Does your country make cars?

2. Do the largest companies in your area export products to many different countries?

3. How many people do you work or study with?

4. Do you know any internationally famous products from your country?

5. Does your home town have a university?

Exercise 2

Martin and Javier meet in a hotel bar in Paris. Match the questions to the correct picture a–h.

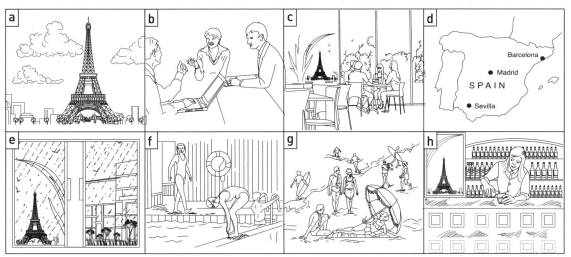

1. Do you come from Spain?
2. What time does the bar close?
3. Do you have an umbrella?
4. Do you have a meeting tomorrow?
5. Do you know a good restaurant?
6. Does the hotel have a swimming pool?
7. Do you often come to Paris?
8. Where do you usually go on holiday?

Exercise 3

Write questions for the answers on the right.

1. Where/from? **Where do you come from?** — I come from Santiago, in Chile.

2. Where/work? — I work for Papeleras Valles.

3. What/Papeleras Valles/make? — The company makes paper. We're a paper processing company.

4. How many people/your company/employ? — About 750.

5. Have/just one plant? — No, we have two, both near Santiago.

Transfer

Prepare five or six questions to ask a friend about his/her work or studies. Use the present simple tense.

UNIT 9

The Present Continuous vs. The Present Simple

See also	
Units 1, 2	**Be**
Units 3, 4, 5, 6	The present continuous
Units 6, 7, 8	The present simple
Unit 20	The present tenses and the past tenses

A Sample sentences

Luc: Brigitta, what do you do?

Brigitta: I work as a marketing director in Heidelberg, but at the moment I'm working in Osnabrück.

Luc: So, where do you live?

Brigitta: My family lives near Heidelberg, but at present I'm staying in a hotel in Osnabrück.

B Form

Remember these differences between the present continuous and the present simple:

The present continuous		The present simple	
Positive	**to be** + infinitive …*ing*	Positive	infinitive(s)
Negative	**to be** + **not** + infinitive …*ing*	Negative	**don't/doesn't** + infinitive
Question	**to be** + subject + infinitive …*ing*	Question	**do/does** + subject + infinitive

C Uses

We use the present continuous to talk about:

1. activities at or around the time of speaking:

Jamila: Are you producing a report this year?

Mohammed: Yes. At present we are checking the facts.

2. temporary activities in the present:

Mary: What are you doing?

Sylvie: I'm writing a report.

We use the present simple to talk about:

1. a general or permanent activity:

John: Do you still play golf?

Karl: No, I don't have time now.

2. how often an activity is done:

Mario: How often do you meet?

Irena: Usually we see each other once or twice a year.

Exercise 1

Read the dialogue below. A journalist is talking to a representative of Chemco Ltd. Put the verb forms in sentences 1–7 into the correct box. The first has been done for you.

J: What plans does Chemco have now? (1)
C: Chemco processes oil and makes paints. (2) We're also planning to make plastics. (3)
J: Are you already working in that area? (4)
C: We're not selling any plastics at the moment. (5)
J: Does the company plan to merge with Sidon Ltd? (6)
C: No, we don't want to join another company. (7)

	Statement	Negative	Question
Present continuous			
Present simple			1

Exercise 2

Complete the dialogue below between a consultant and a marketing manager.

C: Which export markets **do you sell to** (sell to)?
M: We _____ (deal) mainly with Germany, France and Sweden.
C: And _____ (negotiate) with Japanese customers at the moment?
M: No, not at the moment.
C: _____ (plan) to enter any new markets?
M: Yes, Italy. We _____ (launch) a range of products there later this year.
C: And Sweden? _____ (sell) much there?
M: Yes, we often _____ (get) big orders from Swedish manufacturers.

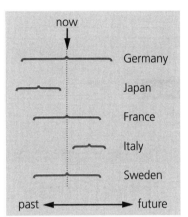

Exercise 3

Complete the spaces in the short dialogue below about a bank, Credit Bank International. Use the correct form of a verb from the box.

like happen open come operate have

A: What _____?
B: We _____ 10 new branches in Argentina and Chile.
A: _____ the bank currently _____ branches only in Buenos Aires and Santiago?
B: Yes.
A: But not Brasilia?
B: No, we _____ in Brazil yet.
A: _____ Pablo Hernandez _____ here this week?
B: Yes, he _____ these meetings.

Transfer

Write five sentences about your own current activities. Use both the present simple and the present continuous.

UNIT 10   Positive and Negative Imperatives

See also
Unit 56   Commands – positive and negative

A Sample sentences

- **Please arrive fifteen minutes before the meeting.**
- **Don't forget your mobile phone.**
- **Buy two tickets and get one ticket free.**

B Form

The positive imperative has one part:
  infinitive

Positive imperative
go
make
do
discuss
be

The negative imperative has two parts:
  don't + infinitive

Negative imperative
don't go
don't make
don't do
don't discuss
don't be

C Uses

We use the positive imperative to tell one or more people what they must do or they can do:

Fasten your seatbelts. The plane is ready for takeoff.   (you must)

Please take a copy of our brochure as you leave.   (you can)

We use the negative imperative to tell one or more people what they must not do:

 Don't park here.

 Please don't smoke here.

Note
We can use **please** with imperatives to make them more polite.

Exercise 1

Underline positive imperatives and ⟨circle⟩ *negative imperatives in the following instructions to visitors to a factory.*

Please arrive at 10 o'clock prompt. Present your identity papers to the security officer at the gate. Do not park your car in the staff car park. Please go where the security officer tells you. He will give you an official pass. Walk to the reception. Present your official pass to the receptionist. Do not enter the office block. A guide will come to meet you. Please wait in reception. Do not smoke. Do not take photographs.

Exercise 2

Give an imperative (positive or negative) for each of the following. Use the verb in brackets.

1.

(use)

2.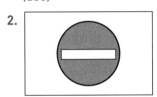

(enter)

3.

(take photographs)

4.

(wear)

5.

(eat)

6.

(consume food or drink)

7.

(walk)

8.

(put in)

9.

(call Freephone 0800)

Exercise 3

Put the verbs in the box into the correct positive or negative imperative form.

knock	park	arrive	photocopy	take photographs	enter

1. *You must* _____ *at 9 o'clock.*

2. *Military airport:* _____ .

3. *This material is copyright.* _____ .

4. *Please* _____ *here. Garage in use.*

5. *Welcome! Please* _____ *and* _____ .

Transfer

What imperatives, positive and negative, have you seen recently in your home town or in the place where you live and work?

UNIT

11

The Past Simple Positive

See also	
Unit 12	The past simple negative
Unit 13	The past simple question

A Sample sentences

- **Last year we opened an office in Berkeley.**
- **The company released its report a few weeks ago.**
- **Sales increased by 40% in the first half of last year.**

B Form

The past simple positive has one part:
    past tense

Subject	Past tense
I	made
you	presented
he/she/it	called
the company/the department (= it)	prepared
the manager/the boss (= he/she)	read
we	met
you	looked
they	visited
the companies/the departments (= they)	did
the managers/the workers (= they)	wrote

C Uses

We use the past simple to talk about an activity at a definite time in the past:
We started the business about a year ago.
He bought the company in 2001 for $5 billion.
Last year he joined the company as marketing manager.

Note
We use the past simple with these expressions:

last... night, week, month, year, century
... ago two hours ago, three weeks ago, four months ago, etc.
yesterday ... morning, afternoon, evening
in ... 2010, the 1980s, the 18th century

TASKS

Exercise 1

Give the past simple form of the following verbs.

> increase   give   help   run   supply   receive   deliver   meet
> order   lose   break   climb   come   read   write   speak

Exercise 2

Below is part of a report from Baxmer, a pharmaceutical company. Underline six mistakes and correct them.

stopped

> On 25 April this year we <u>stop</u> production of Arpol, a treatment for migraine. Arpol production begin in 2004 and early sales was very impressive. However, Belpharm Ltd did launch the Calpem range three years ago. This product was taking a 30% market share in the first two years. At first we agree to continue with Arpol. Now the situation is different.

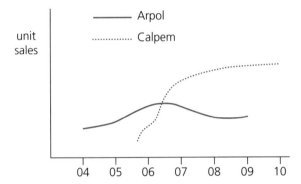

Exercise 3

Look at the time line below showing events over ten years for Metfan S.A., a Swedish furniture maker. Make sentences with the verbs given.

Example:
Metfan started business 11 years ago.

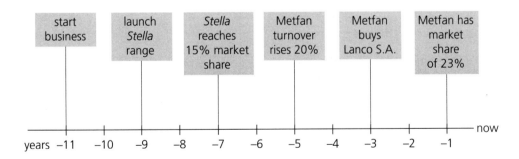

Transfer

Make five sentences about a business you know well or businesses in your country.

UNIT 12

The Past Simple Negative

See also	
Unit 11	The past simple positive
Unit 13	The past simple question
Unit 31	**Do**

A Sample sentences

- Last year we didn't sell as many products.
- I was disappointed because I didn't reach the target.
- In 2002 the company didn't have the skills it needed to do this.

B Form

The past simple negative has two parts:

didn't + infinitive

Subject	didn't	Infinitive
I	**didn't**	live
you	**didn't**	work
he/she/it	**didn't**	produce
the organisation (= it)	**didn't**	employ
the director (= he/she)	**didn't**	discuss
we	**didn't**	meet
you	**didn't**	know
they	**didn't**	like
the teams (= they)	**didn't**	prefer
the employees (= they)	**didn't**	make

C Uses

We use the past simple to talk about an activity at a definite time in the past:

The business didn't grow much last year.
This product didn't exist two years ago.
I didn't go to work yesterday because I wasn't well.

Note

We use the past simple with these expressions:

last... night, week, month, year, century
... ago two hours ago, three weeks ago, four months ago, etc.
yesterday... morning, afternoon, evening
in... 2010, the 1980s, the 18th century

Exercise 1

Underline the past simple negatives in the following.

> I joined this company five years ago. It was a difficult time. The company was not in a very good state. We didn't have a clear management structure. Our local markets were not very good. Our marketing didn't include America or the Pacific regions. We didn't have any clear marketing strategy. Now, things are very different.

Exercise 2

Read the text below. Change the past simple positives to negative. Then make the negatives positive.

> New products were cheap to develop. We spent a lot of money on research. Our market share increased in the early 2000s. The company made many good products. Chemco didn't buy the company. There wasn't a big change in the organisation. The new management didn't want to change everything. Most of the old management didn't leave. Things didn't improve. Now, we are very optimistic.

Exercise 3

*Look at the delivery schedule for an order with Interfood nv, a Dutch frozen foods company. Unfortunately the order went wrong: on January 15, Interfood did not prepare the order. Complete the sentences below. Write what **did not happen**.*

> **Delivery schedule for Espofrigo S.A., Vitoria, Spain**
> **Order number: ESP325/0797**
>
> Jan. 15   Prepare order
> Jan. 16   Send goods to Rotterdam Warehouse by train
> Jan. 17   Load goods onto ship to Bilbao
> Jan. 18   Goods arrive Bilbao. Carretera Trasportes take goods by truck to Vitoria
> Jan. 19   Espofrigo to confirm arrival

1. *On January 15, Interfood **didn't prepare the order**.*

2. *On the next day they* _____.

3. *On January 17 they* _____.

4. *On the next day the goods* _____.

5. *Carretera Trasportes* _____.

6. *So Espofrigo* _____.

Transfer

List things that you did not do ... yesterday/the day before yesterday/last Saturday/last week/last month/three years ago/in 2005/when you were young.

UNIT 13

The Past Simple Question

See also	
Unit 11	The past simple positive
Unit 12	The past simple negative
Unit 31	**Do**
Units 53, 54, 55	Questions

A Sample sentences

- **Did you see that promotion for the new product?**
- **Where did you buy your new computer?**
- **Why did you leave the company?**

B Form

The past simple question has two parts:
   did + infinitive
We put the subject between part 1 and part 2:

did	Subject	Infinitive
did	I	present?
did	you	make?
did	he/she/it	solve?
did	the computer (= it)	analyse?
did	the consultant (= he/she)	reach?
did	we	compete?
did	you	look?
did	they	visit?
did	the specialists (= they)	fix?
did	the machines (= they)	prepare?

C Uses

We use the past simple question to ask about an activity at a definite time in the past:
When did you arrive in England?
Did you meet the managing director when she was in New York?
How long did you work for the company?
What did you say to her?

Exercise 1

Match the question on the left with the appropriate answer on the right.

1. When did you arrive here?
2. How long did the journey take?
3. Did you come by plane direct from New York?
4. Did you have time to see the city last night?
5. Did you sleep well in the hotel?

a. Yes, it was very comfortable.
b. No, unfortunately I didn't.
c. Last night at 8 o'clock.
d. About 15 hours.
e. No, I changed at Amsterdam.

Exercise 2

Bill Klemens went to Malaysia on a business trip. He is discussing the trip with a colleague, Joelle Kee. Complete the spaces in the dialogue.

Joelle: How many days **did you spend** (spend) in Malaysia?
Bill: Only three.
Joelle: _____ (have) an interesting visit?
Bill: Yes, I made some useful contacts.
Joelle: _____ (see) Mr Keitel?
Bill: No, he was in New York.
Joelle: _____ And (visit) our colleagues in Sabah?
Bill: No, I telephoned, but I didn't have time to visit.
Joelle: _____ (have time) for any tourism?
Bill: Tourism? No ... only work and more work!
Joelle: Don't you like work?
Bill: Of course I do. I love work!

Exercise 3

A manager returns from a trip and asks her assistant about yesterday. Write questions for the items below. Use the words in brackets.

1.

   (the maintenance engineer/ repair/the copier?)

2. **URGENT** – *Caracas Report*
   John: please read immediately.

   (John/read/the Caracas report?)

3. *Write to Kongo Club.*

   (you/write/to the Kongo Club?)

4. Mr Fish phoning about order.

   (Mr Fish/phone?)

5. **VISA APPLICATION**

   (you/send the VISA application?)

6. Larish Ltd to collect order. Pay on collection.

   (Larish Ltd/collect their order?) (they/pay?)

Transfer

Prepare six questions to ask a colleague. Use the past simple tense.

UNIT 14 The Past Continuous

See also

Units 1, 2 **Be**

Unit 20 The present tenses and the past tenses

A Sample sentences

Alison:	**What were you doing last year?**
Silvie:	**We were developing a new product.**
Alison:	**Who was working on this project?**
Silvie:	**Mainly Rachida and Voitek. But they were not working on it full time.**

B Form

The past continuous positive and question have two main parts:
    the past tense of **to be** + infinitive ...*ing*

Positive form				Question form		
Subject	to be	Infinitive ...ing		to be	Subject	Infinitive ...ing
I/he/she/it	**was**	making		**was**	I/he/she/it	making?
you/we/they	**were**	presenting		**were**	you/we/they	presenting?
the company (= it)	**was**	preparing		**was**	the company (= it)	preparing?
the manager (= he/she)	**was**	reading		**was**	the manager (= he/she)	reading?
the departments (= they)	**were**	doing		**were**	the departments (= they)	doing?
the workers (= they)	**were**	discussing		**were**	the workers (= they)	discussing?

The past continuous has three parts in the negative:
    the past tense of **to be** + not + infinitive ...*ing*

Negative form			
Subject	to be	not	Infinitive ...ing
I/he/she/it	**was**	**not**	making
you/we/they	**were**	**not**	presenting
the company (= it)	**was**	**not**	preparing
the manager (= he/she)	**was**	**not**	reading
the departments (= they)	**were**	**not**	doing
the workers (= they)	**were**	**not**	discussing

In spoken language we often use the short forms:

> *I/he/she/it/the company* **wasn't** ...
> *you/we/they/the departments/the workers* **weren't** ...

We sometimes also use them in informal written language.

C Uses

We use the past continuous as a time frame for another activity:

What were you doing at this time last week?
At this time last week I was visiting our factory in Switzerland.

what were you doing?

X

this time last week

Exercise 1

Read the extract from a Director's speech at the Annual General Meeting of Pace PLC.
Underline all forms of the past continuous. Label them positive (P), negative (N), or question (Q).

'What was happening a few years ago? Well, the company wasn't doing very well.
During the 1990s we were competing with many suppliers. We had a small turnover.
Then everyone was thinking about mergers and takeovers. In the early 2000s we were
operating in a very different market. There were only four large companies. All four
were making big profits. We were all doing well...'

Exercise 2

A Safety Officer is talking to a technician about a fire at a factory. Complete the dialogue. Use the
words in brackets.

SO: What **were you doing** (you/do) yesterday morning?
T: From 8 o'clock until 9 o'clock _____ (I/check) the production system.
From 9 o'clock until 10 o'clock _____ (I/repair) a computer.
Then when the fire started _____ (I/not/work).
_____ (I have/coffee).
SO: _____ (your colleagues/drink/coffee) too?
T: No, _____ (they/install) a new printer.
SO: _____ (factory/work/normally)?
T: Yes, _____ (everything/run/perfectly).
SO: Okay. Thanks for your help.

Exercise 3

*Look at the table below which describes Sally Kline's day. Write **where she was** and **what she***
***was doing**.*

	time	place	action
1.	10.30	airport	check in
2.	11.00	duty free shop	buy clothes
3.	11.30	departure gate	wait
4.	12.00	plane	read
5.	2.00	plane	have lunch
6.	5.00	meeting	give a presentation

At 10.30 Sally was at the airport. She was checking in.

Transfer

Make sentences about yourself or a company or institution you know. Begin with phrases like
This time last year... *and* **In the summer....** *Use the past continuous where possible.*

UNIT 15   The Present Perfect Simple

See also	
Unit 16	The present perfect continuous
Unit 17	The present perfect with **for, since, ever** and **never**
Unit 18	The past simple vs. the present perfect simple
Business File 4	British English vs. American English
Business File 6	Irregular verb table

A Sample sentences

Martina: How long have you worked here?

Andrea: I have been here for five years now and Erica has been here since 2001.

Jean: Have you done any work like this before?

Richard: Yes, I've prepared accounts in various jobs before.

B Form

The present perfect simple positive and question have two parts:

has/have + the past participle

Positive form		
Subject	has/have	past participle
I/you/we/they	**have**	lived
he/she/it	**has**	worked
the director (= he/she)	**has**	invited
the employees (= they)	**have**	made

Question form		
has/have	Subject	past participle
have	I/you/we/they	seen?
has	he/she/it	finished?
has	the director (= he/she)	received?
have	the employees (= they)	done?

The present perfect simple negative has three parts:

has/have + not + past participle

Negative form			
Subject	has/have	not	past participle
I/you/we/they	**have**	**not**	prepared
he/she/it	**has**	**not**	helped
the director (= he/she)	**has**	**not**	arrived
the employees (= they)	**have**	**not**	discussed

In spoken language we often use these short forms:

Positive form	Negative form
I/you/we/they/the workers**'ve**	I/you/we/they/the workers **haven't**
he/she/it/the company**'s** ...	he/she/it/the company **hasn't** ...

We sometimes also use them in informal written language.

C Uses

We see the present perfect simple as a tense which links the past and the present.
So we use the present perfect simple to talk about:

1. an activity which started in the past and continues to the *present*:
   I have worked for the bank for five years.

2. an activity which happened at a time in the past – but we don't know exactly when –
   with a result in the present:
   I have visited the US several times. (Present result, *I know many places.*)

Exercise 1

Make sentences from the words below. See the example.
Mr Flaherty has studied economics.

I	have	made	Saudi Arabia.
You	haven't	produced	Belgium.
He/She	has	studied	a profit.
We/You/They	hasn't	developed	a report.
The company	's	increased	economics.
Our department	've	visited	new products.
The government		lived in	taxes.
Mr. Flaherty		been to	its turnover.

Exercise 2

Look at the graph below. It shows the profit performance for four products. Write how long each product has been profitable. Use the verbs in the box.

be profitable	make a profit	do well	(sales) increase

Sales of Product A have increased since 2007

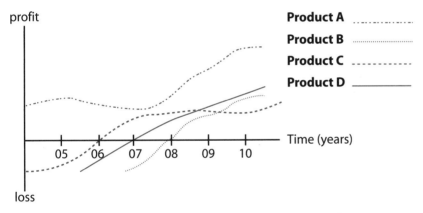

Exercise 3

Answer the following questions. Give long and short answers.

1. Have you ever been to the United States?
No, I haven't been to the USA/No I haven't.

2. How long have you known your best friend?

3. Has your company/school/university made any links with foreign companies?

4. Has your family owned a business?

5. How long have you lived in your present house?

6. Have you worked for an American company?

7. Have you studied for a Masters Degree in Business Administration (MBA)?

Transfer

Ask a friend questions about travel/work/studies/etc. like the ones above. Write down the answers.
He/she...

UNIT

16

The Present Perfect Continuous

See also	
Unit 15	The present perfect simple
Unit 17	The present perfect with **for**, **since**, **ever** and **never**
Unit 18	The past simple vs. the present perfect simple

A Sample sentences

- **Production has been declining since 2000.**
- **The company has been working on this project for several years.**
- **Profits are falling; so we have been looking at ways of cutting costs.**

B Form

The present perfect continuous positive and question have three parts:
has/have + **been** + infinitive . . .*ing* (**has/have been** is the present perfect of **to be**)

Positive form			
Subject	has/have	been	Infinitive . . .ing
I/you/we/they he/she/it	**have** **has**	**been** **been**	living working discussing

Question form			
has/have	Subject	been	Infinitive . . .ing
have **has**	I/you/we/they he/she/it	**been** **been**	producing? studying?

The present perfect continuous negative has four parts:
has/have + **not** + **been** + infinitive . . .*ing*

Negative form				
Subject	has/have	not	been	Infinitive . . .ing
I/you/we/they	**have**	**not**	**been**	doing
he/she/it	**has**	**not**	**been**	helping

In spoken language we often use these short forms:

Positive form	Negative form
I/you/we/they/the workers**'ve been**	I/you/we/they/the workers **haven't been**
he/she/it/the company**'s been** . . .	he/she/it/the company **hasn't been** . . .

We sometimes also use them in informal written language.

C Uses

We use the present perfect continuous to talk about:

1. an activity which started in the past and continues to the present:
   She has been living in London for several years.

2. an activity which happened at a time in the past – but we don't know exactly when
   it happened:
   The company has been doing extra tests on the systems.

In many cases, the meaning of the two present perfect tenses is the same.
He has worked for the airline for 25 years = He has been working for the airline for 25 years.

TASKS

Exercise 1

Match the phrase on the left to a phrase on the right to make six sentences.

You've been looking for	changing my job.
Our exports have been doing well	the performance of our PX range.
The Marketing Department has been studying	for the last ten years.
I've been thinking about	for us since 1995.
Michael has been working	last year's sales figures.
We've been analyzing	a new job.

Exercise 2

Write one sentence for each of the five projects mentioned in the notes below. The first one has been done for you.

Since 2003 we've been expanding our export market.

Start date	Project
2003...	expand/our export market
2006...	use/automated production
2008...	run/training courses
January ...	process orders/with electronic systems
February ...	build/a new warehouse

Exercise 3

Complete the following letter from an Executive of Euro TV, a Paris-based television channel. He is writing to a colleague in Japan.

EuroTV, 170 –174 Rue des Capucins, 2270 Lesigny, FRANCE

Dear Hisashi,

Thank you for your letter. EuroTV _____(develop) links with companies in

other countries. In particular we _____(discuss) programme making with

networks in Belgium and Germany. We _____(talk to) small, private

companies. So far we have not tried to set up links with companies outside Europe.

Many American TV stations _____(examine) ways to work in Europe.

I look forward to meeting you in Paris. We can discuss these developments.

Yours sincerely,

Tom Kitsch

Tom Kitsch

Transfer

Write sentences about four things that you started in the past and which are still continuing.

UNIT 17

The Present Perfect with For, Since, Ever and Never

See also	
Unit 15	The present perfect simple
Unit 16	The present perfect continuous
Unit 18	The past simple vs. the present perfect simple
Business File 6	Irregular verb table

A Sample sentences

A: **Have you ever used this catering company?**
B: **Yes, we have used them since 2000.**
A: **We have never used them. Are they any good?**
B: **Yes, we have had no problems with them for several years.**

B Form

We use the present perfect simple and the present perfect continuous with **for** and **since**:

After *for* we use a period of time:	After *since* we use a point of time:
two days	Tuesday
three weeks	21st April
four months	last month
many years	the beginning of this year
a long/short time	the end of the 90s

I have worked for ABC for many years.   **I have worked for ABC since 1990.**
I have been working for ABC for six years.   **I have been working for ABC since 1st January.**

We use the present perfect simple with **ever** and **never**:

ever	never
at any time in the past	at no time in the past

Have you ever visited the trade fair in Hannover? No, I have never been there.

C Uses

1. With the present perfect both **for** and **since** show the duration of an activity. In both cases it started in the past and continues to the present:

We have been working on this technology for five years. (period of time with **for**)
We have been working on this technology since 2005. (point of time with **since**)

2. We use **ever** in present perfect questions to mean 'at any time up to now':
Have you ever met the president?

3. We use **never** in present perfect statements to mean 'at no time up to now':
The company has never made a profit.

Exercise 1

Match the questions on the left with appropriate answers on the right.

1. How long has she worked for Smith Callman Ltd?

   a. Yes, we made heavy losses in the 1970s.

2. How long have you known Peter Lomax?

   b. Yes, but I've never visited the USA.

3. Have you ever lived in a different country?

   c. She's been with the company since 1994.

4. Has your company ever had major problems?

   d. I've known him for 20 years.

Exercise 2

A shampoo, Shine Plus, is not selling well. The Product Manager is talking to a marketing consultant. Fill the spaces. Use words from the box.

| for | since (2) | ever | never | long | have (2) | has (2) | been |

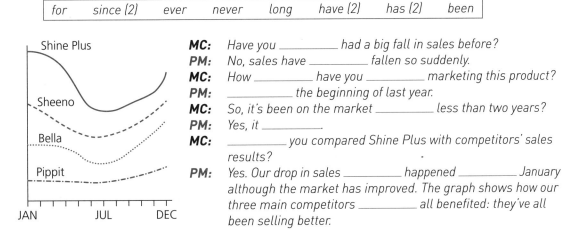

MC: Have you _____ had a big fall in sales before?
PM: No, sales have _____ fallen so suddenly.
MC: How _____ have you _____ marketing this product?
PM: _____ the beginning of last year.
MC: So, it's been on the market _____ less than two years?
PM: Yes, it _____.
MC: _____ you compared Shine Plus with competitors' sales results?
PM: Yes. Our drop in sales _____ happened _____ January although the market has improved. The graph shows how our three main competitors _____ all benefited: they've all been selling better.

Exercise 3

*Kate and Matt meet in an airport departure lounge. They are waiting for their flights. Complete the dialogue below. Use **for, since, ever, never**.*

Kate: How long have you worked for Abacus?
Matt: _____ about four years.
Kate: I see. Have you _____ done business in China?
Matt: No, we've _____ tried the Chinese market.
Kate: Well, our business in China has been rising _____ the beginning of the 2000s.
Matt: And you've been making a profit since then?
Kate: Well, not always. _____ three years, yes.
Matt: Have you _____ visited China?
Kate: Oh yes. Many times. In fact, my husband is Chinese.

Transfer

*Ask someone six questions with **ever** or **how long**. Get answers with **never, for** and **since**.*

The Past Simple vs. The Present Perfect Simple

See also	
Units 11, 12, 13, 14	The past
Units 15, 16, 17	The present perfect
Business File 4	British English vs. American English
Business File 6	Irregular verb table

A Sample sentences

A: **I don't think we have met.**
B: **My name is Dieter Stallkamp. I've only recently arrived from Stuttgart.**
A: **So, when did you join the company?**
B: **I started at the beginning of the year.**

B Form

When we talk about or ask about an activity at a definite time in the **past**, we use:

+	–	?
past tense past simple positive	**didn't** + infinitive past simple negative	**did** + subject + infinitive past simple question

When we talk about or ask about an activity in the past with a link to the **present**, we use:

+	–	?
have/has + past participle present perfect simple positive	**haven't/hasn't** + past participle present perfect simple negative	**have/has** + subject + past participle present perfect simple question

C Uses

Look at this mini-dialogue in the past simple:
A: **So when did you start the company?**
B: **Well, we opened the first sales office five years ago. At first, demand for our products was slow. Then we placed an advertisement in *Euroweekly*.**
A: **And did that help?**
B: **Yes we started to receive enquiries from wholesalers. They didn't want to buy from larger companies because their deliveries were very slow. So, they came to us.**

Now look at this mini-dialogue in the present perfect simple:
A: **In the past three weeks the company has sold 50,000 copies of its anti-virus software.**
B: **And how have they reached their customers?**
A: **They have placed a lot of advertisements online. Have you ever tried online advertising?**
B: **No. We have never found it effective. But we have used an advertising agency for about three years. And they have developed some good campaigns for us.**

Exercise 1

Look at the sentences below. Underline examples of the simple past and circle examples of the present perfect.

1. The company has sold its London offices.

2. The Managing Director resigned three years ago.

3. I have not read the newspaper today.

4. A rival manufacturer has bought the company.

5. The top-selling product made over £3m last year

6. Many shareholders have sold their shares.

7. Market analysts have estimated company turnover at over £40m.

8. Axam Ltd did not improve its sales.

Exercise 2

The graphs below show the turnover, R&D costs and share value for Lander Ltd. Complete the text with the correct form of the words in brackets.

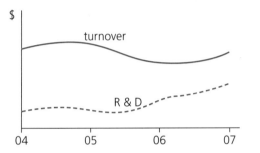

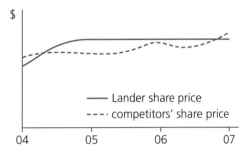

This shows the turnover for Lander. It _____ (decline) between 2004 and 2006 but it _____ (rise) since 2006. The company _____ (spend) more on R&D.

This shows that the value of Lander shares _____ (increase) between 2004 and 2005. It _____ (maintain) the same level since 2005. Competitors' share values _____ (increase). The increase _____ (not/be) very large.

Exercise 3

Complete the email below with the correct form of verbs in the box.

| break   transfer   repair   decide   notice   begin   not/lose   not/read |

Date:	20 May 20 ...
To:	mike.jones@abcplanning.com
From:	t.robson@tkdengineering.com
Subject:	Beta plant closure

Dear Mike

We _____ to close down the Beta plant for three weeks. On Tuesday maintenance inspectors _____ problems with the machines. I _____ the inspectors' report. Yesterday we _____ a detailed study. A few weeks ago we _____ the pump. It is possible that the pump _____ again. We _____ production to our other plant. Fortunately, we _____ much production. I will telephone you next week with more information.

Best regards

Transfer

Write a few sentences describing your recent activities. Use the past simple and the present perfect.

The Past Perfect

See also	
Units 11–13	The past simple
Business File 6	Irregular verb table

A Sample sentences

- He had worked as a marketing assistant for many years. Then he changed jobs.
- Had you used this technology before you came here?
- The club had not made a profit during the five years before the merger took place.

B Form

The past perfect positive and question have two main parts:

had + past participle

Positive form		
Subject	had	past participle
I/he/she/it	**had**	made
you/we/they	**had**	presented
the company (= it)	**had**	prepared
the manager (= he/she)	**had**	read
the workers (= they)	**had**	discussed

Question form		
had	Subject	past participle
had	I/he/she/it	made?
had	you/we/they	presented?
had	the company (= it)	prepared?
had	the manager (= he/she)	read?
had	the workers (= they)	discussed?

The past perfect has three parts in the negative:

had + **not** + past participle

Negative form			
Subject	had	not	past participle
I/he/she/it	**had**	**not**	made
you/we/they	**had**	**not**	presented
the company (= it)	**had**	**not**	prepared
the manager (= he/she)	**had**	**not**	read
the workers (= they)	**had**	**not**	discussed

In spoken language we often use the short form **hadn't**:

*I/he/she/it/the company/you/we/they/the departments/the workers **hadn't**…*

We sometimes also use it in informal written language.

C Uses

We use the past perfect to talk about an activity at a time before the past:

be head of company   sale of company

After he had been head of the company for three and a half years, he sold it.

not call boss   flight to Moscow

He had not called his boss before he flew to Moscow.

Note

We can often use the past simple instead of the past perfect:

I called him after I had arrived in the office = I called him after I arrived in the office.

Exercise 1

Underline examples of the past perfect in the sentences below.

1. After I had shut the door I realised my key was inside.

2. I had finished my sandwich when the phone rang.

3. When I returned I saw that someone had left a package on my desk.

4. Mrs Maw had not finished opening her post when John came in.

5. The work had not been completed before the Vice President arrived.

Exercise 2

Use the words below to make sentences. Include a past perfect tense contrasted with a simple past tense. Use positive (+), negative (-) and question forms (?).

1. The company/test/new products/before/launch/on the market
The company had tested the new products before it launched them on the market. (+)
The company hadn't tested the new products before it launched them on the market. (-)
Had the company tested the new products before it launched them on the market? (?)

2. The engineers/visit/the plant/before/the accident/happen

3. The company/publish/the sales results/before/the share price fall

4. The research team/complete/the report/the management/cut/investment

5. When/the deadline/come//she/finish/the report

Exercise 3

Fred has problems with a photocopier. Complete the dialogue.

Tom: What happened?
Fred: Before the machine broke down, I _____ (made) 100 copies.
Tom: Then what?
Fred: When I _____ (done) 100, the paper jammed.
Tom: What did you do?
Fred: When I _____ (clear) the paper, I pressed the start button.
Tom: Then?
Fred: I thought I _____ (solve) the problem. But I _____ (not/notice) another problem.
Smoke was coming out of the back.
Tom: So then what happened?
Fred: After I _____ (see) the smoke, I telephoned you.

Transfer

Write sentences contrasting events affecting your work or studies.

Example:
When I arrived in Tanzania I had already learnt Swahili.

UNIT 20   The Present Tenses and The Past Tenses

See also	
Units 3–9	The present tenses
Units 11–14	The past tenses
Units 15–18	The present perfect
Unit 19	The past perfect
Business File 6	Irregular verb table

A Sample sentences

John: Where do you come from, Diane?

Sonia: I was born in Scotland, but I live in Finland now.

John: That's interesting. My brother has lived in Finland for five years. How long have you lived there?

Sonia: I moved there three years ago.

John: And do you like it?

Sonia: Yes. But unfortunately, I don't live in the capital. I commute to the office every day. It takes about an hour. So, we are looking for a flat near the centre. Have you ever been to Finland?

John: Yes, many times. In fact I prepared a big construction project there two years ago. But while I was working on it, the client went bankrupt. Fortunately, we had not invested too much money.

B Form

Remember these different forms for the present tenses and the past tenses:

The present, past and present perfect continuous		The present simple	
Positive	**to be** + infinitive …ing	**Positive**	infinitive(s)
Negative	**to be** + **not** + infinitive …ing	**Negative**	**don't/doesn't** + infinitive
Question	**to be** + subject + infinitive …ing	**Question**	**do/does** + subject + infinitive

Present forms of **to be** = **am/is/are**
Past forms of **to be** = **was/were**
Present perfect forms of **to be** = **have been/has been**

	The past simple	The present perfect	The past perfect
Positive	past tense	**have/has** + past participle	**had** + past participle
Negative	**didn't** + infinitive	**haven't/hasn't** + past participle	**hadn't** + past participle
Question	**did** + subject + infinitive	**have/has** + subject + past participle	**had** + subject + past participle

C Uses

Look at the differences in meanings between the following sentences:

I usually work with clients in the catering industry, but at present I am working with a music company.
(present simple vs. present continuous)

I was surfing the Internet, when I saw your website.
(past continuous vs. past simple)

How long have you lived in Jerusalem, Joel? I moved here three years ago.
(present perfect vs. past simple)

Before I moved to Austin, I had never visited Texas.
(past simple vs. past perfect)

TASKS

Exercise 1

Look at the following extract from a newspaper report. Label the tenses as follows:
present simple (PresS), present continuous (PresC), past simple (PastS), past continuous (PastC),
present perfect simple (PPS), present perfect continuous (PPC), past perfect (PastP).

Global slow down

The world economy is slowing down. The World Bank has published a report. It says that the global economy is growing at 2% per year. Last year growth was 2.8%. The report contrasts with a study by the OECD last year. This had suggested that prospects were improving for developing countries. According to Credit Bank International, the world economy has been slowing down for a year.

Exercise 2

Use the prompts below to make a dialogue.

A

1. **Peter/where/work?**

Peter, where _____ ?

2. **how long/there?**

How long _____ ?

3. **where/before/Frobo?**

Where _____ before Frobo?

4. **why/change?**

Why _____ ?

5. **why/choose/Frobo?**

Why _____ Frobo?

B

I _____ Frobo Ltd.

I _____ two years.

Allen Brothers.

Because the markets _____ falling and the company _____ going bankrupt.

I _____ (work) there before I joined Allen Bros.

Exercise 3

Maria is showing a visitor round her distribution company, Largo S.p.A. Make sentences using the prompts below.

1. Maria: _____
_____
(from January until June last year/build/ new office block)

2. Visitor: _____
_____
(how much/cost?)

3. Maria: _____
_____
(cost/$250,000m)

4. Maria: _____
_____
(in December/buy/new lorries)

5. Maria: _____
_____
(unfortunately/one/break down)

6. Maria: _____
_____
(this delivery/go/Spain)

Transfer

Prepare some questions to ask a friend about his/her work or studies. Together, discuss what you have both done and are doing now.

UNIT 21

The Future with Will and Shall

See also	
Unit 22	The future with **going to** vs. present continuous
Unit 23	The future with **will** vs. **going to** vs. present continuous

A Sample sentences

- **I'll meet you after work.**
- **I think they will sell the insurance company.**
- **What shall we call the new product?**

B Form

The future with **will** has two parts:
   the modal **will** + infinitive

Positive form		Negative form	Question form
I/you/we/he/she/it/they **will organise** the meeting		I/you/we/he/she/it/they **will not go** to the meeting	**will** I/you/we/he/she/it/they **prepare** the agenda?
Short forms	**'ll**	**won't**	

We often use the short forms in spoken language; we sometimes use them in informal written language:
I'll check the figures this afternoon.
Sales won't recover before next year.

The future with **shall** has two parts:
   the modal **shall** + infinitive
We only use it after **I** and **we**.
I shall see you tomorrow after the meeting.

The short form of the negative is **shan't**:
We shan't pay any invoices before the beginning of next month.

C Uses

1. We use the future with **will** to talk about future facts:
Prices will rise by 3.3% next month. (*not*: *will to rise*)
When will the product be available in stores?
The company said it won't perform tests on animals.

2. We can use the future with **shall** after **I** and **we**:
I shan't stay long. (*not*: *shan't to stay*)
What shall we do tomorrow?

3. We use the question forms **shall I**? or **shall we**? to make suggestions:
Shall I call you tomorrow?
Shall we go home now?

Exercise 1

Look at the following sentences. Link each one to a picture a–e.

1. Shall we go in?

2. I'll call you again tomorrow.

3. We'll write to you next week.

4. Shall I call the technician?

5. John'll be here at 10 o'clock.

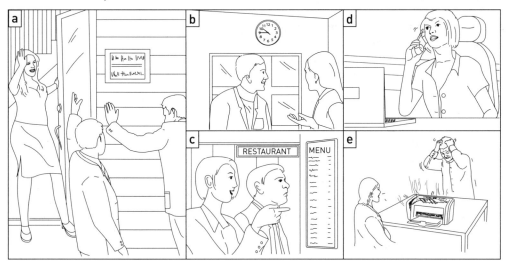

Exercise 2

*Below is part of a presentation by Tom Kip, from LMF Ltd, a food manufacturer. Tom is describing the day's programme to a group of visitors from France. Put the sentences in the correct order. Underline any uses of **will** or **shall**. The first has been marked **(1)** for you.*

a. We'll have lunch in a local restaurant at about 1 o'clock.

b. We'll finish at about 4 o'clock.

c. After this introduction, we'll have a short tour of the plant.

d. So, shall we begin the tour?

e. Then before coffee we'll show you a film about our distribution system.

f. We'll have coffee at 11, then we'll have a meeting with Ken Levins, our Product Manager.

g. Right, now I'll explain the programme for the day. **(1)**

h. After lunch we'll discuss future plans.

Exercise 3

*Complete the exchanges below. Use a form of **will** or **shall** in your answer.*

1. Fred: *I need a taxi.*
Martin: *(phone)* **I'll phone for one.**

2. John: *I'll be in my office tomorrow.*
Marie: *(call you)* _____.

3. Jacob: *I need to see the report.*
Hisashi: *(get it)* _____.

4. Pierre: *Who'll tell us the answer?*
Imogen: *(not/Erik)* _____.

5. Juan: *What about lunch?*
Amy: *(go/Gigi's Restaurant?)* _____.

Transfer

*Answer the following questions about your work. Use a form of **will** or **shall**.*

What do you plan to do tomorrow?

Where are you going on Saturday?

Who won't you see this evening?

What about getting a big pay rise next year?

What'll you talk about tomorrow?

If the company has problems, will you lose your job?

UNIT 22

The Future with Going To vs. Present Continuous

See also	
Unit 21	The future with **will** and **shall**
Unit 23	The future with **will** vs. **going to** vs. present continuous

A Sample sentences

- **When are you going to give us a decision?**
- **We are going to discuss marketing strategy.**
- **I am leaving for Europe at the end of the week.**
- **We are not selling as much to Asia.**

B Form

The future with **going to** has three parts in the positive and question:
to be + **going to** + infinitive

Positive form					Question form			
Subject	to be	going to	Infinitive		to be	Subject	going to	Infinitive
I	am	**going to**			**am**	I	**going to**	
you/we/they	are	**going to**	negotiate		**are**	you/we/they	**going to**	agree?
he/she/it	is	**going to**			**is**	he/she/it	**going to**	

The future with **going to** has four parts in the negative:
to be + **not** + **going to** + infinitive

Negative form				
Subject	to be	not	going to	Infinitive
I	am	**not**	**going to**	
you/we/they	are	**not**	**going to**	come
he/she/it	is	**not**	**going to**	

For the forms of the present continuous (positive, negative and question), see Units 3–5.

C Uses

1. We use the future with **going to** to talk about intentions:
   I am going to do $2000 in sales today. (It is my intention.)
   The company is going to build 1000 cars a year. (It is our company's intention.)

2. We use the future with the present continuous to talk about personal fixed plans or schedules:
   Next month we are launching a new online service. (It is our fixed plan.)
   When are you flying to Jakobsberg? (When have you fixed to fly there?)

Note
It is important to specify a future time, when you use the present continuous with a future meaning.
When are you flying to Jakobsberg?
I'm flying there tomorrow morning.

Exercise 1

*Read the text below. Underline <u>once</u> any uses of **going to** + infinitive (intention) and underline <u>twice</u> any examples of the present continuous tense (fixed plans).*

> Q: What are you working on for the next few weeks?
>
> A: We're setting up a new distribution network in Asia. We're not using our own staff. We're going to use local agents. We're going to recruit top quality experts. We're examining some possible applicants next week. We're going to run psychometric tests as part of the recruitment procedure. I'm meeting colleagues later today to finalise plans.

Exercise 2

A customer is telephoning a mobile phone rental company. Complete the conversation.

Caller: Well, we **'re having** (have) a conference in three months. I need some phones.
PhoneCo: Fine. How many people _____ (come)?
Caller: Well, _____ (send out) 50 invitations this week.
PhoneCo: That's fine. _____ (hire) phones for everyone?
Caller: No, just about half, I think.
PhoneCo: And _____ (need) anything else, faxes or modems?
Caller: No, _____ (not/plan) anything complicated.

Exercise 3

*Look at the project plan for a joint venture between two companies, KJE Ltd and Weisskopf GmbH. Complete the memo below. Use the correct form of the words in the box. Put them into the present continuous or the **going to** form.*

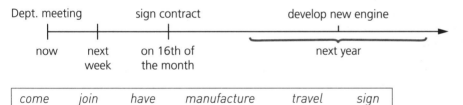

| come | join | have | manufacture | travel | sign |

> **Memo**
> **To:** HJ   **From:** KP
>
> **Re:** KJE/Weisskopf Joint Venture
>
> As you know, we _____ a new engine with Weisskopf GmbH. We _____ a Department meeting next week and I _____ to Bremen on the 16th. We _____ contract then. _____ to the meeting?
> That's all. Good luck.
>
> P.S. Helen _____ (not) the design team. She is too busy.

Transfer

Write sentences on (a) your intentions, and (b) your fixed plans.

UNIT 23

The Future with Will vs. Going To vs. Present Continuous

See also	
Unit 21	The future with **will** and **shall**
Unit 22	The future with **going to** vs. present continuous

A Sample sentences

A: When are you going to launch the new product?
B: It won't be ready before June.
A: When are you going to fix the price?
B: For the rest of this year we are offering them at a special price. This will increase demand.
A: Are you going to appoint a marketing director?
B: Yes, we are interviewing the candidates in two weeks.

B Form

Remember

1. There is no **to** after **will** or **shall**.

2. You need the verb **to be** before **going to** and the present continuous forms.
For more information on the forms, see Units 21 and 22.

C Uses

Look at the differences in meanings between the following pairs of sentences:

What are you going to do tomorrow? (What do you intend to do?)
(future with **going to**)

What are you doing tomorrow? (What are your fixed plans?)
(future with present continuous)

We are going to launch a new cable channel at the end of this year. (We intend to launch…)
(future with **going to**)

The official launch will take place in New York on Friday. (The launch date is a fact.)
(future with **will**)

Now look at this mini-dialogue:
A: When will the report be ready?
B: I'm going to work on it this afternoon.
A: I'm seeing the MD tomorrow morning. We're going to review the sales figures.
B: OK, it'll be finished by 4 o'clock.

TASKS

Exercise 1

Read the dialogue below. Number the future forms 1–6. Then write the numbers in the box.

Fixed plans/*present continuous*	Intentions/*going to*	Facts/specific times/*will*

A: What are we going to do about the promotional material for the exhibition?
B: I'm taking it to the printer's this afternoon. They told me it'll be done by Monday.
A: Okay. Tell them I'll pick it up at 10 o'clock.
B: It's not necessary. They're coming here about something else.
A: Okay. Now, I'm going to find out who can do some translations for us ...

Exercise 2

A journalist is interviewing a director of a paints manufacturer, Byant Ltd. The company is in trouble because last week chemicals polluted a local river. Complete the dialogue with appropriate future forms of the words in brackets.

Journalist: <u>**Are you going to close**</u> *(close)* the factory?
Byant: Of course we _____ *(not/close)* the factory. 800 people work here.
We _____ *(instal)* a new purification system next summer.
Journalist: People think your new system _____ *(not/be)* enough.
Byant: I'm sure it _____ *(be)*.
Journalist: _____ *(invest)* more in environmental protection?
Byant: We _____ *(increase)* spending on this by 25% this year and next year.
Journalist: Is that too little, too late?
Byant: No, certainly not. We _____ *(spend)* a lot of money. And now, we can promise you something else. The river _____ *(be)* clean again by the end of this week.

Exercise 3

Complete the email below. Use the verbs in the box in appropriate future forms.

tell explain move happen come have look round

To:	ricardo.benato@eurosales.com
From:	jeanclaude.isias@papin.com
Subject:	Visit from Harkes Ltd

Dear Ricardo,

Representatives of Harkes Ltd _____ next week. They _____ the plant and then we _____ a meeting at 2 o'clock. We _____ our plans for the next five years. They know we _____ our Sales Division to Brussels. They don't know that this_____ in December this year. I _____ them before the meeting.

Best Regards
Jean Claude Isias (Papin S.A.)
(1) 4577 3371

Transfer

Discuss future plans, intentions and events with a colleague. Ask him/her questions.

47

UNIT

24

Conditional I

See also
Unit 25   Conditional II

A Sample sentences

- **If we get ten new accounts, the company will pay a bonus.**
- **The company will not survive, unless a buyer comes to its rescue.**
- **Businesses will return to the country, if political conditions improve.**

B Form

A conditional sentence has two parts:
    the **if** clause + the main clause
In conditional I sentences, we use:

If clause	Main clause
present simple	future with *will*

If we send the mailshot this week, it will arrive next week.

We can use **unless** for **if ... not**:
Unless we merge our two companies, we will not be competitive. (If we don't merge ...)

C Uses

A conditional I sentence shows a real possibility:
If Ahmed leaves now, he will be back in Glenvale before lunch.
(We don't know if Ahmed will leave now; but if he leaves now, there is *a real possibility* that he will be in Glenvale before lunch.)

Now look at these conditional I sentences:
If labour costs increase, we will manufacture abroad.
Unless we move our production abroad, our competitors will take our market share.
Our workers will strike if we don't offer higher wages. =
Our workers will strike unless we offer higher wages.

Note
There is no rule about the comma between the **if** clause and the main clause. If there is a pause between the two clauses, we write a comma; if not, we don't.

Exercise 1

*Label the main clauses (MC) and underline them with a continuous line (_____). Label the **if** clauses (IC) and underline them with a dotted line (.........). The first one has been done for you.*

1. <u>We will buy Axam PLC</u> (MC) if the price is right. (IC)

2. If we are successful our share price will go up.

3. If the market declines we won't buy Axam.

4. One of our competitors will buy Axam if we don't.

5. We can take our time, unless Chemco makes a sudden offer for Axam.

Exercise 2

Make conditional sentences based on these prompts.

1. we/pollute the river//have to pay a fine
If we pollute the river we'll have to pay a fine.

2. the computer/crash//we lose the data

3. our market share/increase//we/give a pay rise

4. they/send the goods today//they arrive tomorrow

5. sales/fall//we/raise prices

6. unless/we/have/good weather//we/not make a profit

Exercise 3

Moda PLC is a fashion clothes manufacturer. Here is an email on plans for next year. Complete the spaces with appropriate clauses from the box.

unless the economy recovers	our products won't sell	we will do better
we will produce	If we have	

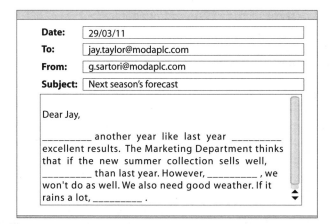

Date: 29/03/11

To: jay.taylor@modaplc.com

From: g.sartori@modaplc.com

Subject: Next season's forecast

Dear Jay,

_____ another year like last year _____ excellent results. The Marketing Department thinks that if the new summer collection sells well, _____ than last year. However, _____ , we won't do as well. We also need good weather. If it rains a lot, _____ .

Transfer

*Make four conditional sentences about your work or your studies. Use **if** and **unless**.*

UNIT 25 Conditional II

See also
Unit 24   Conditional I

A Sample sentences

- **If ITCorp accepted our offer, both companies would benefit.**
- **The results would improve, if we spent more time on planning.**
- **What would you do if you lost your job?**
- **Unless you left now, you would not arrive in time.**

B Form

A conditional sentence has two parts:
   the **if** clause + the main clause
In conditional II sentences, we use:

If clause	Main clause
past simple	conditional with **would**

If we sent the mailshot this week, it would arrive next week. (= conditional II)

If we didn't send the mailshot this week it wouldn't arrive in time. (= conditional II negative; here we can't use **unless**)

C Uses

A conditional II sentence shows a remote possibility:
If Ahmed left now, he would be back in Glenvale before lunch. (We don't know Ahmed's plans, but there is only *a remote (small) possibility* that he will leave now.)

Now look at these conditional II sentences:
If we lost that contract, we would be in a terrible mess.
What would you do if you took over as the boss?
I wouldn't employ someone if they didn't do the work properly.

Note
In conditional I we see the event or action as a *real possibility*; in conditional II
we see the event or action as a *remote possibility*:
If we increase our prices, our profits will rise. (*a real possibility* that we will increase our prices)
If we increased our prices, our profits would rise. (*remote possibility* that we will increase our prices)

Exercise 1

*Underline three conditional II sentences in the extract of a report below. Label the **if** clauses (IC) and the main clauses (MC) in the three conditional II sentences.*

> If we sell Mago in Asia it will help to establish our brand name. But if we set up our own
>
> distribution network it would cost too much. Unless we spent millions, we wouldn't make any
>
> money. If we use local people it will be much cheaper. If Mago does well in Asia, then we'll
>
> expand there in the future. If it failed of course, we'd be in trouble.

Exercise 2

Make conditional II sentences with these prompts.

1. the factory/burn down//the insurance/pay
If the factory burned down the insurance would pay.

2. someone/steal/the plans//it/be/a total disaster

_____

3. sales/collapse//people/lose/their jobs

_____

4. the plane/crash//we/miss/the meeting

_____

5. Mary/be/happy//Fred/resign

_____

6. we/increase/the R&D budget to $500m//we/be/the market leader

_____

Exercise 3

Two colleagues are on a business trip. They are discussing travelling for work. Complete each sentence by adding a clause from the box.

> | I would get a different job | if we didn't go first class | If we spent less on hotels |
> | ~~we'd save money~~ | I would like travelling | My company wouldn't use this hotel |

1. *If we didn't stay in expensive hotels **we'd save money.***

2. _____ *the company would pay more tax.*

3. *Travelling would be harder work _____.*

4. _____ *if I didn't have to wait for hours in airports.*

5. *If I didn't like the travelling _____.*

6. _____ *unless it was really good.*

Transfer

Think of some remote possibility events in your work or personal life. Write five conditional II sentences.

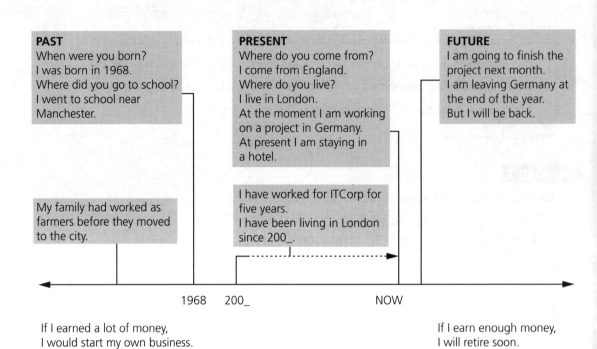

PAST
When were you born?
I was born in 1968.
Where did you go to school?
I went to school near
Manchester.

PRESENT
Where do you come from?
I come from England.
Where do you live?
I live in London.
At the moment I am working
on a project in Germany.
At present I am staying in
a hotel.

FUTURE
I am going to finish the
project next month.
I am leaving Germany at
the end of the year.
But I will be back.

My family had worked as
farmers before they moved
to the city.

I have worked for ITCorp for
five years.
I have been living in London
since 200_.

1968   200_   NOW

If I earned a lot of money,
I would start my own business.

If I earn enough money,
I will retire soon.

Exercise 1

Match the question on the left to the correct answer on the right. Then put brackets round the part of any answer that could be left out in a short answer. The first one has been done for you.

1. Where do you live?
2. Where are you staying at the moment?
3. What are you working on these days?
4. Where do you work?
5. When did you start your present job?
6. How long have you been doing that?
7. What are you doing this evening?
8. What are you going to do next summer?
9. If you had a completely free choice, where would you work?
10. If you learn English perfectly, how will it help you most?

a. Understanding in meetings will be easier.
b. I'd go to the USA.
c. I work for Ford (UK).
d. I'm staying with a colleague in London.
e. I'm going to Australia with my sister.
f. I'm preparing a customer survey.
g. (I live) near Liverpool.
h. I've been doing it for about two weeks.
i. I'm meeting a friend in a bar.
j. I began in January this year.

Exercise 2

Imagine you are interviewing someone for a job. You have to complete the following personal details form. What questions would you ask? Begin with the given word on the right.

Personal Details	Questions
Name:	1. What ...
Address:	2. Where ...
Date of birth:	3. When ...
Present position/occupation:	4. Where ...
Length of service:	5. How long ...
Previous position:	6. Before that, ...
Current project(s)	7. At the moment ...
Future intentions/ambitions:	8. In the future, what ...

Transfer

Write a paragraph about yourself with similar information to the personal details above. Include answers to the following questions.

If you go on holiday next year, where will you go?

If you started your own business, what kind of business would it be?

UNIT 27 — Tense Review 2

See also

Units 1 to 25   All tense forms

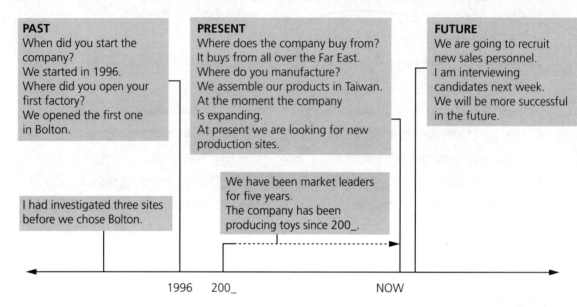

PAST
When did you start the company?
We started in 1996.
Where did you open your first factory?
We opened the first one in Bolton.

PRESENT
Where does the company buy from?
It buys from all over the Far East.
Where do you manufacture?
We assemble our products in Taiwan.
At the moment the company is expanding.
At present we are looking for new production sites.

FUTURE
We are going to recruit new sales personnel.
I am interviewing candidates next week.
We will be more successful in the future.

I had investigated three sites before we chose Bolton.

We have been market leaders for five years.
The company has been producing toys since 200_.

1996   200_   NOW

If another toy company was for sale, I would buy it.

If we invest in new markets, our sales will increase.

Exercise 1

Read the following dialogue between a journalist and Sydney J. Clement, Vice-President of Axoil Inc, an American oil company. Write the sentence numbers in the correct box below.

	Positive	Negative	Question
present			
past			
future			

Journalist: What level of turnover does Axoil have? (1)
Sydney: Next year our turnover will be $870m. (2) It's increasing by 5% every year. (3)
Journalist: So when did the company start trading in oil? (4)
Sydney: We started in Arizona in 1935. (5)
Journalist: Were you only looking for oil in those days? (6)
Sydney: Well, no, we weren't only looking for it. (7) We've been processing oil since 1935. (8) Now we're working in all five continents of the world. (9) In the next ten years we're going to develop interests in the automotive sector. (10)
Journalist: If that goes well, will you continue to grow? (11)
Sydney: I don't see any problem about that. (12) We'll never stand still. (13)

Exercise 2

Use the information below to complete sentences about Ardanza Pascual, a Spanish foods manufacturer. Use the given prompts.

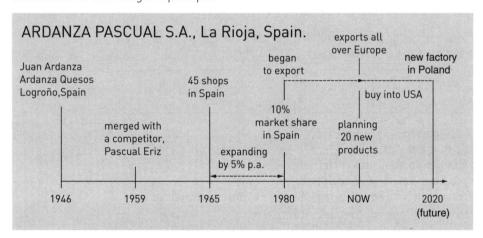

In 1946 Juan Ardanza started Ardanza Quesos in Logroño.
In 1959 Ardanza Queeoe merged with Pascual Eriz.

The two companies _____ competitors.
In 1965 Ardanza Pascual _____.
Between 1965 and 1980 the company _____.
Since 1980 the company _____.
Now the company _____.
The company _____ the US market.
In 2020 it _____.

Transfer

Write one or two paragraphs about the history and the present and future activities of a company you know well.

UNIT 28   Infinitive + To

See also
Unit 30   Infinitive + **to** or verb …**ing**

A Sample sentences

- **I would like to have a career in hotel management.**
- **The company agreed to lease the building for 20 years.**
- **It is important to listen to employees.**

B Form

The infinitive + **to** is a form of the verb. It is two words:
to + infinitive, e.g. **to help, to produce, to negotiate**, etc.

C Uses

We use this infinitive form:
— after some verbs
— after some adjectives.

1. With verbs:
They want to reduce costs.
The firm plans to spend £600 million on a new processing plant.
We hope to advance in the market by providing a better service than our rivals.

Note
We usually link two verbs in this way, but see also Unit 29.
We use an infinitive + **to** after these verbs:

plan	*want*	*intend*	*agree*	*decide*	*wish*
promise	*refuse*	*expect*	*arrange*	*hope*	

2. After some adjectives:
I am pleased to meet you.
We will be glad to do business with them.
I was sorry to hear about your accident.
It is dangerous to drive and use a mobile phone at the same time.

Note
We often link an adjective and a verb in this way, but see also Unit 29.
We use an infinitive + **to** after these adjectives:

glad	*happy*	*pleased*	*sad*	*sorry*	*important*
difficult	*easy*	*possible*	*necessary*	*convenient*	

Exercise 1

*Underline the infinitives + **to** in the following extract from a letter.*

> I was pleased to talk to you on the telephone last night. We will be glad to see you in Washington next month, but I am sorry to hear that Sam is not coming. Tell him, of course, we'd like to meet him another time...

Exercise 2

*Match the phrases on the left with a suitable infinitive + **to** on the right.*

1. I was sorry ...	to do well next year.
2. It will be good ...	to spend more on advertising next year.
3. We plan ...	to see you again.
4. We always want ...	to hear that John was not well.
5. We expect ...	to give a good service.

Exercise 3

*Here is part of a speech to the Annual General Meeting of the Bramwell Group, by the Chairman, William Foss. He is leaving the company after 20 years. Fill the spaces with the infinitive + **to**. Use the verbs in the box.*

know	thank	follow	see	play	leave	have	come

"Friends, I am pleased _____ the opportunity to speak again at our Annual General Meeting. I am glad _____ so many old friends. It is difficult _____ what to say after 20 years as Chairman of the Group. I will be sad _____ the company after so long. The good news is that I plan _____ more golf next year! But also, I hope _____ to the AGM next year. I expect it will be difficult not _____ the news about the company. Now, of course, I would like _____ the many people who have helped me in 20 years ..."

Transfer

*What do you think? Complete the following with an infinitive + **to**.*

I am always glad ...
I expect ...
I am always sad ...
It is never easy ...
It is necessary ...

Verb . . . ing

| See also | |
| Unit 30 | Infinitive + **to** or verb . . .**ing** |

A Sample sentences

- **The company will start producing the screens next year.**
- **Please stop sending me unwanted emails.**
- **60% of employees say they are interested in receiving more information and training.**
- **The firm interviews several candidates before making a decision.**

B Form

Verb . . .*ing* is a form of the verb with one part:
   infinitive + *ing*, e.g. **living, working, helping, producing**, etc.

You can see this form in:
   — continuous verb forms e.g. I am/was/have been **going**. (see Units 3, 4, 5, 14 and 16)
   — noun forms e.g. we are interested in **expanding**.

C Uses

We use the verb . . .*ing* form:
   — after some verbs
   — after prepositions.

1. With verbs:
   They enjoyed working with each other.
   The company announced that it will stop selling the drug next year.
   He suggests advertising in a local newspaper.

Note
We sometimes link two verbs in this way, but see also Unit 28.
We usually use a verb . . .*ing* after these verbs:

| *avoid   enjoy   stop   finish   suggest   regret* |

2. After prepositions:
   He is interested in negotiating a deal. (*not*: in negotiate)
   I look forward to meeting you. (*not*: to meet, because **to** here is a preposition)
   Before hiring any specialist, a check on background and experience is necessary.
   (*not*: before to produce)

Note
We always use verb . . .*ing* after a preposition.

Exercise 1

*In the email below, underline four examples of the verb ...**ing** used after a verb or a preposition.*

Date:	12.1.2010
To:	george.macdonald@advertiseme.com
From:	sophie.allen@advertiseme.com
Subject:	Shello sales campaign

Dear George

We are planning a meeting next week. We are interested in hearing colleagues' views on the sales campaign for the Shello range. Before attending the meeting, please read the interim report, Shello Advertising SA/JD 3421JD. I suggest inviting the marketing group to attend the meeting, but we should avoid having long discussions about individual markets.

Regards
Sophie Allen

Exercise 2

*Look at these sentences from five different letters. Complete the spaces with appropriate verb ...**ing** forms.*

1. Before _____ to the meeting, please read the attached report.

2. Thank you for _____ the Oakham 50 Printer. On _____ the box, please make sure all the contents are complete.

3. If you are interested in _____ more, please contact us on 0800 600600.

4. We hope you enjoyed _____ us. Please come again!

5. *Don't stop _____ about quality!*

Exercise 3

*Ben Massey is asking for advice from a colleague. Complete the spaces with the verb ...**ing** form. Choose from the verbs in the box.*

know meet take talk learn sign

Ben: Claude, listen. Before _____ a decision on the Combo advertising, I would appreciate _____ your views on the agency we are working with, Kinetics.

Claude: Well, avoid _____ the contract this week. Tell them we're interested in _____ more about their plans.

Ben: Good. Thanks. I'll tell them we're looking forward to _____ them again soon to discuss things in more detail.

Claude: Yes. And ask them to stop _____ about television advertising. We said it was too expensive.

Transfer

*Write sentences about yourself or your work with verb ...**ing** forms after the following words:*
interested in, before, after, regret, suggest, avoid, stop.

UNIT 30 — Infinitive + To or Verb ...ing

See also

Unit 28   Infinitive + **to**

Unit 29   Verb ...**ing**

A   Sample sentences

- **Do you like working at the hotel?**
- **Do you like to work on new projects?**
- **We will continue to introduce new products.**
- **We will continue introducing new products.**

B   Form

After some verbs we can use:

Verb ...*ing* or infinitive + **to** e.g.: I have started **writing** my report.

I have started **to write** my report.

C   Uses

Sometimes the meaning is the same; sometimes it is different.

1. The same meaning

We can use both forms after these verbs:

> *begin   start   continue   intend   prefer*

A: **I prefer paying cash.**

B: **I prefer to pay cash.**

2. A different meaning

We can use both forms after these verbs, but with a different meaning:

> *remember   forget   try   like*

Please remember to lock the gate. (Don't forget.)

I remember locking the gate. (I locked it and I remember it.)

We like spending time here. (We enjoy it.)

We like to follow up and make sure our staff are achieving high standards.

(It is a good thing to do.)

Note

We would like to launch our new range in the autumn. (*not*: we would like launching)

Exercise 1

Choose the correct alternative to complete the sentences below. In two cases, both are possible.

1. We continue *to promote/promoting* the use of recycled materials in our factory.

2. Would you like *seeing/to see* our latest products?

3. I tried *to phone/phoning* you yesterday.

4. Our Overseas Director intends *to visit/visiting* all our subsidiaries this year.

5. I remember *meeting/to meet* you in Madrid last year.

Exercise 2

Read the sentences given here. Then choose which meaning is the correct one.

1. I like drinking coffee.
    a. I want to drink some coffee.
    b. Coffee is what I like to drink.
    c. This coffee is very good.

2. I forgot to telephone Mr James.
    a. I do not remember calling him.
    b. I did not call him.
    c. I do not want to call him.

3. Try calling him in the evening.
    a. If you call in the evening, it is possible that you will reach him.
    b. Only call him in the evening.
    c. It is difficult to call him but you should make the effort.

Exercise 3

Harry Cox is a purchaser for a British manufacturer. Here is part of an email he wrote to a friend while sitting in a bar near the Colosseum in Rome. Complete the spaces with the correct form of a verb from the box.

> bring   arrive   hear   do   go   come   see   check

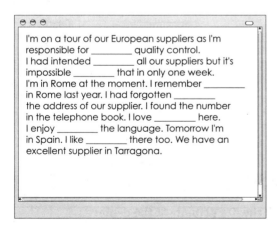

I'm on a tour of our European suppliers as I'm responsible for _____ quality control.
I had intended _____ all our suppliers but it's impossible _____ that in only one week.
I'm in Rome at the moment. I remember _____ in Rome last year. I had forgotten _____ the address of our supplier. I found the number in the telephone book. I love _____ here.
I enjoy _____ the language. Tomorrow I'm in Spain. I like _____ there too. We have an excellent supplier in Tarragona.

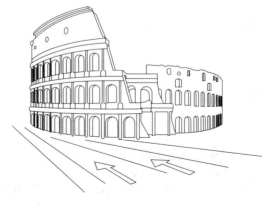

Transfer

Make sentences about a colleague or about yourself using the following verbs:
start, love, intend, hate, try, remember.

UNIT 31

Do

See also	
Units 7, 8	Present simple negative and question
Unit 10	Positive and negative imperatives
Units 12, 13	Past simple negative and question
Unit 46	**Make** vs. **do**
Unit 52	Negative statements

A Sample sentences

A: Does Mr Zimmerman work for your company?
B: No, Mr Zimmerman doesn't work here any longer.
A: Why did he leave?
B: He didn't fit into our corporate culture.

B Form

The auxiliary **do** has two main tenses:
  the present and the past. (See also Unit 46 for the full verb **do**.)

We use the auxiliary to form questions and negatives in the present simple and past simple:
Where do you work?
When did you join the company?
He doesn't work here.
He didn't like the atmosphere.

The forms of the auxiliary **do** are:

Present simple					
Question form		Negative form			
Verb	Subject	Subject	Verb	not	Short form
do	I/we/you/they?	I/we/you/they	**do**	**not**	**don't**
do	the sections?	the sections	**do**	**not**	**don't**
does	he/she/it?	he/she/it	**does**	**not**	**doesn't**
does	the boss?	the boss	**does**	**not**	**doesn't**

Past simple					
Question form		Negative form			
Verb	Subject	Subject	Verb	not	Short form
did	I/we/you/they?	I/we/you/they	**did**	**not**	**didn't**
did	the sections?	the sections	**did**	**not**	**didn't**
did	he/she/it?	he/she/it	**did**	**not**	**didn't**
did	the boss?	the boss	**did**	**not**	**didn't**

C Uses

We use the auxiliary **do** in:

1. present simple questions:
   Where do you live?

2. present simple negatives:
   The company doesn't announce products until they're actually at the dealers.

3. past simple questions:
   When did you join the family business?

4. past simple negatives:
   We didn't get financial help.

5. negative imperatives:
   Please don't mention this to Fred.

Exercise 1

Choose the correct alternative in the sentences below.

1. *Do he/Does he* come here often?

2. Does he *work/works* here?

3. *Works she/Does she work* for your company?

4. Did they *came/come* from Osaka yesterday?

5. He *don't/doesn't* like flying so he *did come/came* by train.

6. We *don't/didn't* sign the contract yesterday.

7. Please *don't speak/not speak* so fast.

Exercise 2

1. *Make the following sentences negative.*
    a. He likes his job.
    b. We sell computer software.
    c. He works for RYG.

2. *Make the following sentences into questions.*
    a. He lives in the city centre.
    b. She speaks Arabic.
    c. You liked California.

3. *Put these sentences into the past simple.*
    a. Jo goes to Oslo every week.
    b. He doesn't like the hotel.
    c. I don't understand.

Exercise 3

Write appropriate questions and answers for the prompts below.

1. _____ fly here yesterday?

No, _____. I came by train.

2. _____ you export to the USA?

No _____.

3. _____ your company make computers?

Yes, _____.

4. _____ spend a lot on R&D?

Yes, _____.

Transfer

*Ask a friend three questions using **do** or **did**. Write four sentences about yourself using **don't** or **didn't**. Tell a friend not to do something.*

UNIT 32   Will and Would

See also	
Unit 21	The future with **will** and **shall**
Unit 23	The future with **will** vs. **going to** vs. present continuous
Units 24, 25	Conditionals I and II

A   Sample sentences

A: **Would you help me, please?**
B: **Yes, certainly.**
A: **Will you fill in this form and return it to us as soon as possible?**
B: **Of course.**

B   Form

Will and **would** are modal verbs.
Would is the past tense form of **will**.
After **will** and **would**, we use the infinitive without **to**:
We will send the goods immediately. (*not*: we will to send)
Would you sit down, please. (*not*: would you to sit down)

The positive short forms are:

will	I'**ll**	he'**ll**/she'**ll**/it'**ll**	we'**ll**/you'**ll**/they'**ll**	the company'**ll**
would	I'**d**	he'**d**/she'**d**/it'**d**	we'**d**/you'**d**/they'**d**	the partners'**d**

We'll look at your application and call you back.

The negative short forms are: **won't** (= will not) and **wouldn't** (= would not)
The order won't be ready before Friday.

C   Uses

We use **will** and **would**:

1. to talk about the future:
   Forecasters say profits will fall by 10% this year. (See Units 21–23 on the future.)

2. to express conditions:
   If the plan wins approval, we will begin building next year.
   If high unemployment occurred, wages would fall. (See Units 24–25 on the conditionals.)

3. to express willingness and make offers:
   A: I'll pick you up at your hotel at half past seven. (I offer to pick you up.)
   B: OK, I'll be ready. And the contract? (I am willing to be ready.)
   A: More discussion, I'm afraid. They wouldn't accept our terms. (They were not willing to.)

4. in requests for action or information:
   Will you sign these papers, please? (I request you to sign.)
   Would you ask Dino to call me, please? (**would** is more polite than **will**)

Exercise 1

Read the following sentences. Say if they are examples of the future (F), conditions (C), offers or willingness (O) or requests (R).

1. Will you send me more details?

2. If I'm interested I'll call tomorrow.

3. I'll post you our price list.

4. John'll visit you early next week.

5. The contract will be ready in March.

6. I'll meet you at the airport.

7. Would you reduce the price if I ordered 20?

8. Will you help with these figures, please?

Exercise 2

*Complete the following negotiation between a buyer and a supplier. Use appropriate positive or negative forms of **will** or **would**. Use short forms, where possible.*

Tom: I _____ like to discuss our situation.

Bill: If I can, I _____ help you. If it's a small problem, we _____ agree.

Tom: _____ you give me a bigger discount?

Bill: Sorry, Tom, I _____ drop the price any more. We _____ lose money.

Tom: No, you _____. If you sell more, you _____ make a bigger profit.

Exercise 3

A customer phones the After Sales Department of AXK Ltd with a problem. Choose the correct line from the box to complete the dialogue.

> **a.** I'm not sure if that will be possible. Will you hold on please?
> **b.** Okay. We'll sort it out.
> **c.** Right, I'll ask an engineer to visit you.
> **d.** Okay. If you use the emergency switch on the back, the light will come on.
> **e.** Hello again. Someone'll be there at 2 p.m. tomorrow.
> **f.** Will you give me your address, please?

AX: Hello, After Sales Department.

PC: Hello. Peter Cord from Leeds, here. I'd like some help with an AX20. The power isn't working.

AX: _____

PC: No, it won't. There's no power.

AX: _____

PC: Will you send someone today?

AX: _____

PC: Certainly.

AX: _____

PC: Okay, thank you.

AX: _____

PC: Yes, it's Beta Foods Ltd, 350 Otley Road, Leeds.

AX: _____

PC: Thank you. Goodbye.

Transfer

*Write sentences which include a form of **will** or **would** and which are:*
an offer to help, a request, a conditional, a reference to the future.

UNIT
33
May and Might

See also	
Unit 34	**Can** and **could**
Unit 36	**Mustn't**, **needn't**, **don't have to** and **haven't got to**

A Sample sentences

A: May I ask a question?
B: Of course you may. Go ahead.
A: The new software might not work. What will we do then?
B: Don't worry, Sarah. The engineers can't leave until the whole system is operating.

B Form

May and **might** are modal verbs.
Might is the past tense form of **may**.
After **may** and **might**, we use the infinitive without to:
We may send the goods immediately. (*not*: we may to send)
When might you be in Paris? (*not*: might you to be)

We use **may** and **might** after all subjects; they do not change.
There are no positive short forms of **may** and **might**.
The short form of **might not** is **mightn't**:
I'm worried. They mightn't deliver the goods on time.

C Uses

We use **may** and **might** to talk about:

1. possibility and impossibility:

A: How are plans for the new project going?
B: Not too well. We may not have the technology to do it.
A: That's a pity. Then we might need to postpone it for a while.
B: Yes, we might.

2. permission and prohibition:

May/might I ask a question?   **You may smoke here.**   **You may not smoke here.**
Yes, of course you may.

(See also **can't** in Unit 34 and **mustn't** in Unit 36.)

Notes

In C1, **may** is a stronger possibility than **might**.
In C2, we may use **may I** or **might I** to ask for permission; **might I** is more polite.
In C2, we normally use **may** rather than **might** to express permission and prohibition.

Exercise 1

Correct any mistakes in the following dialogue.

A: May I ask you something?
B: Of course you might.
A: May I deliver the report next week?
B: You mayn't. The meeting is tomorrow.
A: Well, I might to arrive late.

Exercise 2

*Read the sentences below. Write **may (not)**, **might (not)** or **may/might (not)** on the right, depending on the meaning of each sentence.*

1. *It is possible that the goods won't arrive.*   _____
2. *Please can I help you?*   _____
3. *You can't smoke here.*   _____
4. *It's possible that we'll have a drink in the bar.*   _____
5. *It's possible that the lift is not working.*   _____
6. *It is possible that the bank will help us.*   _____

Exercise 3

Answer the following questions with the prompts below. The first is done for you.

1. How will you go to New York?

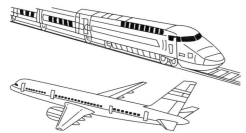

I'll probably fly, but I **might** go by train.

2. Can I fly first class?

No, you _____

3. When are you going to finish the research?

File Tools Pictures Search View Options Help	
Calendar	
Thursday 20th	Saturday 22nd
Friday 21st	Sunday 23rd

I'll probably finish it by Friday but it _____ ready by Thursday.

4. May I smoke outside?

Yes, of course _____

Transfer

Write sentences about probability that affect you.
Example: **I might go to London next year.**

UNIT
34
Can and Could

See also	
Unit 33	**May** and **might**
Unit 36	**Mustn't**, **needn't**, **don't have to** and **haven't got to**

A Sample sentences

> **A:** Can I help you?
> **B:** My name is Nancy Farmer. Could I speak to Mr Kumar, please.
> **A:** I'm sorry, but he's not available at the moment. Can he call you tomorrow?
> **B:** No, he can't reach me tomorrow, but he could call me on Friday.

B Form

Can and **could** are modal verbs.
Could is the past tense form of **can**.
After **can** and **could**, we use the infinitive without **to**:
We can send the goods immediately. (*not*: we can to send)
Could you repeat your name, please? (*not*: could you to repeat)

We use **can** and **could** after all subjects; they do not change.
There are no positive short forms of **can** and **could**.
The negative short forms are: **can't** (= can not) and **couldn't** (= could not)
I can't hear you. Please speak up.

C Uses

We use **can** and **could**:

1. to talk about ability and inability:
> **A:** When can you deliver my washing machine?
> **B:** I think we could manage it before the end of the week.

2. to talk about possibility and impossibility:
> **A:** What can we do to speed up the process?
> **B:** I don't know. But things couldn't be slower!

3. to talk about permission and prohibition:
> **A:** If you've finished, you can leave.
> **B:** But I haven't finished.
> **A:** Then you can't leave.

(See also **may/may not** in Unit 33 and **mustn't** in Unit 36.)

4. in requests for action:
> **A:** Can/could you give the name and phone number of your sales manager, please?
> **B:** Of course. It's Fintan Mullane, and his number is 0576 345980.

Notes
In C1, **could** is a weaker ability than **can**; in C2, can is a stronger possibility than **could**.
Normally, we don't use **could** for present permission.

Exercise 1

*Use phrases with **can**, **can't**, **could** and **couldn't** to replace the underlined words.*

1. A: <u>Is it possible for you to</u> come at 3 o'clock?
   B: <u>It is possible</u>, but 4 o'clock would be better.

2. A: Her appointment is today.
   B: Yes, but she phoned yesterday to say <u>she was not able to</u> come.

3. A: When you saw the figures, <u>did you</u> understand them?
   B: No, <u>I didn't</u>.

4. A: <u>Do you know how to</u> speak German?
   B: No, <u>I don't</u>.

Exercise 2

Look at the pictures below. Choose the sentence from a–c which matches each picture.

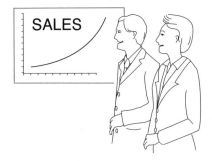

1. a. We can't have a pay rise.
   b. We could have a pay rise.
   c. We can definitely have a pay rise.

3. a. We can see a big increase in sales here.
   b. Couldn't we increase our advertising a little?
   c. I can't see any improvement here.

2. a. We could all lose our jobs.
   b. Can we build a bigger factory?
   c. We can pay the workers more.

4. a. Can you explain these results?
   b. We can sell everything.
   c. You can have a pay rise.

Exercise 3

*Complete the sentences below using **can**, **can't**, **could** and **couldn't**.*

1. '_____ help you?' 'Yes, I need some advice.'
2. '_____ come in?' 'Of course.'
3. 'Sorry, _____ understand.'
4. 'The plane _____ take off.' 'It was too foggy.'
5. 'My car has broken down. I _____ be very late.'

Transfer

*Make sentences which express ability/inability, possibility/impossibility, permission/prohibition, and requests for action. Use forms of **can** and **could**.*

Must, Have To and Have Got To

See also	
Unit 36	**Mustn't, needn't, don't have to** and **haven't got to**
Unit 37	**Should** and **ought to**

A Sample sentences

- **We must receive your comments on or before May 4th.**
- **In many European countries, men have to complete a period of military service; they've got to do at least a year.**
- **Last year China had to increase wheat imports because of a sharp drop in domestic production.**

B Form

Must is a modal verb; after **must** we use the infinitive without **to**:
We must raise extra capital. (*not*: we must to raise)
Have to is a present tense form; **have got to** is a present perfect tense form.
Had to is the past tense form of **have to**; we also use it as the past tense of **must** and **have got to**:
Last year all drivers first had to report to reception; now we have (got) to deliver the goods straight to the warehouse.

We use **must** after all subjects; it does not change. There is no short form of **must**.
Here are the forms of **have (got) to**:

Present Positive			Question	
Subject	Verb	Verb	Subject	Verb
I/you/we they	**have (got) to**	**do**	I/you/we/they	**have to?**
he/she/it	**has (got) to**	**does**	he/she/it	**have to?**
the company	**has (got) to**	**does**	the company	**have to?**
the directors	**have (got) to**	**do**	the directors	**have to?**

Past Positive			Question	
Subject	Verb	Verb	Subject	Verb
I/you/we they	**had to**	**did**	I/you/we/they	**have to?**
he/she/it	**had to**	**did**	he/she/it	**have to?**
the company	**had to**	**did**	the company	**have to?**
the directors	**had to**	**did**	the directors	**have to?**

The question forms of **have got to** are: **have** I/you/we/they **got to** …, **has** he/she/it **got to**…
There is no short form of **have to**.
The short forms of **have got to** are: I**'ve**/you**'ve**/we**'ve**/they**'ve got to**, he**'s**/she**'s**/it**'s got to**.

C Uses

We use **must** and **have (got) to**:

1. to talk about obligations – what you must do:
   A: We must do something. The situation is critical.
   B: I know. There has to be a simple solution.
   A: What did we do last time?
   B: We had to go to the bank and explain the situation.
   A: And then we had to pay back the money?
   B: Then we've got to do the same now.
   A: And how soon did we have to repay the loan?
   B: We had to repay it within six months.

2. to express certainty:
   The new government wants to introduce reform. So change must soon be on its way.
   (= It is certain that there will soon be change.)

Exercise 1

Read the following dialogue. Then mark the sentences 1–6 below true (T) or false (F).

Sue: I've got to go to a meeting. I must telephone John before I go. You have to stay here.
Bill: Okay. Wait! You've got to take the report with you.
Sue: Why? Have I got to present it in the meeting?
Bill: No, but Fred wants it today. He said he must have it.

1. It is not necessary for Sue to go to the meeting. ☐
2. She has to telephone John. ☐
3. Bill has to go to the meeting. ☐
4. It is not necessary for Sue to take the report. ☐
5. She must present the report in the meeting. ☐
6. Fred thinks it is not necessary for him to have the report. ☐

Exercise 2

Correct the mistakes in the following sentences.

1. We got to pay more tax this year.
2. We have not to spend too much on special promotions.
3. Last year we have to advertise a lot on television.
4. Our competitors are in trouble. They had got to reduce their prices.
5. We must to plan our marketing carefully.

Exercise 3

*Complete the sentences for the following pictures. Use **must**, **have to** or **have got to**.*

1.

'We _____ buy some more trucks.'

3.

'You _____ present a business plan.'

2.

'I've no money. I'll _____ borrow
some from the bank.'

4.

'There's only one problem. We _____
pay the money back.'

Transfer

Make sentences about obligations for yourself, your friends, or a company you know.

Mustn't, Needn't, Don't Have To and Haven't Got To

See also	
Unit 35	**Must, have to** and **have got to**
Unit 37	**Should** and **ought to**

A Sample sentences

- **You mustn't remove anything from the property.**
- **Thanks to mp3 players you needn't be at home to listen to your favourite music.**
- **It was Saturday and I didn't have to go to work.**
- **The museum is free. You haven't got to pay to get in.**

B Form

Mustn't is the negative of the modal verb **must**; after **mustn't** we use the infinitive without **to**:
You mustn't touch these chemicals. (*not*: you mustn't to touch)

Needn't is also a negative modal verb. After **needn't**, we also use the infinitive without **to**:
You needn't pay this bill before the end of next month.

Don't have to is a present tense form; **haven't got to** is a present perfect tense form.
Remember to use:
  — **doesn't have to** after **he/she/it** or a singular noun
  — **hasn't got to** after **he/she/it** or a singular noun.
We don't have to work harder; we just have to work smarter.
The company hasn't got to grow; it's just got to become more profitable.

C Uses

We use these verbs in talk about what is prohibited and what is not necessary.

1. Prohibited:

You mustn't enter this building.   **You mustn't park your car here.**
(See also **may not** in Unit 33 and **can't** in Unit 34.)

2. Not necessary:
You needn't do anything at all.
(It is not necessary that you do anything.)

You don't have to pay us now.
(It is not necessary that you pay us now.)

I'm glad we haven't got to go there.
(It is not necessary to go there.)

Exercise 1

Make the sentences below negative.

1. We have to design new products.
We don't have to design new products.

2. Companies must pay a minimum wage.
3. We need to meet health and safety regulations.
4. Our competitors had to reduce their prices.
5. We've got to advertise in national newspapers.

Exercise 2

Change the underlined words in the sentences below. Use the correct form of the words in brackets. Do not change the meaning.

1. <u>It is not necessary that we</u> pay staff a minimum wage. (have to)
We don't have to pay staff a minimum wage.

2. <u>You do not have to have</u> a visa to go to Poland from Germany. (need)
3. <u>You don't need to</u> pay by cash. (have got to)
4. <u>We hadn't got to</u> increase production. (need)
5. <u>He hasn't got to</u> learn a new software program. (have to)

Exercise 3

*Nordic Business, a newspaper, wrote a report on a successful Danish company, Larssen S.A. Here the Chairman of the company, Bo Johannessen, writes a letter to the newspaper. Complete the spaces with appropriate forms of **have to, need, must**.*

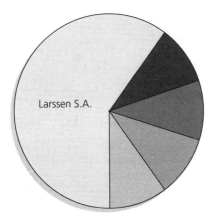

Larssen S.A.

Dear Sir,

You reported last week that Larssen S.A. had a strong market position. Then you said that the company _____ think about its competitors. This is not true. We _____ believe that our market share is permanent. We _____ worry about our jobs today, but we certainly cannot forget about our competitors. A year is a short time in business.

Yours faithfully,

Bo Johannessen
Chairman Larssen S.A.

Transfer

*Write three sentences about yourself and three about where you work. Include **mustn't**, **needn't**, **don't have to** and **haven't got to**.*

UNIT
37

Should and Ought To

See also
Unit 35　　　**Must, have to** and **have got to**

A Sample sentences

- **You should meet him. He's a very interesting person.**
- **The company ought to spend some time and money doing market research.**
- **Inflation should slow further next year.**
- **You shouldn't buy what you don't need.**

B Form

Should is a modal verb; after **should** we use the infinitive without **to**:
You should recycle all paper and glass. (*not*: you should to recycle all paper and glass)

The negative of **should** is **shouldn't**; the negative of **ought to** is **oughtn't to**.
We use **should**, **shouldn't**, **ought to** and **oughtn't to** after all subjects; they do not change.
There is no past tense form of **should**, **shouldn't**, **ought to** or **oughtn't to**.

C Uses

1. We use **should I/we** to make suggestions:
  A: Everybody is here now. So, should we start the meeting? (I suggest that we start.)
  B: And should I take the minutes? (I suggest that I take the minutes.)

2. We use **should** and **ought to** to give advice:
  Customers should leave a cash tip if they want the money to go to their waiter. (It is our advice.)
  They ought to use profits to expand their business. (It is our advice.)
  You shouldn't use a headhunter; it is very expensive.
  (It is our advice not to use a headhunter.)

3. We use **should** and **ought to** to express probability:
  Rotarongan Airways are very reliable; the plane should be on time.
  (It is probable that the plane will be on time.)
  You ordered the goods last week. Then they should arrive tomorrow.
  (It is probable that they will arrive tomorrow.)

Note
They must be home by now. (It is certain.)
They should be home by now. (It is probable.)

Exercise 1

Choose the correct alternative from the words in italics below.

A: *Should we/ought we to* have a meeting?
B: We *oughtn't to/shouldn't* have one today. We *should/ought to* wait a few days.
A: *Should/ought* we?

Exercise 2

Two colleagues are discussing high bank charges. Label each sentence as a suggestion (S), advice (A) or a probability (P).

Jim: Should we discuss the problem with the bank?
Alice: I don't know. You ought to talk to Jeremy first.
Jim: Well, the bank charges ought to come down next year.
Alice: Maybe we should close the account.
Jim: First, I think I ought to write to the bank.

Exercise 3

*Use the prompts below to make sentences using **should** or **ought to**.*

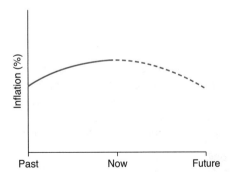

1. *(advice) see a doctor*
   You _____ see a doctor.

3. *(suggestion) cut our prices*
   We _____ cut our prices.

2. *(probability) arrive tomorrow*
   The truck _____ arrive tomorrow.

4. *(probability) inflation fall*
   Inflation _____ fall soon.

Transfer

Write sentences about yourself, your friends or a company you know. Include some examples of talking about probability, some suggestions and some advice.

Examples:
The company should make a profit again this year.
The boss ought to have a pay rise.

UNIT
38

Question Tags

See also	
Units 1, 2	**Be**
Unit 31	**Do**
Units 32, 33, 34, 35, 36, 37	Modal verbs

A Sample sentences

- **The tables are made of pine, aren't they?**
- **They make electric shavers, don't they?**
- **You won't forget, will you?**
- **They can't both be right, can they?**

B Form

A question tag has two parts:
   modal or auxiliary + subject
We normally form question tags with opposite polarity:

positive verb	–	negative tag
negative verb	–	positive tag

We are meeting next week, aren't we?
positive verb   negative tag

We aren't meeting next week, are we?
negative verb   positive tag

Look at the following positive–negative polarities:

Positive	can	could	will	would	shall	must	might	is	are	has	have
Negative	can't	couldn't	won't	wouldn't	shan't	mustn't	mightn't	isn't	aren't	hasn't	haven't

Look at the following negative–positive polarities:

Negative	doesn't	don't	can't	couldn't	won't	wouldn't
Positive	does	do	can	could	will	would

Negative	shan't	mustn't	mightn't	isn't	aren't	hasn't	haven't
Positive	shall	must	might	is	are	has	have

If the verb doesn't have an auxiliary or modal, we use a form of the auxiliary **do**:

A: Prices increased last year, didn't they?
B: Well, prices increase every year, don't they?
The tense of the tag is the same as the tense of the main verb.
The subject is normally a pronoun, i.e. *I, you, he, she, it, we, they* or *there*:
The food was very expensive, wasn't it?

C Uses

A tag turns a statement into a question.
We use tags when we want confirmation or agreement from the other person:

A: The project was cancelled, wasn't it?
B: Yes, it was. It's a shame isn't it?

A: You haven't forgotten, have you?
B: Well, next time you can remind me, can't you?

A: You've done a lot of work, haven't you?
B: Yes, the project should go smoothly shouldn't it?

Exercise 1

Match the statement on the left with the correct tag on the right.

1. Business is important,
2. Businesses have to make a profit,
3. Profit creates jobs,
4. People will always have new ideas,
5. Most companies have improved working conditions,
6. Companies haven't always spent much on training,
7. Businesses cannot forget their customers,
8. Government must help businesses,

can they?
haven't they?
mustn't it?
don't they?
isn't it?
doesn't it?
won't they?
have they?

Exercise 2

Passman plc is trying to buy a competitor, BKD Ltd. A Director of Passman plc is leaving a meeting. Journalists want to talk to him. Write tags and short answers for the text below.

1. The company has agreed to buy BKD Ltd, **hasn't it?**   No, it **hasn't.**

2. You can't tell us the price of BKD, _____?   No, I _____.

3. You're going to London now, _____?   Yes, I _____.

4. There will be another meeting in the morning, _____?   Yes, there _____.

5. So discussions are still continuing, _____?   Yes, _____.

6. But you haven't agreed a price, _____?   Not yet. Goodbye.

Exercise 3

Complete this conversation in a hotel bar.

A: This _____ a good hotel, _____?

B: Yes, it's fine. You _____ stayed here before, _____?

A: No, this is my first time.

B: It's 8 o'clock. We _____ have dinner, _____?

A: Yes, I'm hungry. Oh dear! I didn't book a table.

B: We _____ need to, _____?

A: I don't know. We'll find out, _____?

Transfer

Write a conversation with a friend. Use ten different tags.

UNIT 39   Active

See also
Unit 40 — Passive
Business File 6 — Irregular verb table

A Sample sentences

- **We are discussing the terms of the agreement.**
- **Mr Uno accepted the job.**
- **They compete all over the world.**
- **Profits have steadily increased.**

B Form

Every active sentence has at least two parts:
    a subject + an active verb form
We normally put the subject in front of the verb:
The Finance Director travels to America every year.
        subject   +   verb

The active verb is **transitive** or **intransitive**.
After a transitive verb we put a direct object.

Peter	took	the minutes	at the last meeting.
The participants	**made**	**three decisions.**	
They	will change	the forecasts.	
subject	+ transitive verb	+ direct object	

After an intransitive verb we can't put a direct object. But we can put a phrase with an adverb or preposition.

Sales	**are increasing.**	
subject	+ intransitive verb	
Sales	**are increasing**	**rapidly.**
subject	+ intransitive verb	+ adverb
Sales	**are increasing**	**in Central Europe.**
subject	+ intransitive verb	+ prepositional phrase

(For more information on adverbs and prepositions, see Units 65, 67–70 and 81–84.)

C Uses

We use the active verb form in speech and writing to describe actions and events. In general, the active form is more personal than the passive. (See Unit 40.)
Look at the following sentences with active transitive verbs:

A: **When did you meet him?**
B: **I met him three years ago.**
A: **And when are you going to see him again?**
B: **I'll see him next week, I think.**

Now look at the following sentences with active intransitive verbs:

A: **Russ, when are you going to retire?**
B: **I'll retire next year, I think. We are moving to a new house at the beginning of the year.**
A: **And are you moving out of town?**
B: **No, my wife is still working.**

Exercise 1

Make sentences out of the words below.

1. yesterday/left/Mr Miller/the office
Mr Miller left the office yesterday.

2. last night/flew/he/to Miami
3. with him/took/he/his laptop
4. he/to finish/on the plane/wanted/the report/writing
5. in Miami/to Head Office/will give/he/it

Exercise 2

Match a transitive verb in the first box with a typical direct object from the box below.

rent	accept	appoint	design	investigate	write	borrow	pay	quote
a price	a problem	money	an invoice	a car	an offer	a secretary	a new product	a letter

Exercise 3

Complete the following sentences with a verb from the box.

improved	recovered	risen	reduced	fell

1. *Our prices have* _____ *this year.*

2. *Last year our sales* _____ .

3. *We* _____ *our prices.*

4. *We have also* _____ *our products.*

5. *Our sales have* _____ .

1.

	old price	new price
Product A	$2.99	$3.50
Product B	$9.99	$11.50

2.
Sales (£)

4.
Mobile Phone of the Year Awards
2008
"Poor performance"
2010
"Recommended"

5.
Sales ($)

3.
Product no. 3166
£45.00
£39.99
9 781857 585711

Transfer

Write simple sentences about a local employer. Use the verbs in the box.

make	employ	sell	export	train	make a profit	go bankrupt

Example:
A factory in my town makes sports equipment.

UNIT 40 Passive

See also

Units 1, 2	**Be**
Unit 39	Active
Business File 6	Irregular verb table

A Sample sentences

- **Any remaining money is distributed to shareholders.**
- **Kwan's work has been accepted for publication.**
- **This issue was discussed in Chapter 6.**
- **The contract will be signed at the end of the year.**

B Form

The passive verb form has two parts:

to be + past participle

Prices	**are**	**increased**	**each year.**

to be + past participle

subject   passive verb

We can only make passive verb forms from transitive verbs. (See Unit 39.)
Look at the following passive verb forms:

	Simple	Continuous
Present	the design **is chosen** the designs **are chosen** **to be** (present) + past participle	the design **is being chosen** the designs **are being chosen** **to be** (present) + **being** + past participle
Past	the design **was chosen** the designs **were chosen** **to be** (past) + past participle	the design **was being chosen** the designs **were being chosen** **to be** (past) + **being** + past participle
Present perfect	the design **has been chosen** the designs **have been chosen** **to be** (present perfect) + past participle	
Past perfect	the design **had been chosen** the designs **had been chosen** **to be** (past perfect) + past participle	
Infinitive	(to) **be chosen** (to) **be** + past participle	(to) **be being chosen** (to) **be** + **being** + past participle

We use a phrase with the preposition **by** to indicate the doer.

These figures		**have been checked**		**by**		**our accountant.**
subject	+	passive verb	+	preposition	+	doer

C Uses

Look at the use of passive verbs and the preposition **by** in the following mini-dialogue:

A: Has the trip to the US been arranged yet?
B: Yes, it was arranged by our office in Florida.
A: And are all the details given in an email?
B: Yes. On your arrival in Orlando you will be met by one of our representatives.

TASKS

Exercise 1

*Make passive sentences from these words. Write sentences in the present simple, the past simple and the future with **will**.*

Staff are organised in project teams.
Staff were organised in project teams.
Staff will be organised in project teams.

Staff	*invest*	*a company newsletter.*
New products	*organise*	*in our laboratories.*
Customers	*base on*	*in new projects.*
Company policy	*test*	*in project teams.*
Profits	*send*	*quality.*

Exercise 2

Use the passive to describe the process shown here. Use the prompts given.

1. *orders/take/by telephone*

3. *the goods/load/into vans*

2. *the information/send/to the warehouse*

4. *they/deliver/to shops*

Exercise 3

Tim Hall, an airline manager, is talking about what happens before a plane takes off. Complete the spaces with passives.

There are many important activities before take-off. The fuel tanks _____ (fill) and the aircraft systems _____ (check). Food _____ (bring) on board. All the baggage _____ (load) in the hold. The captain and the co-pilot _____ (inform) of runway conditions and other details about take-off. When everything is almost ready, passengers _____ (invite) to board the plane.

Transfer

Describe any process you know. How is bread made? How is tea made? How is a car made?

UNIT 41 Active vs. Passive

See also	
Unit 39	Active
Unit 40	Passive
Business File 6	Irregular verb table

A Sample sentences

A: How often do you upgrade your computer system?
B: Our system is upgraded every year.
A: And when are you going to do the next upgrade?
B: The next upgrade will be carried out by our IT consultant in October.

B Form

For the active verb form, see Unit 39; for the passive verb form, see Unit 40.
Now look at the relationship between the active and the passive sentences below:

The company		**closed**		**the plant**	**last year.**	(active sentence)
subject	+	active verb	+	direct object		

The plant		**was closed**		**by**	**the company**	**last year.**	(passive sentence)
subject	+	passive verb	+	preposition	+ doer		

The verb **close** is transitive. (See Unit 39.)

C Uses

We use the active verb form in speech and writing to describe actions and events:
They are launching a budget range of software disks next month.
First they will take part in an IT exhibition in Birmingham.

We can use the passive in the following situations:

1. We are not interested in the doer:
The first cars were delivered to distributors last month.
The name of the person who delivered the goods is not relevant, so we can't use an active sentence.

2. In process descriptions:
First the door is primed, then rubbed down using sandpaper.
This is the typical style for the description of the steps in a process. Again, we are not interested in the doer. The corresponding active sentence would be:
First you prime the door, then you rub it down using sandpaper.

3. In impersonal language:
The building site is dangerous; hard hats must be worn at all times.
This is the typical style of a written order or instruction. The corresponding active sentence would be:
The building site is dangerous; wear hard hats.

TASKS

Exercise 1

Read the text below about security of information in Chemco PLC. There are six verb forms in the text. Mark them A (active) or P (passive).

Computers and Security

Users <u>should change</u> their password every week. All confidential information <u>should be stored</u> on computer hard disk. Users <u>should copy</u> confidential information on to DVDs. DVDs <u>should be placed</u> in the safe in the Finance Office. Confidential information <u>should not be removed</u> from Chemco PLC without the permission of a Department Manager. <u>Report</u> all security incidents to an appropriate manager.

Exercise 2

Complete the sentences for each situation below. Use the given verb in the active or passive.

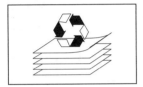

1. *recycle*

    Paper should _____ .

3. *leave/coats and bags, etc.*

    Visitors should _____ *here.*

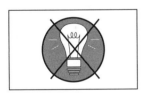

2. *switch off/lights*

    Please _____ .

4. *wear*

    Eye protection must _____ .

Exercise 3

Below are notes for a welcome presentation for visitors to Eastern Water by Sam Weal, the Public Relations Manager. Write the beginning of his presentation. Use the seven verbs given here. Put each verb into an appropriate active or passive form.

| have dinner | distribute | treat | give | go on | see (2) |

First, see a film about Eastern Water.

Then Managing Director talk on history and future for EW.

Then a tour of the factory.

Demonstrations of water distribution, and water treatment processes.

Then dinner.

Transfer

Describe some actions in your normal day. Then describe a process you know.

UNIT
42

It Is/They Are vs. There Is/There Are

See also	
Units 1, 2	**Be**

A Sample sentences

A: It is not possible to approve these figures. They were wrong last year and they are still wrong.
B: But there was a mistake in the program then.
A: There are still many mistakes in the program. It isn't right yet.
B: It is a very complex program.

B Form

We can use **it** or **there** with the verb **be** in the following main tenses:

	Present	Past	Future	Present perfect	Past perfect
it	it **is** (it**'s**) they **are** (they**'re**)	it **was** they **were**	it **will be** they **will be**	it **has been** (it**'s been**) they **have been** (they**'ve been**)	it **had been** (it**'d been**) they **had been** (they**'d been**)
there	there **is** (there**'s**) there **are**	there **was** there **were**	there **will be** there **will be**	there **has been** (there**'s been**) there **have been** (there**'ve been**)	there **had been** there **had been**

Note
The most common short forms are shown in brackets.

C Uses

Look at the following mini-dialogues:

A: Have you seen their new house?
B: Yes. It is lovely. (the house)

A: Have you seen their new house?
B: Yes. There's a large kitchen and then there are two small lounges.
(= there exists ...there exist)

A: Have you visited their new house?
B: No. It has been impossible to arrange a visit. (To arrange a visit has been impossible.)
In fact it was a mistake to try. (To try was a mistake.)

In the first exchange, **it** refers to information that has already been identified, i.e. the new house. In the second exchange, **there** introduces new information, i.e. the kitchen and the lounges. In the third exchange, we use 'the empty **it**' before the adjective (*impossible*) and the noun (*a mistake*). The **it** has no meaning; but in this way we can postpone the important information to the end of the sentence.
It is difficult to develop a marketing plan has more impact than **To develop a marketing plan is difficult.**

Note
We can put either a singular or a plural verb after **there**. The form depends on the subject.
There is one important reason for our decision.
There are three main points in my presentation.

84 | Pre-Intermediate Business Grammar

Exercise 1

Make eight questions or sentences from the words below.

Examples:
Are there a lot of museums here?
It isn't cheap.

It	is	French.
There	are	a good restaurant here.
They	it	good quality.
Are	they	expensive.
Is	aren't	cheap.
	isn't	many tourists here.
	there	a lot of museums.

Exercise 2

Choose the correct alternative to complete the dialogue below.

A: *There is/There are/It is* many good hotels in Tokyo. I like the Tokyo Hilton.
  There is/It is in the centre of the city.
B: *Is there/Are there/Is it* many small family hotels?
A: No, *there aren't/it isn't.*
B: I imagine *they is/they are/there are* very expensive.
A: In Tokyo? Yes, *there is/is it/it is* an expensive city.

Exercise 3

Maria is at Düsseldorf railway station. She wants to go to Münster. Look at the notes from the timetable. Complete the spaces in the dialogue below. Use the phrases in the box.

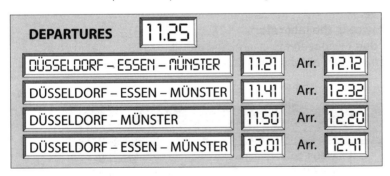

there is (2)
is it
there was
it's (2)
there are
it isn't
~~is there~~
are there

Maria: __Is there__ a train to Münster?
Clerk: Yes, _____ many trains. Now _____ 11.25. _____ a train at 11.20.
  The next one is at 11.41.
Maria: _____ direct?
Clerk: No, _____. It goes via Essen. _____ a train to Münster via Essen every 20 minutes.
Maria: _____ direct trains to Münster?
Clerk: Yes, _____ a direct train at 11.50. _____ direct to Münster.

Transfer

*Make a dialogue using **is there/are there/there is/there are/it is/they are** about your town.*

UNIT
43

Have and Have Got

See also	
Units 15, 16, 17	Present perfect
Units 35, 36	**Have to, have got to,** and **haven't got to**
Unit 44	**Get** and **have got**

A Sample sentences

A: Do you have an office in Tokyo?

B: No, we've only got a representative office there. We don't have enough sales there. Has your company got an agent in Japan?

A: Yes. In fact until last year we had two, but one didn't have regular contact with us. So we had to cancel our agency agreement.

B Form

Have is both a full verb and an auxiliary.

1. For the auxiliary **have**, see Unit 15 (present perfect) and Unit 19 (past perfect).
2. Below are the forms of the full verb **have**:

Present statement			Present question		
Subject	Positive verb	Negative verb	Verb	Subject	Verb
I/you/we/they	have	don't have	do	I/you/we/they	have?
he/she/it	has	doesn't have	does	he/she/it	have?
the company	has	doesn't have	does	the company	have?
the directors	have	don't have	do	the directors	have?

Past statement			Present question		
Subject	Positive verb	Negative verb	Verb	Subject	Verb
I/you/we/they	had	didn't have	did	I/you/we/they	have?
he/she/it	had	didn't have	did	he/she/it	have?
the company	had	didn't have	did	the company	have?
the directors	had	didn't have	did	the directors	have?

We sometimes use **'s** and **'ve** as the short forms in positive statements:

We've a new measuring device in the laboratory.

We form the negative with **don't** or **doesn't** (present) and **didn't** (past).

They don't have the equipment yet; at least they didn't have it last week. (*not*: haven't/hadn't)

3. Below are the present forms of the verb **have got**:

Present statement			Present question		
Subject	Positive verb	Negative verb	Verb	Subject	Verb
I/you/we/they	have got	haven't got	have	I/you/we/they	got
he/she/it	has got	hasn't got	has	he/she/it	got
the company	has got	hasn't got	has	the company	got
the directors	have got	haven't got	have	the directors	got

The past forms of **have got** are **had got** (positive verb), **hadn't got** (negative verb) and **had ... got** (question).

The short forms of **have got** are I'**ve**/you'**ve**/we'**ve**/they'**ve got**, he'**s**/she'**s**/it'**s got**

C Uses

1. Sometimes **have** and **have got** have (got) the same meaning:

Sixty insurance companies have (got) their headquarters in the city.

2. Sometimes we use **have** in fixed phrases:

On fine evenings, we usually have a barbecue.

Come and have a coffee while we discuss what you should do.

Exercise 1

Label **have** in the following text as auxiliary (AUX), full verb (V) or part of **have got** (HG).

> I didn't have a very good job last year. Now I've got a new position in the company.
> I've taken control of export sales. We've many new clients in America and Asia.
> Have you seen our product brochure? We've had a new one printed this week.
> Mary, have you got a copy?

Exercise 2

Match the following to the correct picture a–f.

1. We've got a problem.
2. The company has stopped trading.
3. I've bought a new car.

4. Have you got a light?
5. They've sold the factory.
6. I have a cup of coffee after lunch.

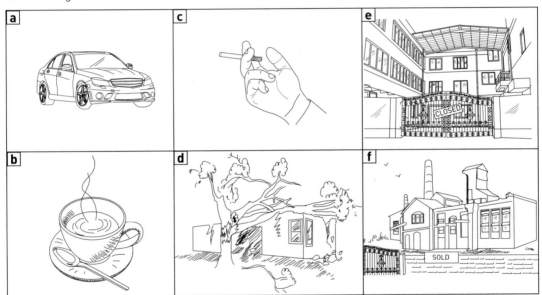

Exercise 3

Fumi Wang is talking to Mike Winters, of Trans World Systems, a software company.
Complete the following conversation. Use forms of **have** or **have got**.

Fumi: How many employees _____?
Mike: _____ about 2,000.
Fumi: _____ many sales reps?
Mike: About 300. _____ 30 in the Far East.
Fumi: _____ worked in Malaysia?
Mike: Yes, I _____. And we _____ three big customers there.
Fumi: What about Indonesia?
Mike: No, we _____ any customers there.

Transfer

Write a short dialogue about a company you know well. Use sentences with **have** and **have got**.
Include the following words.

employees	sales representatives	offices	customers	agents	products

UNIT 44   Get and Have Got

See also

Unit 43   **Have** and **have got**
Business File 4   British English vs. American English

A   Sample sentences

A: How often do you get financial updates?
B: I get new information every week.
A: And when did you get the latest information?
B: I got a report yesterday. I've got it here. Have you got time to look at it?

B   Form

Get is a full verb (see Business File 6: Irregular verb table.) The form **have got** is the present perfect of **get** (see Unit 43 for the forms of **have got**).

C   Uses

1. We use **get** in the present and past to mean 'receive':
   A: Did you get the message?
   B: Yes, I got it yesterday.

2. We use **get** in phrases to mean 'become':
   It is getting harder to find a good builder.
   Both men got rich in 2005 when they sold the company.

3. We use **get to** to mean 'arrive':
   I got to his house at 8 o'clock.

4. **Have got** means **have**, i.e. with a present meaning:
   They have got a new client. (= they have)
   Has he got a job?

Note
We have got the keys. (We have them now.)
We got the keys last week. (We received them last week.)

Exercise 1

*Underline and label six forms of **get** (G) and **have got** (HG) in the following text.*

A: Did you get my letter yesterday?
B: I didn't get it yesterday. It came today. I've got it here on my desk.
A: The problem is getting serious, but I haven't got time to discuss it now. I'll call later.
B: Well, I've got a meeting this afternoon.
A: Okay. I'll call you before lunch.

Exercise 2

Match the following to the correct picture a–f.

1. Fred's getting fat.
2. I've got a fax from Expoil.
3. It's getting late.

4. The company is getting bigger.
5. I've got a headache.
6. I got your email.

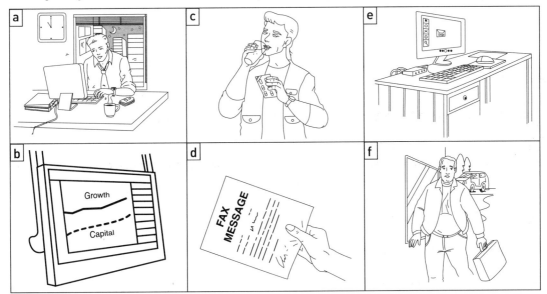

Exercise 3

*Complete the following exchanges. Choose a form of **get** or **have got** from the box. Use the correct tense.*

get (2)   get easier   get better   have got (2)   not/get

1. James: How are things?
    Beth: _____ . We had a difficult spring, but the summer has been good.

2. Mike: What _____ you _____?
    Alice: It's the annual sales report.

3. Peter: Bad news. We _____ the contract.
    Sue: Oh, that's a pity.

4. Amy: _____ you _____ the money? We posted it on Monday.

5. Syd: Yes, I _____ yesterday. Thank you very much.

6. Alice: I _____ a new job and it's really difficult.

7. Billy: It'll _____ , I'm sure.

Transfer

*Write sentences about yourself with **get** or **have got**. Include positive, negative and question forms.*

UNIT 45

Say vs. Tell

A Sample sentences

A: What did head office say about the branch manager?
B: They didn't say a lot. They told us that he hadn't been very helpful.
A: And what did they say about the appraisals?
B: They always tell us that the appraisals are outside their responsibility.
A: Next time, please tell them that we are worried.

B Form

Infinitive	Past tense	Past participle
say	said	said
tell	told	told

C Uses

Say

Many people say that the city is safer now than it was ten years ago.
(*not*: Many people say us that the city is safer now than it was ten years ago.)
A: **What did he say to you?** (*not*: What did he say you?)
B: **He said to me that he will make a very important speech at the conference.**
    (*not*: He said me that he will make a very important speech at the conference.)

Tell

Please tell Jane that I will call her later.
(*not*: Please tell to Jane ...)
I will tell my friends to stay at your hotels.
(*not*: I will tell to my friends ...)
He told us the history of the city. (*not*: He told the history of the city.)

Exercise 1

Two colleagues are in a restaurant. Match a sentence on the left to an appropriate reply on the right.

1. What did you say?	**a.** I've told him already.
2. Tell me which you prefer.	**b.** No, I said I would this time.
3. Tell me about the work in India.	**c.** What shall I say?
4. Say anything you like.	**d.** Have I told you about Mr Singh?
5. Tell the waiter you want another knife.	**e.** I said I would like fish.
6. Let me pay.	**f.** I prefer white wine with fish.

Exercice 2

A purchaser from Delta Hospital Services wants to buy some equipment from a supplier, Langer. There are four mistakes in the conversation. Identify them and correct them.

Delta: Tell to me again, how much do you want?
Langer: I said $20,000.
Delta: But tell me a lower price.
Langer: I am telling our lowest price.
Delta: What did you say me last week about terms of payment?
Langer: I tell you 60 days' payment.

Exercise 3

Complete the email below with **say**, **said**, **tell** *or* **told**.

To:	k.brand@abcsolutions.com
From:	r.patel@abcsolutions.com
Subject:	Your meeting with Dennie Flowers (Axis Ltd) Tuesday 20 March

Dear Karen,

What did Ms Flowers _____ about the delivery last week?
I saw her on Monday. She didn't _____ anything about it.
Did she _____ you anything about the invoice?
On the telephone I _____ her we would give a 10% discount. In fact
I forgot. Please phone her. _____ her I made a mistake. _____ we
can send a new invoice.
Note: I have _____ all our sales reps to offer a 10% discount.

Best Regards
Rajiv

Transfer

What have you said today? Who did you tell something? What has someone told you?

UNIT

46

Make vs. Do

See also	
Unit 31	**Do**

A Sample sentences

A: What do you do?
B: I work as a receptionist for Arnison and Naylors.
A: And what do Arnison and Naylors make?
B: They don't make anything; they sell houses.

B Form

Make and **do** are full verbs. (See Business File 6: Irregular verb table.)
Do is also an auxiliary verb. We use it in the negative and question forms of the present and past simple tenses. (See Unit 31.)

Look at the following sentences:

Who	**do**	**you work for?**
	(auxiliary)	
We	**do**	**business all over the world.**
	(full verb)	
We	**made**	**a profit last year.**
	(full verb)	

C Uses

Make and **do** often have similar meanings. Sometimes we use **make** and sometimes we use **do**. There are no fixed rules. So you should learn some of these phrases.

Do				
business	damage	an exercise	good	a job
repairs	research	well badly better	work	wrong

make				
an appointment	an arrangement	a budget	a choice	a complaint
a decision	a loss	a mistake	money	an offer
a profit	progress	a report	sure	a trip

Now look at the following dialogue with **make** and **do**:
A: So, how did your company do last year?
B: We did very well. We made a profit of $1.2 billion.
A: How did you make so much money?
B: We did a lot of work on our forecasts.
A: So you didn't make any mistakes in your budgets?
B: No, we didn't.

Exercise 1

Choose the correct verb in the following sentences.

1. I did/made an appointment for next week.

2. Sarah has too much work to do/make.

3. We are doing/making a good profit.

4. Pablo did/made a plan for the South American market last week.

5. The storm did/made a lot of damage.

6. Unfortunately the RAMA 20 is doing/making a loss.

7. Can you do/make a list of possible target markets?

8. Make/Do me a favour. Send Angela a copy of this report.

Exercise 2

*Two colleagues are discussing a meeting. Their company has produced a new product, BIGGO. Fill the spaces in the dialogue with an appropriate form of **do** or **make**.*

Amy: Was it a good meeting?
Leo: Yes, we _____ a decision. We are going to increase production of BIGGO.
Amy: What about the costs?
Leo: We _____ a new budget. We think we will _____ more business next year. We'll _____ a profit of £200,000.
Amy: Good. Do you know that Rospa Ltd. have _____ a complaint about our BIGGO promotion?
Leo: Yes, they are _____ a big mistake. We have _____ nothing wrong. We have _____ our research. Rospa know that BIGGO is going to _____ money. With good marketing we will _____ sure that we _____ better than Rospa next year.

Exercise 3

*Complete the sentences below. Replace the underlined words with a new verb phrase using **make** or **do** in the correct tense.*

1. *We <u>work</u> with a lot of companies in France.* — We _____ business in France.

2. *<u>There is</u> a mistake here.* — You are _____ a mistake.

3. *We are very happy. <u>They worked well</u>.* — They _____ a good job.

4. *The meeting was very long but <u>it has been useful</u>.* — We _____ progress.

5. *They <u>suggested a price</u> but it was too low.* — They _____ an offer, but it was too low.

6. *We had <u>to choose</u>: to cut production or to cut the price.* — We had to _____ a choice.

7. *Our engineers have <u>studied the problem</u>.* — They _____ the research.

Transfer

What did you do yesterday? What are you doing today? Have you made anything recently?

UNIT 47 Used To

A Sample sentences

A: Do you travel a lot in your job?
B: I used to go abroad twice a month.
A: I'm sure that was very tiring.
B: Not really. At that time I was used to travelling, but now I'm used to working in the office.

B Form

There are two different verb phrases with the form **used to**:

1. **used to** + infinitive
   I used to work for ITCorp. (I worked for ITCorp in the past, but I don't work there now.)
   We use **used to** to talk about a past habit.

2. **to be used to** + infinitive ...*ing* or **to be used to** + noun

We	**are**		**used to**		**hearing**	**about bankruptcies.**
	to be	+	**used to**	+	infinitive ...*ing*	
They	**are**		**used to**		**these problems.**	
	to be	+	**used to**	+	noun	

   We use **to be used to** to talk about a general habit.
   We can use it in any tense.

C Uses

These two verb phrases have different meanings.

1. **used to** + infinitive

   We use this phrase to talk about a past activity or habit that is **not** a present activity or habit.
   We used to stock 36 different kinds of steel pipes. (In the past we regularly stocked 36 types of steel pipes, but now we don't.)
   In the past we used to design everything by hand; today we use computers.

2. **to be used to** + infinitive ...*ing* or **to be used to** + noun

   We use this phrase to talk about a general habit – normally in the present, but possibly in the past or future.
   Is it still strange, or are you used to it now?
   He was used to the journey as he had done it several times.
   I'm sure Peter will soon be used to the new computer system.

Note
The following sentences have different forms but similar meanings:
We were used to working until 7 or 8 pm.
(= past general habit)
We used to work until 7 or 8 pm. (= past habit)

Exercise 1

*Underline six examples of **used to** in the dialogue. Label them as PH (past habit) or GH (general habit).*

Peter: Do you travel a lot?
Janis: Yes, but I am used to working away. I am away more than I am at home.
Peter: That is hard. What about your husband?
Janis: He's used to it. He looks after our children.
Peter: Have you always worked?
Janis: I used to stay at home when the children were very young. Now they are at school, I am always travelling. The children are used to a 'weekends only' mum.
Peter: I hope you like flying.
Janis: I used to hate it, but it's okay now. My husband hates flying. He used to be a pilot.

Exercise 2

*Write sentences, based on the prompts below, about Michael Ross, Chairman of Kelfield PLC. Use **used to** and the words in brackets.*

1. *He has lived abroad.*

He _____ (live/in Italy).

2. *He attends international meetings.*

He _____ (make/presentations).

3. *He likes going for walks.*

When he was young _____ (go for walks/with his father).

4. *He works long hours.*

He _____ (work/late).

5. *He likes going out with friends.*

He _____ (eat/in restaurants).

6. *Michael has a new car.*

He _____ (have/a motorbike).

Exercise 3

*Complete the following sentences using appropriate forms of **used to**.*

Ann: I always drive to work. It takes an hour.
Peter: How awful!
Ann: I don't mind. I _____ it.
Peter: Have you always driven to work?
Ann: No, I _____ go by train.
Peter: Is this your first job?
Ann: No, I _____ work for RYG. You ask so many questions!
Peter: I _____ it. I'm a journalist!

Transfer

*Write five sentences about yourself and your work or studies in the past and now. Use **used to**.*

UNIT 48 Rise vs. Raise

See also
Unit 85   Describing trends

A Sample sentences

A: The government is going to raise taxes next year.
B: So, taxes will rise again. They raised taxes last year.
A: And the level of unemployment rose.

B Form

Rise and **raise** are different verbs, but they have similar meanings.

Infinitive	Past tense	Past participle
rise	rose	risen
raise	raised	raised

So **rise** is an irregular verb and **raise** is a regular verb. The other difference is that **rise** is intransitive and **raise** is transitive. (See Unit 39.)
Prices rose last year. (intransitive)
We raised prices last year. (transitive)

C Uses

We use both verbs to indicate an upward movement:

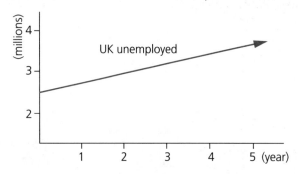

Unemployment is rising at the moment.
We intend to raise the quality and standard of work.
Demand has risen recently.
Train companies have raised ticket prices by up to 30%.

Exercise 1

*Underline examples of **rise** and **raise**. Mark them as intransitive (I) or transitive (T).*

> In the first half of the year prices rose by 10%. Wages rose at the same time. The government raised taxes and the banks raised interest rates. Inflation continued to rise.

Exercise 2

Choose the correct sentence from the alternatives given.

1. a. Sales raise by 10%.
   b. The company raised.
   c. Sales rose by 10%.

2. a. We rised our advertising budget.
   b. The advertising budget has risen.
   c. The advertising budget has been rised.

3. a. Costs will probably be risen.
   b. Costs will probably rise.
   c. We will probably raise costs.

4. a. The number of unemployed workers rose this year.
   b. This year the number of unemployed workers raised.
   c. The company raised the numbers of unemployed workers this year.

5. a. Electricity companies rise their charges.
   b. Electricity companies have raised their charges.
   c. The charges by the electricity companies have raised.

6. a. Bank charges will rise next year.
   b. Bank charges will raise next year.
   c. Banks will rise their charges next year.

Exercise 3

Write sentences 1–5 for the pictures a–e. Use the given prompts.

1. *The National Telephone Company _____ the price of making a call.*

2. *The R+D budget _____ next year.*

3. *In summer prices _____ .*

4. *Inflation _____ in 2008.*

5. *The Company will _____ agents' commissions.*

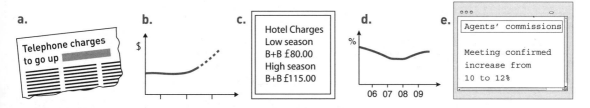

a. Telephone charges to go up

b. $

c. Hotel Charges
Low season
B+B £80.00
High season
B+B £115.00

d. %   06 07 08 09

e. Agents' commissions

Meeting confirmed increase from 10 to 12%

Transfer

*Write four sentences about your work or studies. Use appropriate forms of **rise** or **raise**.*

UNIT

49

Verb + Preposition

See also	
Unit 29	Verb ...**ing**
Business File 6	Irregular verb table

A Sample sentences

- **They are preparing for a conference in London next week.**
- **Do you approve of spending so much?**
- **Our success depends on regular orders from big companies.**
- **The company has succeeded in reducing costs.**

B Form

A verb + preposition phrase has two forms:

verb	+	preposition	+	noun phrase
I've heard		**about**		**the vacancy in the Marketing Department.**

verb	+	preposition	+	verb ...*ing*
Are you thinking		**of**		**applying?**

Typical prepositions are:

about	at	for	in	of	on	to	with

Here are some common verb + preposition phrases:

agree with	apologise for	ask for	care for	consist of	depend on	hear about
hope for	look forward to	pay for	rely on	succeed in	think of	wait for

Note
We always use verb ...*ing* after a preposition:
Excuse me for interrupting. (*not*: excuse me for interrupt)

C Uses

Now look at these sentences with verb + preposition phrases:
I look forward to seeing you soon. (*not*: I look forward to see you soon.)
Here **to** is a preposition.
Dealers are waiting for prices to fall.
He apologised for being late.
The department asked for a 13% increase in its budget.

Exercise 1

Match a verb on the left with a preposition on the right.

succeed	to
ask	on
hear	for
depend	with
consist	in
look forward	about
agree	of

Exercise 2

Complete the letter below with an appropriate tense of the correct verb and preposition from the box.

| talk about | succeed in | look forward to | depend on |
| | consist of | agree to | invest in |

Dear James,

Thank you for_____ attend our meeting on 28 October. We will _____ our marketing strategy for next year. The agenda will _____ just three points: recruitment, training, advertising and promotion. I think we will _____ reaching our target of a 10% increase. For our Sales Staff, obviously we need to _____ training. We cannot _____ our present reputation.

I am _____ seeing you on 28 October.

Yours sincerely

P Jones, Chairman

Exercise 3

Two colleagues, Sam and Paula, go out for an evening after a successful negotiation with a supplier. Complete the dialogue with an appropriate verb and preposition combination. Choose a verb from the box. Put it in the correct tense.

| wait for   pay for   manage to   hope for   rely on   ask for   depend on |

Sam: The meeting was really good. We got almost all we were _____.

Paula: Yes, in fact, I was surprised we _____ obtain a very low price.

Sam: Also, we got good terms. We don't have to _____ the goods until January.

Paula: That's true. I think they have lost some business recently. They were _____ getting the contract from us. We got a good deal because they knew we have other suppliers. We were not _____ them. Also, we weren't in a hurry. We can _____ smaller companies to supply us.

Sam: But obviously, we were _____ a quick deal.

Transfer

Write a paragraph about yourself and/or your company or studies. Include examples of verb and preposition combinations.

Verb + Adverb (Phrasal Verb)

See also

Business File 6   Irregular verb table

A Sample sentences

- **Always switch off the light when you leave the room.**
- **The office didn't make its sales targets, and the company eventually shut it down.**
- **You must fill out a form if you want to claim expenses.**
- **Why did you give up marathon running?**

B Form

A verb + adverb phrase is also called a phrasal verb.

1. **We   have marked   down   the prices   on all our furniture.**
   verb   +   adverb   +   object

2. **We   are going to give   small gifts   away   at our stand.**
   verb   +   object   +   adverb

3. **The company is in financial difficulties.   We   must turn   it   round.**
   verb   +   object   +   adverb

4. **I can't hear you.   Please   speak   up.**
   verb   +   adverb

If the phrasal verb takes an object, then we can put the object after the adverb (sentence 1) or between the verb and the adverb (sentence 2). But if the object is a pronoun, then we must put the pronoun between the verb and the adverb (sentence 3).
Sentence 4 shows a phrasal verb without an object.

Typical adverbs in phrasal verbs are:

about	*across*	*along*	*around*	*away*	*back*	*down*	*forward*	*in*	*off*
on	*out*	*over*	*round*	*through*	*up*				

C Uses

Sometimes a phrasal verb keeps the meaning of its parts:
A: Let's bring forward the date of the meeting.
B: No. I think we should put the date back.

Sometimes a phrasal verb has a different meaning from its parts:
A: We have a lot to discuss. We're getting behind schedule.
B: We can make up some time, if we call the meeting off.
   (**make up** = gain; **call off** = cancel)

TASKS

Exercise 1

Match the verb on the left with a phrasal verb on the right with the same meaning.

return (goods) =	close down
reduce (production) =	call off
abandon (plans) =	take over
buy (a company) =	cut back
go out of business =	switch on
start (a machine) =	send back

Exercise 2

Match the pictures a–d with the correct sentences 1–4 below. Underline the phrasal verb in each sentence.

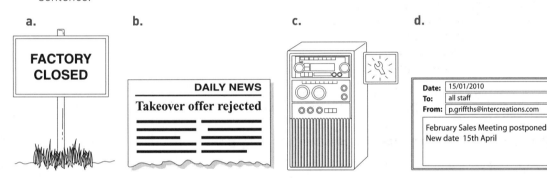

a.

FACTORY CLOSED

b.

DAILY NEWS
Takeover offer rejected

c.

d.

Date:	15/01/2010
To:	all staff
From:	p.griffths@intercreations.com

February Sales Meeting postponed
New date 15th April

1. The meeting has been put back two months.

2. AD Industries closed the plant down ten years ago.

3. We've called in the suppliers to fix the machine.

4. AGCO has turned down an offer of $800,000 for the company.

Exercise 3

Replace the underlined words in the conversation below with a phrasal verb from the box.

build up   set up   put up   send back   cut back   turn down

Boris: If we cannot sell all the goods we have, we must <u>reduce</u> production.
Susan: Yes. Our agents want to <u>return</u> goods they cannot sell. But I also think we should <u>establish</u> an agency network in Asia.
Boris: But we <u>rejected</u> that idea last year.
Susan: I think the Board should find ways to <u>develop</u> our reputation for quality service.
Boris: Certainly. That would be better than <u>increasing</u> prices again.

Transfer

*Have you **given up** anything?*
*Do you want to **set up** anything?*
*Have you **put back** any plans?*
*Have you **taken away** anything?*
*Do you **look back** on things?*
*Have you **taken out** anything?*
*What would you like to **cut down** or **call off**?*

101

UNIT 51

Positive Statements

See also	
Unit 3	The present continuous positive
Unit 6	The present simple positive
Unit 11	The past simple positive
Unit 52	Negative statements

A Sample sentences

- **He reports to the group vice president.**
- **Capacity at European plants is expanding.**
- **Last year the company opened ten new retail stores.**
- **I have just returned from a visit to the training centre.**

B Form

A positive statement has at least two parts:

subject	+	positive verb form
The market		**is booming.**
		will improve.
		has increased.

In positive statements, we usually put the subject before the verb:

The caretaker   **lives**   **on the top floor.**
   subject   +   positive verb
On the top floor lives the caretaker is possible but not common.

We can put the verb into one of the following tenses:

present simple	past continuous	past perfect simple
present continuous	present perfect simple	past perfect continuous
past simple	present perfect continuous	

If the verb is transitive, we can use an active or passive form:

   We   **launch**   **new products each year.**
subject + active verb

New products   **are launched**   **each year.**
   subject   +   passive verb

We can also make a verb phrase with a modal verb:

   We   **can increase**   **sales.**
subject + modal verb phrase

The modal verbs are:

will   would   may   might   shall   should   can   could   must

C Uses

We use positive statements to give positive information.
Here are some positive statements with different verb phrases:
The seminar will start at 2pm.
We have five points on the agenda.
In the meeting they discussed the future of the company.
Shareholders must vote on this offer.
Both issues should be decided soon.

Exercise 1

Read the text below. Underline and label the subject of each sentence (S) and the verb phrase (VP).

> *Sales (S) have been very disappointing (VP) this year. Our costs are rising every day. Clearly, our marketing team need to market our products better. But our R&D Department are confident. They are developing a brilliant new product. It will need support from the bank. A new business plan is being prepared at the moment.*

Exercise 2

The text below gives the history of Keele Brothers Ltd. Put the sentences into the correct order. The first two have been done for you.

a. Now United Electric exports all over the world. ☐

b. In 2000 Keele Brothers was taken over by United Electric Inc. ☐

c. In those days Keele Brothers made bicycles. 2

d. Between 1980 and 2000 the main products were pumps and small engines. ☐

e. The name of the company was changed to United Electric (UK) Ltd. ☐

f. Keele Brothers Ltd was started in 1970. 1

g. Since then the company has developed an international market. ☐

Exercise 3

Complete the sentences below taken from the annual report of Hebden plc, a manufacturing company. Put the verbs in the correct form.

1. In 2009 Hebden _____ an international consortium to develop a new aircraft. (join)

2. Since 2004 the company _____ continual growth. (realise)

3. Our products _____ all over the world for many years. (export)

4. Our production _____ highly automated systems. (use)

5. Our market share in our home market _____ now 12%. (be)

6. 7,000 people _____ by the Hebden group. (employ)

7. The annual report _____ details for our 21 different product areas. (contain)

Transfer

Write six positive statements about yourself or a company you know. Use different verb phrases.

UNIT
52

Negative Statements

See also	
Unit 4	The present continuous negative
Unit 7	The present simple negative
Unit 12	The past simple negative
Unit 31	**Do**

A Sample sentences

- **We aren't increasing our advertising budget this year.**
- **The company doesn't have any South African operations.**
- **They haven't sold the stock yet.**
- **We can't wait until next year.**

B Form

A negative statement has at least two parts:
subject   +   negative verb form
Quality   isn't improving.

The negative verb form has a modal or auxiliary + **not** + verb.
In negative statements, we usually put the subject before the verb:
The members   didn't   agree   on this point.
   subject   +   auxiliary + not   +   verb
On this point the members didn't agree is possible but not common.

We can put the verb into one of the following tenses:

present simple	past continuous	past perfect simple
present continuous	present perfect simple	past perfect continuous
past simple	present perfect continuous	

If the verb is in the present simple or past simple, we use a form of **do** to make the negative.
(See Unit 31.)
We   don't produce   the A5687 in England; we   produce   it in the Far East.
   negative verb form   positive verb form

If the verb is transitive, we can use an active or passive form:
We   don't choose   a new president each year.
subject   +   active verb
A new president   is not chosen   each year.
   subject   +   passive verb

We can also make a verb phrase with a modal verb:
We   can't increase   prices.
subject   +   modal verb phrase

The modal verbs are:

will   would   may   might   shall   should   can   could   must

C Uses

Look at the negative statements in this mini-dialogue:
A: The situation doesn't look good.
B: I don't agree. We didn't make a loss last month.
A: Yes, but we haven't made a profit for six months.
B: But we mustn't always focus on the past.

Exercise 1

Underline negative statements in the text below. Label subjects (S) and negative verbs (NV).

To:	nick_fox@jdloughman.com
From:	maria_aubert@jdloughman.com
Subject:	Ibros S.A. negotiation

Dear Nick

We did not have a meeting with Ibros S.A. because we rejected their offer. The offer did not come by email. We received a fax on Thursday. We understand that the Managing Director of Ibros, Mr Kalkis, will not sign the contract. We have not accepted the present proposals. At the moment we are not planning to continue production of the Alisia range. Last year we didn't reach agreement immediately. Now, I think it will not be easy to find a solution.

Exercise 2

Make the following statements negative. Use short forms, where possible.

1. We will finish our business tomorrow afternoon.
2. The meeting was planned to last three days.
3. We can go home tomorrow.
4. We should go to the Castle restaurant tonight.
5. It opens every night.
6. Friday is a good night to go.
7. They cook fish on Fridays.
8. I have eaten a lot of fish recently.
9. The Castle restaurant has been recommended to us.
10. We went there last time.

Exercise 3

*Write negative statements for the pictures a–f below. Use an appropriate modal or auxiliary + **not**.*

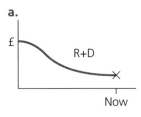

a.

b.

1. *we/not/increase/R+D spending*
   We have not increased our R+D spending.

2. *inflation/not/rise/in the near future*

3. *Sol's market share/not/increase in ten years*

4. *the sales volume/not/improve between 2004–6*

5. *actual sales/not reach/forecast sales/in 2009*

6. *Hammond Ltd/not be/taken over/next year*

d.

2003 2004 2005 2006 2007

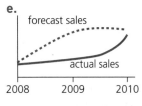

e.

forecast sales

actual sales

2008   2009   2010

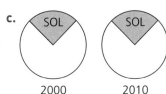

c.

2000   2010

f. **Definitely no takeover of Hammond**

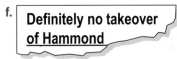

Transfer

Write six negative statements about yourself, your work or your studies, or about an institution or company you know.

Questions: Yes/No

See also	
Unit 5	The present continuous question
Unit 8	The present simple question
Unit 13	The past simple question
Unit 31	**Do**
Units 54, 55	Questions

A Sample sentences

- **Do you still play golf?**
- **Didn't we discuss this yesterday?**
- **Has Marija finished the calculations yet?**
- **Can't we do this another time?**

B Form

A **yes/no** question has at least two parts:
    question verb form + subject

The question verb form also has at least two parts:
       Do   **you**   **agree?**
verb part 1   +   subject   +   verb part 2
The question verb form has a modal or auxiliary in verb part 1.

In **yes/no** questions, we put the modal or auxiliary before the subject:
   Have   **they**   **moved**   **to new offices?**
auxiliary   +   subject   +   verb part 2

We can put the verb into one of the following tenses:

present simple	past continuous	past perfect simple
present continuous	present perfect simple	past perfect continuous
past simple	present perfect continuous	

If the verb is in the present simple or past simple, we use a form of **do** to make the question. (See Unit 31.)
   Did   **we**   **meet**   **our production targets?**
form of do   +   verb part 2

We can also make a verb phrase with other modal verbs:
Should   **we**   **make**   **these components or buy them?**
 modal   +   verb part 2

The modal verbs are:

will	*would*	*may*	*might*	*shall*	*should*	*can*	*could*	*must*

We can make **yes/no** questions in positive and negative forms:
Have we met somewhere before? (it's possible)
Haven't we met somewhere before? (I think so, but I'm not sure)

C Uses

Look at these **yes/no** questions:

A: **Can you supply 1,000 electric motors?**
B: **Do you need them this week?**
A: **Yes. Didn't you promise delivery of the electric motors on Friday?**
B: **Yes, haven't you received them yet?**

TASKS

Exercise 1

*Underline the **yes/no** questions in the following dialogue.*

A: Do you live near your company?
B: No, it's about 25 km to the office.
A: So how do you travel to work?
B: I go by train or sometimes by car.
A: Is it quicker by train?
B: Yes – and I can work on the train.
A: Isn't it crowded?
B: No, not usually. It's okay.

Exercise 2

Paulo Introini wrote an email to his company's Marketing Department. He received the email message printed on the right. Match the correct answers (a–f) on the right to the questions (1–6) on the left.

To: Marketing Department
From: pauloin@incap.co.de
Subject: ARGOS Ltd.

Dear All

Here are six questions.
1 Has all the research been completed?
2 Was the rate of response good?
3 Was the feedback satisfactory?
4 Are we planning to repeat the survey?
5 Will you send me a report?
6 Are changes recommended in our selling technique?

Kind regards
Paulo

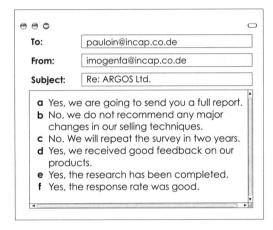

To: pauloin@incap.co.de
From: imogenfa@incap.co.de
Subject: Re: ARGOS Ltd.

a Yes, we are going to send you a full report.
b No, we do not recommend any major changes in our selling techniques.
c No. We will repeat the survey in two years.
d Yes, we received good feedback on our products.
e Yes, the research has been completed.
f Yes, the response rate was good.

Exercise 3

*Look at the prompts below. Write a **yes/no** question for each one.*

1. you/call/Fred/yesterday?
   Did you call Fred yesterday?
2. Mandy/meet/Joanne/next weekend?
3. Alex/be back/from Nairobi tomorrow?
4. Tom/usually/rent/a car for trips abroad?
5. be/you/prepared/for your presentation/next week?
6. Rolf/go/New York/in June last year?

Transfer

*Prepare eight **yes/no** questions to ask a friend about his/her work.*

UNIT
54

Questions: Wh-

See also

Units 5, 8, 13	Questions in present and past
Unit 31	**Do**
Units 53, 55	Questions

A Sample sentences

- **Who are you going to hire?**
- **What did you learn from your experience yesterday?**
- **When does his train arrive?**
- **Why have they ordered the new equipment?**

B Form

A **wh**-question has at least three parts:
  wh-question word + verb + subject

The main **wh**-question words are:

who?	whom?	what?	which?	where?	when?	why?

(We will look at **how** in Unit 55.)

The verb may be either a positive verb form or a question verb form:
Who(m) did you meet at the airport? (question verb form)
Who met you at the airport? (positive verb form)
The difference depends on the grammatical function of **who**. In the first sentence **who(m)**
is the object; in the second, the subject.
Only **who**, **what** and **which** can be either a subject or object.
For more information on question verb forms, see Unit 53.

C Uses

Look at these **wh**-questions:

1. asking about people – **who, who(m)** or **which** + personal noun:

   Who built this tower? (**who** is the subject of the verb)
   Who(m) did he choose for the role? (**who(m)** is the object of the verb)
   Which candidates came to the interview? (**which candidates** is the subject of the verb)
   Which candidate will you appoint? (**which candidate** is the object of the verb)

   Note
   In spoken language we usually use **who** for the object; in formal written language we use **who(m)**.

2. asking about things – **what, which** + impersonal noun:
   What exactly are we going to do?
   Which department will have responsibility for technology issues?
   (**which department** is the subject)
   Which department will you put in charge of technology issues?
   (**which department** is the object)

3. asking about the time – **when**:
   When did you resign as the CEO of the bank?

4. asking about the place – **where**:
   Where have they come from?

5. asking about the reason – **why**:
   Why do they need permission for that?

Exercise 1

*Underline the **wh**-question words in the sentences below. Match the questions on the left to the correct answer on the right.*

1. When did you get here?
2. Where are you staying?
3. Do you plan to stay long?
4. What kind of business are you in?
5. Which bank?
6. Why are you in New York?
7. Who is the senior Vice-President of CBI?
8. Have you been here before?

a. For a meeting with our partners.
b. Roland K. Saxman.
c. No, this is my first visit.
d. I came on Monday.
e. At the Crescent hotel.
f. I work for a bank as a financial adviser.
g. Credit Bank International.
h. Just two days.

Exercise 2

*Complete the questions below with **wh**-question words.*

Q: _____ lorry is going to Belgium?

A: The one on the left.

Q: _____ is the other one going?

A: To Greece.

Q: _____ are they carrying?

A: One's carrying fruit. The other is carrying meat.

Q: _____ one is carrying meat?

A: The one for Greece.

Q: _____ is our client in Greece?

A: Kalkos S.A.

Q: _____ are they based?

A: In Saloniki.

Q: _____ is the driver?

A: Maggie Farnham. She always goes to Greece.

Exercise 3

At Compo Ltd the Marketing Department have a meeting to talk about a new idea.
Write questions about the underlined words in the sentences below.

1. John had a good idea.
2. He decided to increase the budget.
3. We need to advertise in a newspaper.
4. You wrote a report.
5. They gave the report to her secretary.
6. Ms Theo said the report was excellent.
7. We explained the reasons for supporting the idea.
8. We agreed the date the project could start.
9. He named the office which will control the project.

Who had a good idea? (have)
_____? (decide)
_____? (advertise)
_____? (write)
_____? (give)
_____? (said)
_____? (be)
_____? (start/project)
_____? (office/control/project)

Transfer

*Ask a colleague questions using **who, whom, what, which, where, when, why**.*

109

UNIT

55

Questions: How

See also	
Units 5, 8, 13	Questions in present and past
Unit 31	**Do**
Units 53, 54	Questions
Units 77, 78, 79	Quantifiers

A Sample sentences

- **How did they become such big brands?**
- **How many people will lose their jobs?**
- **How long has the company been in business?**
- **During the past month, how often have you spent time alone with your husband or wife?**

B Form

We form a question with **how** in the same way as a **wh**-question. It has at least three parts:
how + verb + subject
The main **how**-question words are:

how?	how much/many?	how long?	how far?	how often?	how big/small?

The verb is always a question verb form:

How much	**did**	**they**	**pay**	**for the company?**
How-question word	verb part 1	subject	verb part 2	
How often	**should**	**we**	**check**	**the stock levels?**
How-question word	verb part 1	subject	verb part 2	

For more information on question verb forms, see Unit 53.

C Uses

Look at these **how**-questions:

1. asking about manner – **how**:
   How do you calculate the market value of a company?
   How can they ensure consistent quality during the manufacturing process?

2. asking about quantity and amount – **how much**, **how many**:
   How much do I owe you? (how much = how much money)
   How much housing is needed?
   How many products does the company export successfully?

3. asking about the length of time – **how long**:
   How long have you lived in Florida?

4. asking about the distance – **how far**:
   How far is it from Edinburgh to London?

5. asking about the frequency – **how often**:
   How often do they call?

6. asking about the dimensions – **how big**, **how small**, etc.
   How big is your office?
   How small does the digital camera have to be?

7. asking about the extent of a quality – **how busy**, **how hot**, etc.
   How busy are you after lunch?
   How hot does it get in summer?

Exercise 1

Form six questions from the jumbled words.

1. exhibition/the/how/came/many/people/to?
2. often/exhibitions/do/attend/how/you?
3. do/promotion/company/you/the/how/of/organise/your?
4. last/long/exhibition/did/the/how?
5. fair/a/cost/a/much/stand/how/at/does?
6. big/trade/the/how/Paris/fair/is?

Exercise 2

*Complete the email below by asking the question for the given answers. Use a question phrase with **how**.*

Date:	18/10/2010
To:	k.r.nijran@amtel.com
From:	marketing@amtel.com
Subject:	RE: AMTEL MARKET SURVEY

Dear Kevin,

_____ are we going to spend? *US $450,000*
_____ people will get questionnaires? *3,000*
_____ will the research take? *two months*
_____ do we need to repeat this survey? *every two years*
_____ will the survey extend? *all over Japan*
_____ is the consultancy which is carrying out the research? *the 4th biggest in Japan*
_____ will they analyse the result? *by computer and personal interview*

Answers by Monday please! Thanks.

Exercise 3

Ben Kamal is Managing Director of Aranco Ltd. He is talking about insurance with a friend, Willy Hoos. Complete the dialogue with appropriate questions.

Willy: <u>How do you decide</u> (decide) which insurance company to use?

Ben: We choose an insurance company on the basis of cost and service.

Willy: _____ (employee insurance/cost)?

Ben: Employee insurance costs about 10% of the salaries.

Willy: _____ (employees/have)?

Ben: Around 850.

Willy: _____ (they/stay/with Aranco)?

Ben: Normally if they stay, they stay for a long time.

Willy: _____ (make/a detailed study of employee insurance)?

Ben: We make a detailed study very often. Every year. It's very important.

Willy: _____ (be/Aranco's turnover)?

Ben: Our turnover is £30m. This is increasing by between 3% and 6% every year.

Transfer

How many people live in your town? How big is the largest company? How often do you travel abroad? How far is the local airport? How long does it take to get to the nearest seaport?

UNIT

56

Commands – Positive and Negative

See also
Unit 10   Positive and negative imperatives
Unit 38   Question tags

A Sample sentences

- **Make sure that your work is presented neatly.**
- **Don't place anything wet on a wooden table.**
- **Please send your order to this address.**
- **Sit down, will you!**

B Form

We form a positive command using an infinitive (the positive imperative form):
Call   this number right now.
infinitive

We form a negative command with **don't** + infinitive (the negative imperative form):
Don't wait   until tomorrow.
don't + infinitive
For more information on imperative verb forms, see Unit 10.

We can put **please** before or after the command to make it more polite.
Call me before 10 o'clock, please. (written with a comma)
Please don't phone me after 10 o'clock at night. (written without a comma)
We can put the tag **will you** after a command to make it more emphatic, but this is not very polite.
Correct these figures, will you?

C Uses

Look at these commands:

1. positive commands:
   Take the train to Nagoya and then call me from the station.

2. negative commands:
   Don't forget your glasses.
   Don't sign documents without reading them.

3. polite commands:
   Please leave a message on my voicemail.
   Don't use the swimming pool, please; it needs cleaning.

4. emphatic commands:
   Read the instructions first, will you?

Exercise 1

Underline positive commands once and negative commands twice in the following extract.

> Please arrive at about 8.30. Register with reception. You will be given a key. You may relax until 9.30. At 9.30, please meet at the Main Entrance. Don't go directly to the Seminar Room. Wait for your group leader. He/she will give you instructions. Please don't telephone the office except in an emergency. Further information can be obtained by email or letter.

Exercise 2

Match the commands below to the correct picture a–h.

1. Do not run on the walkways.

2. Please do not use mobile phones in this area.

3. Building work in progress. Please wear protective headgear.

4. Danger of radiation. Do not enter this area.

5. Turn on your headlights in the tunnel.

6. Do not touch. Danger of electric shock.

7. Caution. Do not light fires.

8. Switch off engine. Do not smoke.

a.   **c.**   **e.**   **g.**

b.   **d.**   **f.**   **h.**

Exercise 3

Jane Callow has a new Personal Assistant. Jane is in London on business. She leaves instructions for her Personal Assistant. Complete her instructions with positive commands for the tasks marked (✓) and negative commands for the tasks marked (✗). Use verbs in the box.

> book/tickets (✓)   accept (✗)   ~~check (✓)~~   listen to (✓)   write (✓)   fix/appointments (✗)

First, please check all the post. *Then* _____ *voicemail.* _____
_____ *for Friday or Monday.* _____ *to Munich.* _____ *Kelso and TBM,*
and finally _____ *Jade & Co.'s offer on Monday.*

Transfer

Write three positive commands for a regular visitor to your home or company. Write three negative commands for the same person.

Sentence Types: Simple vs. Complex

A Sample sentences

- **Prices have gone up.**
- **House prices will increase but wages won't rise.**
- **Expenses are high because he has to travel a lot.**
- **Organizations which need to save money often cut jobs.**

B Form

A simple sentence has only one clause, i.e. contains one verb phrase.
We call this a **main clause**.

We   must deliver the goods by Friday.
          verb phrase

                    main clause

A complex sentence has more than one clause, i.e. contains more than one verb phrase:

We   can borrow   from the bank   or   raise   capital from the shareholders.
          verb phrase 1   verb phrase 2

          main clause 1   main clause 2

We   are moving   to a new office because the present building   is   too small.
          verb phrase 1   verb phrase 2

          main clause   subordinate clause

In the first complex sentence the two clauses are joined with **or**. We call **or** a **co-ordinating conjunction**. A co-ordinating conjunction joins two main clauses. There are three co-ordinating conjunctions: **and, but, or**.

In the second complex sentence the two clauses are joined with **because**. We call **because** a **subordinating conjunction** because it depends on the main clause. A subordinating conjunction joins a main clause and a subordinate clause. Typical subordinating conjunctions are: **because, when, though, if, that, who/which**.

C Uses

1. A simple sentence can be a statement, a question, or a command:
   When are you going to see him? (question)
   The committee's next meeting is scheduled for August 22. (statement)
   Don't forget to send a copy of the report to everyone. (command)

2. Co-ordination is often more vague than subordination. Look at the following sentences:
   Finally, we appointed Susanne Schneider and we think that she'll be a good Research Director.
   Finally, we appointed Susanne Schneider, who we think will be a good Research Director.
   Finally, we appointed Susanne Schneider because we think that she will be a good Research Director.
   They have similar meanings, but the final sentence is the most informative.

3. Subordination shows the relationship between the main clause and the subordinate clause:
   A: OK, the green light, *which* you can see here, is the first indicator.
      (relative clause makes specific)
      Don't press the button *until* the green light goes on. (indicates time)
   B: But what do we do *if* the green light doesn't go on? (indicates condition)
   A: This shows *that* the machine is not ready. (subordinate clause after the verb to explain 'show')

Exercise 1

Label the main clauses (MC) and the subordinate clauses (SC) in the following. Underline the co-ordinating conjunctions and circle the subordinating conjunctions.

> The Amco 75 went into production in the Spring. Sales were very good and we quickly established a significant market share. We have begun exporting the Amco 75, though early sales are weak. We will have a satisfactory year if our exports improve. Profit has gone up this year because our domestic sales have increased. Our research has been very productive but costs have risen. Now we have many competitors who are seen as important dangers in some key markets.

Exercise 2

Add appropriate conjunctions in the following dialogue. Choose from the box.

> who   because   or   ~~and~~   though   if

A: We need more office space _____**and**_____ our staff want more computer equipment.
B: Yes, we have agreed to recruit another secretary, _____ we have not decided when.
A: But we need one now. There will be problems _____ we don't get one soon.
B: I think there will be resignations _____ everyone is working too hard.
A: I agree. People will resign _____ they will simply be less effective at work.
B: I'm going to speak to Patrick, _____ will accept that the situation is critical.

Exercise 3

Look at the paragraph below. Hans Koeppel talks about his company. Count the sentences. Are they simple or complex? Below it is the same paragraph, rewritten with fewer sentences. Make them into complex sentences by putting one word in each space.

> I work for Arkop GmbH. Arkop makes car components. The company is based in Kirchheim. Kirchheim is in Southern Germany. This is a good location. Many of our customers are very close. We sell our products all over Germany. We also export a lot. Our domestic market is the most important part of our business.

I work for Arkop GmbH _____ makes car components. The company is based in Kirchheim, _____ is in Southern Germany. This is a good location _____ many of our customers are very close. We sell our products all over Germany _____ we also export a lot, _____ our domestic market is the most important part of our business.

Transfer

Write six simple sentences about a company or institution you know well. Then reduce the number of sentences by rewriting them as complex sentences.

58 Subordinate Clauses

A Sample sentences

- We worked quickly because we had to meet the deadline.
- After the MD presents the figures, you can ask your questions.
- I am going to buy a laptop so that I can work on the train.
- Although the mobile phone market has increased, growth has slowed.
- We have appointed a new Chief Executive, who used to work for ITCorp.

B Form

A subordinate clause depends on a main clause. It cannot stand by itself as a sentence.

We sold the premises because we needed to raise extra capital.

          main clause   subordinate clause

Typical subordinate clauses start with:

1. **that**:
   The MD said *that* the company was making good profits.

2. a subordinating conjunction:
   If sales improve, the company will soon be profitable again.

   The main subordinating conjunctions are:

because if   when   after   while   so that   so   (al)though

3. a **wh**-word or **how**-word:
   We don't know *when* the new product will be launched.

   the main **wh**-words and **how**-words are:

who   which   what   when   where   why   how   how much/many/long etc.

C Uses

Look at the following sentences. Each sentence has a subordinate clause; and each subordinate clause has a different meaning.

1. **because** – cause or reason:
   The business will succeed *because* we have recruited good staff.

2. **if** – condition:
   We will reduce the fee *if* you pay in advance.

3. **although** – contrast:
   Although we have reduced costs, profits have not increased.

   Notes
   We can use *though* or *although*.

4. **so that** – purpose:
   We are changing the way we do business *so that* we can compete more effectively.

5. **so (that)** – result:
   There was enough room *so (that)* we could invite twenty guests.

6. **after** – time:
   After you finish high school, you can go to university.

7. **wh**-word – reported question and relative clause:
   I would like to know *why* you are here. (reported question)
   They jointly own the company *which* will operate the pipeline. (relative clause)

Exercise 1

*Identify nine subordinating conjunctions or **wh**-words in the wordsquare below. There are five horizontal, three vertical and one diagonal.*

B	E	C	A	U	S	E
T	S	B	L	O	L	R
H	E	M	I	I	F	F
O	M	W	H	A	T	W
U	K	W	H	I	C	H
G	T	H	R	D	P	E
H	S	O	O	X	L	N

Exercise 2

Match the main clause on the left with an appropriate subordinate clause on the right.

Main clauses	Subordinate clauses
We will know if there are any problems	so it will need a lot of promotion.
The product will be launched next week	because we need a major new success.
It's a new concept	after the first six months' sales.
We are going to promote it heavily	who have always been our key market.
We will target young people	though at first only in the home market.

Exercise 3

Valbor Metal is trading in a difficult market. In an internal meeting, a member of the Board is talking about the problems. Complete the following text with words from the box.

if   though   so   where   which   because

'We need to increase our prices _____ our costs are rising. Many companies are in a similar position, _____ our costs are especially high. We have a strong export market _____ our sales are still good. We have identified some key problems _____ make the home market very difficult at present. We will have continued problems _____ we do not take some difficult decisions. There is no time to lose, _____ we have to do something quickly.'

Transfer

Write five sentences with subordinate clauses about the major employer in your home town, or about your company.

Relative Clauses with Who and Which

A Sample sentences

- **You need to speak to Chris Brown, who is in charge of marketing.**
- **The person who interviews you will supervise your work too.**
- **Most buyers are looking for a business which can grow.**
- **He applied for the post of sales director, which has been vacant since last month.**

B Form

A relative clause is a type of subordinate clause.
Relative clauses begin with a relative pronoun.
Who and **which** are typical relative pronouns.

I can't find the annual report	**which**	**they sent to us.**
main clause	relative pronoun	
	subordinate clause	

There are two types of relative clauses:
— defining relative clauses
— non-defining relative clauses.
The case *which I left at the airport* **has all my papers in it.** (defining)
Your case, *which has all your papers in it*, **is at the airport.** (non-defining)
A defining relative clause is written without commas; a non-defining relative clause
is written in commas.

C Uses

1. Defining relative clauses give information which is essential to understand the sentence:
   You are the only person who can answer this question.
   The clause **who can answer this question** identifies the person; without this information, the
   sentence has a different meaning.
   This is the machine which can print 25 pages a minute.
   The clause **which can print 25 pages a minute** identifies the machine; without this information,
   the sentence has a different meaning.

2. Non-defining relative clauses give additional, non-essential information:
   Norbert, who(m) we met in New York, is visiting London next month.
   The clause **who(m) we met in New York** gives additional information; we can still identify
   the person without this information.
   I've read all of your papers, which I found very interesting.
   The clause **which I found very interesting** gives additional information; we can still identify
   the papers without this information.

Exercise 1

Underline five relative clauses in the text below. Label them defining clauses (D) or non-defining clauses (ND).

**University College
Salisbury**

Tel: 01722 368359
Fax: 01722 368333

ANTIBIOTICS TODAY

The conference, which will discuss the action of antibiotics on diseases, will be held at University College, which is one of the oldest colleges in the city. People who wish to attend should send an application form to the President of the Society, who is in charge of bookings. Anyone who is presenting a paper at the conference will automatically receive full details.

Exercise 2

Combine the sentences below into single sentences with a relative clause.

1. Our clothes are very fashionable. They are popular with young people.
   Our clothes, which are very fashionable, are popular with young people.
2. The woman said our collection was wonderful. She is the editor of *Style*.
3. We use the best agencies to show our collection. They charge a lot of money.
4. We depend on magazine publicity. This increases our international reputation.
5. Many important magazine editors attend the fairs. They have massive influence.
6. The design team is very experienced. They plan our participation.

Exercise 3

Write sentences with the prompts below. Include relative clauses using the words in brackets.

1. Our company (makes floors) grow/by 10% per year.
   Our company, which makes floors, is growing by 10% per year.
2. The Director (came here yesterday) be/Italian.
3. Our main clients (in Europe) be/sports clubs.
4. In 2008 (record year) we/supply/floors/for the Olympic Games.
5. Our R and D institute (based at Newtown University) develop/new floor materials.
6. The floors (we/send/to Finland/last year) are specially for outdoor use.

Transfer

Write four sentences, including relative clauses, about the town where you live.

UNIT 60

Clauses of Cause or Reason with Because

See also
Unit 58   Subordinate clauses

A Sample sentences

- I am going to do the training because I will learn something from it.
- We spent the money because we needed new equipment.
- I am calling because I would like your help.

B Form

A clause of cause/reason is a type of subordinate clause.
Clauses of cause/reason begin with a subordinating conjunction. (See Unit 58.)
Because is a subordinating conjunction of cause or reason.

We manufacture in SE Asia	because	labour costs are low.
main clause	subordinating conjunction	
	subordinate clause	

C Uses

Clauses of cause or reason answer the question 'why?'; they present the cause or the reason.

A: Why are you leaving early?
B: I'm leaving because I want to catch my train.
A: And why are you joining ITCorp?
B: I am joining ITCorp because they have offered me an interesting job.
   And why are *you* moving to SoftSys?
A: Because I've worked at ITCorp for 15 years and I need a new challenge.

A: Why are profits down?
B: I think they are down because turnover has fallen.
A: And why has turnover fallen?
B: I am sure it has fallen because raw materials are more expensive.
A: And why are raw materials more expensive?
B: In my opinion, it's because we can't buy them from Rotaronga.

Exercise 1

Underline the clauses of cause or reason in the following extract.

> Our financial position changes during the year because our sales are seasonal. They are seasonal because we have always been specialists in winter clothing. This creates problems because in summer we have a shortage of money. We are planning to enter new markets because, if we do not, we will not survive.

Exercise 2

Complete the following by writing clauses of cause or reason based on the prompts below.

1. We need a new factory _____ **because our plant is too old.** _____
(our plant/be/too old)

2. We are going to build one next to the sea _____
(our business/need/sea transport)

3. This is also a good location _____
(we/be/near/train station)

4. We need a large development site _____
(we/build/big warehouse)

5. We do not need many staff _____
(the company/have/an automated process)

6. We will keep costs down _____
(we/plan to employ/few people)

Exercise 3

Use the prompts below to write a paragraph with clauses of cause or reason with **because**.

Example:

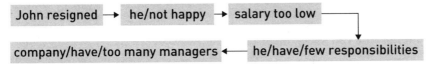

John resigned because he was not happy. He was not happy because his salary was too low. His salary was too low because he had few responsibilities. He had few responsibilities because the company had too many managers.

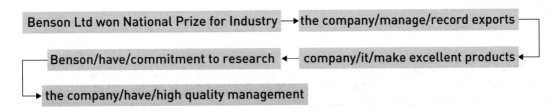

Transfer

Write a paragraph about your recent activities. Include examples of clauses of cause or reason with **because**.

UNIT 61

Singular and Plural Nouns

See also
Unit 62   Countable and uncountable nouns

A Sample sentences

- The company has its main office in Hershey, Pennsylvania.
- The company has branches in 172 countries.
- The Japanese subsidiary is in Nagoya.
- The organisation employs 180,000 people worldwide.

B Form

A noun is a grammatical unit. If we can put **a** or **an** in front of the singular form of the noun, we call it a countable noun. (See Unit 62 for uncountable nouns.)

a company   an account   an agent   a branch   a firm   an employer   a meeting   a magazine

We use **a** if the noun begins with a consonant; we use **an** if the noun begins with a vowel.

a job , a factory   a plant   an agency   an employee   an industry   an organisation an update (but *a union*)

We call these nouns countable because they have a singular and a plural form.

Singular	company	account	branch	firm	employer	meeting	magazine
Plural	companies	accounts	branches	firms	employers	meetings	magazines

After a singular noun we use a singular verb; after a plural noun we use a plural verb.

The   company   makes   cars.
    singular noun   singular verb

Our   Directors   often   travel   abroad.
    plural noun   plural verb

Notes

1. Some countable nouns only have a plural form. The most common is **people**:
There were 20 people at the meeting. (*not*: there was 20 people)

The singular of **people** is **person**:
There is only one person who can solve this problem.

2. Some nouns only have a plural form, but are not countable. Some common ones are:

assets (financial)	contents	funds (money)	headquarters	premises (buildings)	savings

C Uses

Look at the following sentences. Each sentence has at least one countable noun in the singular or the plural.

A: Where is your company based?
B: Our headquarters are in Bentonville, Arkansas, but we have branches all over the world.
A: And what about the market for your products?
B: At the moment the market is expanding and our turnover is increasing.
A: How many people does the company employ?
B: In total there are 3000 staff working for the company.

Exercise 1

Complete the following table. If no singular or plural form is possible, write x.
The first has been done for you.

singular	plural	singular	plural
export	**exports**	fish	
information		turnover	
research			records
	accountants	capital	
figure			sales

Exercise 2

Complete the following text by choosing the correct alternative for each noun.

Every *year/years* the company publishes its annual *account/accounts* in a report for the *shareholder/shareholders*. The main *detail/details* concern the financial report. This contains *information/informations* about *sale/sales*, *turnover/turnovers*, *cost/costs* and *profit/profits*. It also reports the *asset/assets* that are held by the company, and the *liability/liabilities*. These are any *debt/debts* or *cash/cashes* that the company owes. All this *data/datas* is presented in the *profit and loss/profits and losses* account and the balance sheet.

Exercise 3

Complete the dialogue by referring to the pictures a–e.

A: Where is your _____ (a)?
B: It's near Orleans but our _____ (b) is in Paris.
A: How many _____ (c) do you have?
B: About 2,000 including our _____ (d).
A: What's the annual _____ (e)?
B: This year it'll be about £85m.
A: And what will be the _____ (e) on that?
B: Around £5m.

G-Com International

SALES

G-Com
Estimate 4
(Year ending)

Turnover: £85m
Profit: £5m

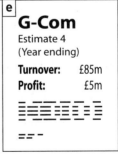

Transfer

Write a short paragraph including the following nouns used either in the singular or in the plural as necessary.

people	office	turnover	profit	work	staff	conditions
	information	money	problem	colleague	report	

Countable and Uncountable Nouns

See also
Unit 61   Singular and plural nouns

A Sample sentences

- We buy all our computers from one supplier. We believe that they make the best equipment.
- Airlines make big profits on transatlantic flights but they lose money locally.

B Form

A noun is a grammatical unit. If we can put **a** or **an** in front of the noun, we call it a **countable** noun. (See Unit 61 for singular and plural nouns.) If we can't put **a** or **an** in front of the noun, we call it an **uncountable** noun.

Countable	machine(s)	detail(s)	suggestion(s)	coin(s)	device(s)	job(s)	case(s)
Uncountable	machinery	information	advice	money	equipment	work	baggage

A countable noun has a singular and plural form; an uncountable noun has only one form.

We would like to buy a   **machine.**
                                     singular countable

We would like to buy 20   **machines.**
                                     plural countable

We would like to buy some   **machinery.**   (*not*: machineries)
                                     uncountable

After an uncountable noun we use a singular verb.

The   **information**   **is**   **in our brochure.**   (*not*: the informations are)
             uncountable noun   +   singular verb

The   **equipment**   **comes**   **from Rotaronga.**
             uncountable noun   +   singular verb

C Uses

Look at the following sentences. They show the use of countable and uncountable nouns.

A: Are you looking for a new job? (*not*: a new work)
B: Yes, my present work doesn't interest me. (*or* my present job)

A: I want to buy some camera equipment.
B: Well, my advice is to hire a camera to begin with. (*not*: my advices)

A: Could you give me some information about your training programmes? (*not*: some informations)
B: Of course, I'll send you some details.

A: Excuse me, sir, is this your baggage? (*not*: your baggages)
B: Yes, I have one suitcase and my wife has two suitcases.

Exercise 1

Read the following extract from a newspaper report. Mark all the nouns countable singular (C), countable plural (CP), uncountable singular (U) or uncountable plural (UP).

CHANGES IN RETAILING

The rationalisation of retailing has been a major characteristic of recent years and many small shops have disappeared. Large chains and supermarkets now dominate the sector. In the UK, 70% of food is sold by just four retailers. Many people have criticised this trend. They say it leaves the consumer with less choice.

Exercise 2

Underline the mistakes in the following sentences. Correct them.

1. Hello. I would like some informations about your products.

    Certainly. How can I help you?

2. How many works have you had since you left school?

    I've had four.

3. I asked my bank manager for an advice.

    What did he say?

    He told me to get a new work.

4. Please can I change this money? I need some coin for the telephone.

    With pleasure.

5. PLEASE DO NOT LEAVE BAGGAGES UNATTENDED

6. We have spent a lot of money on new machines.
   All the equipments in this room are new.

Exercise 3

Complete the following.
1. We don't have enough information. Ring them and ask for more d _____.
2. John works for a company that makes agricultural m _____.
3. We are a financial services company. We give a _____ on insurance, pensions and other aspects of money management.
4. I asked him for a _____. He made two s _____. First, do more advertising and secondly, find a new sales assistant.
5. Please can you help me with these c _____? They are very heavy.
6. John has changed his j _____. He now works for a bank.
7. Many p _____ work in insurance or banking, but most work in commerce.

Transfer

Write sentences using four countable and four uncountable nouns.

UNIT
63

Noun Compounds

See also	
Unit 61	Singular and plural nouns
Unit 62	Countable and uncountable nouns

A Sample sentences

- **The cost of making a telephone call has fallen.**
- **The advertising campaign was a big success.**
- **I went for a job interview today.**
- **He handed me his business card.**

B Form

A noun compound is a phrase with two or more nouns together, e.g.

computer   **software**
 noun   +   noun

1. The first noun is like an adjective; it gives more information about the second noun:
   A: I need some information.
   B: What type of information?
   A: I need some product information.

2. The first noun is normally in the singular:

finance director	*trade fair*	*fax machine*	but ***sales*** *manager*

C Uses

We use noun compounds because:

1. They are shorter:

   A: What about Severcide?
   B: There will be a major product launch in 2012. (*rather than* the launch of the product)
   A: And Herbigrade?
   B: We are shortly going to launch an advertising campaign. (*rather than* the campaign of advertising)

2. They have more impact:

   A: This approach to management development requires a serious commitment by the organization. (*rather than* the development of management)
   B: I agree. We need more training seminars. (*rather than* seminars for training)

3. Usually stress falls on the first word of the compound.

Notes
Some noun compounds are written as one word:
chequebook   taxpayer   newspaper   flowchart   notebook

Some are written with a hyphen:
factory-worker   work-force   air-conditioning   tape-recorder

Some are written as two words:
employment law   insurance claim   adult education   growth rate

Exercise 1

Make nine noun compounds from the following words.

weather	room	satellite	card	identity	clock
credit	alarm	container	hotel	dish	forecast
inflation	market	ship	rate	share	card

Exercise 2

Read the letter below. Rewrite it as a fax, replacing the underlined words with noun compounds.

EJ Metal Co Ltd, Unit 48, Clough Rd Industrial Estate, Hull, HU6 4PY
Tel. 01482 662841   Fax 01482 662800

ARCO Ltd   12 Mar 20...
210 Kingsway
Blaydon NE6 4PR

Dear Sir or Madam,

Please send some <u>information about products</u> and a <u>list of prices</u>. I also need details of your <u>services for customers</u> and <u>terms of payment</u>. In addition, I am interested in a <u>demonstration of your products</u>. I would like to arrange a meeting with one of your <u>representatives concerned with sales</u>. Are your running any special <u>promotions for sales</u> at the moment? Please send <u>message by fax</u> to the above number

Yours sincerely

P.J.O'Rourke

Fax from P.J.O'Rourke EJ Metal Co Ltd
Fax No 01482 662800 Tel 01482 662841
To 0191-484-333129
Attention: Sales Office
*Please send   * _____*
                    * _____*
*and details of   * _____*
*and   * _____*
I would like a _____ and I want to arrange a
meeting with a _____ . Also, do you have any
special _____ at present? Please send a _____
to the above number ASAP.
Thanks
P.J. O'Rourke

Exercise 3

Complete the noun compounds in the following.

1. *When do you eat in the middle of the day? I eat at about* **lunchtime**.
2. *If you apply for a job, you complete and send a j _____ a _____.*
3. *The result of the test is a t _____ r _____.*
4. *When you need to change money to another currency, you ask for the e _____ r _____.*
5. *If a company wants to spend money on advertising, it prepares an a _____ b _____.*
6. *Before getting on a plane, you have to wait in the d _____ l _____.*
7. *People who travel a lot on business make many b _____ t _____.*
8. *We use a lot of computers. We live in an age of i _____ t _____.*

Transfer

Look in an English language newspaper or magazine. Find ten examples of noun compounds.

Genitive Forms

See also
Units 61, 62, 63   Nouns

A Sample sentences

- **I disagree with Mr Bajaj's statement.**
- **The article appeared in today's edition of the Times.**
- **The company's sales fell by 3.8%.**
- **She looked around for the ladies' toilet.**

B Form

We form the genitive of a noun with an apostrophe (') or with the preposition **of**:
this year's results (= the results of this year)
the Directors' decisions (= the decisions of the directors)
the launch of the product
the cost of materials

Note
Where we form the genitive with an apostrophe, we write:
- — **'s** if the noun is singular, e.g. **the company's results** (= the results of the **company**)
- — **s'** if the noun is plural, e.g. **the companies' results** (= the results of the **companies**)

C Uses

1. We typically use the genitive with **'s** or **s'** with the following nouns:
   a. human nouns: **Dr Morton's job**
   b. animal nouns: **the dog's head**
   c. time nouns: **today's newspaper**
   d. location nouns: **America's economy**
   e. organisation nouns: **the Board's decision** (*but* the Chairman of the Board)

2. We use the genitive with **of** when referring to things:
   the Director of Research and Development
   the minutes of the meeting

Exercise 1

Underline genitive forms in the following extract from a speech by Alex Conrad, Chief Executive of Tambo Inc., a food manufacturer.

'Tambo's results are very good. Last year's figures were also pleasing, but now our turnover has improved by 15%. Our competitors' results are not as good. The work of all our staff has been excellent. Our products have answered the needs of our customers. The company's dedication to quality has been total. The decision of the Board to enter new markets was also very important. The former Chief Executive, Bill Machin, made a very big contribution – Bill's ideas made Tambo the success it is today.'

Exercise 2

Choose the correct genitive form for each of the following.

1. **a.** the car of Fred
   b. Fred's car
   c. Freds' car

2. **a.** the car of the Chief Executive
   b. the Chief Executive's car
   c. the Chief Executives' car

3. **a.** the market share of KLP is 12%
   b. KLP's market share is 12%
   c. KLPs' market share is 12%

4. **a.** the paper of yesterday
   b. yesterday's paper
   c. yesterdays' paper

5. **a.** the workers' canteen
   b. the canteen of the workers
   c. the worker's canteen

6. **a.** the design of the computer
   b. the computer's design
   c. the computers' design

Exercise 3

Complete the text below about the future for Frodo, an engineering company. Write appropriate genitive forms to combine the words in brackets.

The **results of the tests** *(results/tests)* were very good. The _____ *(report/Research Director)* was very positive. We hope that all _____ *(customers/Frodo)* will like the new product. We think it will meet _____ *(needs/our customers)*. I agree with _____ *(opinion/John Tudor)*. He thinks _____ *(market share/Frodo)* will increase. With this new product, _____ *(performance/next year)* will be very good. As always, we must focus on the _____ *(quality/our products and services)*. The _____ *(speech/Chairman)* at the AGM will say that quality and new products are most important.

Transfer

Look in an English language newspaper or magazine. Identify ten genitive forms.

UNIT 65

Adjectives vs. Adverbs

See also
Unit 66   Comparison of adjectives

A Sample sentences

- Our researchers are careful; they analyse the data carefully.
- The city has a real problem with crime; it will be really difficult to solve it.
- His claims are complete nonsense; these details are completely wrong.

B Form

Adjectives and adverbs are grammatical units.

1. Here are some typical adjective endings and adjective forms:

-ite	-ful	-al/-ial	-ive	-able/-ible
definite	useful	commercial	expensive	profitable
-less	-ous	-ing	-ed	-ant
useless	ambitious	interesting	interested	important

2. Other adjectives, particularly short ones, do not have special endings:

good   bad   young   old   big   small

3. Most adverbs are formed by adding **-ly** to the adjective:

Adjective	definite	useful	commercial	real	total
Adverb	definitely	usefully	commercially	really	totally

4. Some adjectives have the same form as adverbs:

hard   early   late   fast   straight
He is a hard worker. (adjective)
He words hard. (adverb)

C Uses

We use an adjective:

1. to give more information about a noun:

We need   skilful   managers.
          adjective   +   noun
What type of managers? *Skilful* **managers.**

2. after the verb be:
She is fluent in English. (*not*: fluently)

We use an adverb:

1. to give more information about a verb:

She speaks   English   fluently.
     verb   +   adverb

How does she speak English? *Fluently.*

2. to give more information about an adjective:

The sales forecast was completely   wrong.
                    adverb   +   adjective
How wrong is the sales forecast? *Completely* **wrong.**

3. to give more information about an adverb:

He chose his words   *extremely*   carefully.
                      adverb   +   adverb

4. to give more information about a sentence:
***Firstly,* I'd like to apologize.**

Exercise 1

Label eight adjectives (adj) and seven adverbs (adv) in the following extract from a report on MODO, a clothing company.

> Excellent results have helped MODO. In an unusually wet summer, the company did really well. The fashionable clothes were popular with young consumers. Now the company will definitely increase its production. Staff are busily planning an equally successful range for next year, but the market will be very competitive.

Exercise 2

Complete the crossword with adjectives and adverbs using the clues below.

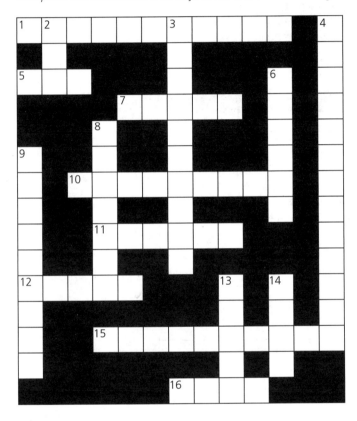

Across
- **1** competes well (11)
- **5** one left over; not even (3)
- **7** not right (5)
- **10** the same (9)
- **11** intelligent (6)
- **12** not late (5)
- **15** often (10)
- **16** difficult or not soft (4)

Down
- **2** not young (3)
- **3** new for the market (10)
- **4** more or less (13)
- **6** not going fast (6)
- **8** fundamental (7)
- **9** every three months (9)
- **13** obvious (5)
- **14** arriving when the plane has left (4)

Exercise 3

Complete the following dialogue. Two managers are discussing plans. Choose the correct alternative.

Alan: The changes in the market are going to affect the company quite *serious/seriously*.
Helga: We need to make some *quick/quickly* decisions.
Alan: We *urgent/urgently* need a new marketing strategy.
Helga: *Fortunately/fortunate*, the products are *excellent/excellently*.
Alan: I agree *absolute/absolutely*, but we have to get people *interesting/interested*.
Helga: I'm *confidently/confident* that we will do that.
Alan: Good, because our sales have fallen *dramatic/dramatically*.

Transfer

*Describe a business you know well. Describe its activities and trading performance. Use words like **good**, **big**, **usually**, **modern**, **quickly**, **absolutely**, etc.*

Comparison of Adjectives

See also
Unit 65   Adjectives vs. adverbs

A Sample sentences

- Prices are higher than in July last year.
- Train services are getting more expensive.
- Networking is the most effective way to find a job.
- Japan's crime rate is the lowest of any industrialized country.

B Form

Many adjectives have three forms: positive, comparative and superlative:
Last year Manson had *high* profits. (positive adjective)
Last year Burton had *higher* profits than Manson. (comparative adjective)
Checkout had *the highest* profits. (superlative adjective)

1. If the positive adjective has one syllable, we form the comparative
   by adding **-er** and the superlative by adding **-est**:

Positive	Comparative	Superlative
long	longer	longest
high	higher	highest
cheap	cheaper	cheapest

If we compare two objects, we use **than** in the comparative:
Burton's profits are higher *than* Manson's.
If we compare more than two objects, we use **the** in the superlative:
Checkout has *the* highest profits.

2. If the positive adjective has two syllables and ends in **-y**, **-ow** or **-le**, we form the comparative by
   adding **-er** and the superlative by adding **-est**. (If the adjective ends in **-y**, the **y** changes to **i**; if
   it ends in **-le**, we add **-r** and **-st**):

Positive	Comparative	Superlative
easy	easier	easiest
narrow	narrower	narrowest
simple	simpler	simplest

3. For other adjectives with two syllables or more, we form the comparative with **more** and
   the superlative with **most**:

Positive	Comparative	Superlative
modern	more modern	most modern
expensive	more expensive	most expensive
competitive	more competitive	most competitive

4. There is a small group of adjectives with irregular comparative and superlative forms:

Positive	good	bad	little	much	far
Comparative	better	worse	less	more	farther/further
Superlative	best	worst	least	most	farthest/furthest

C Uses

1. If we compare two objects, we use **than** in the comparative:
   Burton's products are more expensive *than* Manson's, but their profits are higher.
2. If we compare more than two objects, we use **the** in the superlative:
   Checkout has *the* most expensive prices and *the* highest profits.

Exercise 1

Complete the following table.

Positive	Comparative	Superlative
cheap		
strong		
modern		
	more useful	
	worse	
		most experienced
near		
	more comfortable	
weak		
		most difficult
		most
	less	

Exercise 2

Look at the graph. Mark the sentences true (T) or false (F).

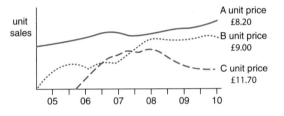

unit sales

A unit price £8.20
B unit price £9.00
C unit price £11.70

05   06   07   08   09   10

1. Product B is the most successful. ☐

2. Product A has sold more than product B. ☐

3. Product C is the least expensive. ☐

4. Product B is cheaper than product A. ☐

5. Product A is the oldest. ☐

6. Product B is newer than product C. ☐

Exercise 3

Look at the table below comparing three banks.

	Capital reserves ($)	Market share %	Branches
Rotobank Ltd (RB)	1,200m	4	750
Credit Bank Int (CB)	1,955m	9	1470
Gold Bank Inc (GB)	11,000m	2	620

*Write sentences comparing the three banks. Use forms of **small**, **big**, **much** (2), **strong**.*

Gold Bank has **the fewest** branches. It has a _____ market share than Rotobank Ltd.
Gold Bank has _____ capital reserves. It is _____ bank. In terms of branches, Credit
Bank International is _____ than the other two banks. It has many _____ branches. It
also has _____ capital reserves than Rotobank Ltd.

Transfer

Compare your country with another country you know. Write six sentences.

UNIT 67   Adverbs

See also
Unit 65   Adjectives vs. adverbs

A Sample sentences

- **Firstly, we offer information and advice.**
- **The computer will be delivered soon.**
- **Please check your order carefully.**
- **Government spending is slightly higher than forecast.**

B Form

1. Most adverbs are formed by adding **-ly** to the adjective, e.g. **quick – quickly**. (See Unit 65.)
2. Some adjectives have the same form as adverbs, e.g. **hard**, **late**. (See Unit 65.)
3. Some adverbs have no adjective form, e.g. **very**, **soon**, **outside**.
4. The adverb of **good** is **well**.

C Uses

1. There are three types of adverbs:

   a. Adverbs of place answer the question **where?**:
   Her husband was working abroad. (Where was her husband working? Abroad.)
   You can eat outside if you want to. (Where can you eat? Outside.)
   I'm afraid Dr Fleischer has gone home. (Where has Dr Fleischer gone? Home.)

   b. Adverbs of time answer the question **when?**, **how long?** or **how often?**:
   Can we talk about this tomorrow? (When can we talk about this? Tomorrow.)
   I have always lived in Boston. (How long have you lived in Boston? Always.)
   We never sell any of our mailing lists. (How often do you sell you mailing lists? Never.)
   (See Unit 67.)

   c. Adverbs of manner answer the question how?:
   The unemployment rate rose steadily. (How did it rise? Steadily.)
   I am very pleased by the progress we made. (How pleased? Very pleased.)
   The company is performing quite well. (How is the company performing? Well. How well? Quite well.)

2. Position of adverbs
   We can often put adverbs in different positions in a sentence. The three main positions are:

At the beginning	In the middle	At the end
Soon profits will increase.	Profits will *soon* increase.	Profits will increase *soon*.

   The position of the adverb in the middle depends on the verb:
   I often travel abroad. (before the verb where there are no auxiliaries)
   I have often travelled abroad. (after the first auxiliary)
   I am usually at my desk by 8 o'clock. (after the verb **be**)
   Where there is both an adverb of place and an adverb of time at the end of a sentence, you put place before time, e.g. **He went abroad yesterday.** (*not*: yesterday abroad)

Exercise 1

Label the adverbs below place (P), time (T) or manner (M).

> fast   abroad   never   quietly   soon   on time
> currently   late   outside   tomorrow   hard   since Monday

Exercise 2

Mr Roach had to go to a business meeting at 2 o'clock. Look at the pictures below. Complete the sentences using words from the box.

> calmly   yesterday   suddenly   fortunately   urgently
> just in time   too late   very fast   early   immediately

1. _____ Mr Roach got up _____.

2. He had a coffee, then _____ began to read the paper.

3. _____ he noticed the time.

4. _____ he ran out of the house.

5. He looked _____ for a taxi.

6. The taxi went _____ to the airport.

7. He was _____ for the plane.

8. _____, he was not _____ for the meeting.

Exercise 3

Complete the following short dialogue. Use the words in the box.

> immediately   ~~out~~   back   carefully   well   later   tomorrow

A: Is Mrs King there?
B: No, sorry. She is **out**.
A: When will she be _____?
B: Perhaps she'll be back _____ today.
A: OK. I'll phone _____.
B: Can I take a message?
A: Well, yes please. Tell her the meeting with Blanchard went very _____. We have to prepare a contract _____, but it must be done _____. The details are very important.
B: OK. Thanks. Goodbye.

Transfer

How long have you lived in your town?
How well do you speak English?

When do you normally have a holiday?
Where do you go after work?

A Sample sentences

- **How often do you see her?**
- **We always keep cash for emergencies.**
- **He rarely goes out to dinner.**
- **The industry holds a trade exhibition twice a year.**

B Form

We can divide expressions of frequency into indefinite frequency and definite frequency.

1. Indefinite frequency

These phrases tell us approximately how often something happens:

most often

always
usually/normally
often
sometimes
rarely/seldom
never

least often

We usually sell our products through a network of agents.
They never offer our competitors' products.

2. Definite frequency

These phrases tell us more precisely how often something happens in a period of time:

Frequency	Time
once	a minute
twice	an hour
three times	a day
four times	a week
five times	a month
many times	a year

Frequency	Time
every	minute
every	morning
every	night
every	year
every	Monday
every	July

Frequency
hourly
weekly
monthly
quarterly
annually
yearly

We review our sales figures twice a year.
We print a new brochure annually.

C Uses

1. Questions about frequency:
How often do you go to head office?

2. Statements about frequency:
We normally charge £25 for replacing cards which have been lost or stolen.
(See Unit 67 C2 for position of adverbs.)
Usually the employer pays a certain number of dollars per hour. (special emphasis)
We launch new products twice a year. (normal position)
Once a year we carry out a customer survey. (special emphasis)

Exercise 1

Make frequency adverbs from the following jumbled letters. Then number them 1–7, in order of frequency.

tofne	yerlar	yasclinloaoc	reenv	sawyal	queenfrytl	emositsem
				always		
				1		

Exercise 2

Complete the following phrases with an expression of frequency, based on the word(s) in brackets.

1. *I go to London _____ (January and June).*

2. *We have meetings _____ (Monday, Tuesday, Wednesday, etc.).*

3. *Our share price changes _____ (1 p.m., 2 p.m., etc.).*

4. *I write a sales report _____ (Friday afternoon).*

5. *We report to Head Office _____ (Monday, Wednesday and Friday).*

6. *Our Sales Report is published _____ (December).*

7. *I _____ go to America on business (zero).*

Exercise 3

Two people are in an airport department lounge in Amsterdam. They are waiting for a flight to New York. Complete part of the conversation with frequency expressions from the box.

> always   how often   frequently   usually(2)   times a day
> twice   normally   sometimes   rarely   never

Wim: _____ do you go to New York?

Maurice: _____ We have an office there, so I have to go about once or _____ a month.

Wim: Do you _____ fly with KLM?

Maurice: Well, I _____ use KLM because my partner works in Amsterdam. I _____ visit him before I go to New York, but I _____ fly British Airways from London.

Wim: Are there a lot of flights to New York from London?

Maurice: Oh yes. There's one about six _____.

Wim: Well, before the flight, I'll get some Duty Free. I _____ get something.

Maurice: Really? I _____ do. I don't smoke and I _____ drink so I don't buy anything from Duty Free.

Transfer

Write sentences about what you do and do not do. Use frequency adverbs to say how often.

Degree with Very, Too and Enough

See also	
Unit 67	Adverbs

A Sample sentences

- It is very difficult to estimate the size of the market.
- There is too much work for one person.
- The building is not big enough for our needs.

B Form

Very, too and enough are adverbs. (See Unit 67.)
We put **very** and **too** before an adjective or adverb:
Rotaronga is a very industrial region.
                        adjective
In fact, industry has grown too quickly.
                        adverb
We put **enough** after an adjective or adverb:
Social services have not increased fast enough.
                        adverb

Note
We put **enough** before a noun:
The area already has enough factories.
                        noun

C Uses

1. **Very** makes the meaning of an adjective or adverb stronger:
   A: **All his staff are intelligent.**
   B: **Yes, and some of them are very intelligent.**
   A: **They answered our questions quickly.**
   B: **Yes, but they didn't answer them very accurately.**

2. **Too** means more (or less) than necessary; **enough** means acceptable:
   A: **Our manufacturing time is too slow.**
   B: **I agree, it is not fast enough. But our workers are well paid.**
   A: **Yes, but they think their wages are not high enough. They think they are paid too little.**

3. Now look at the following dialogue:
   A: **Sales were not very good this year.**
   B: **I know, and the costs are too high.**
   A: **Our customer service is not fast enough.**
   B: **I agree. We must do something very quickly.**

Exercise 1

Add **very**, **too** or **enough** to the following phrases.

_____ time   _____ dangerous   _____ difficult

not big _____   strong _____   _____ important

_____ beautiful   _____ profitable   _____ many people

Exercise 2

Complete the comments on these dishes in a restaurant.

1. 'There's _____ much on the plate.'   **4.** 'I can't eat this! It's _____ hot!'

2. 'I'm hungry! This isn't _____.'   **5.** 'This looks _____ good.'

3. 'The table's _____ small.'   **6.** 'The meal was _____ expensive.'

Exercise 3

Complete the following exchanges with appropriate words.

A: There's a lot of traffic on the roads.
B: Yes, I agree. There's _____ much.
A: The Chien Andalou restaurant is one of the best in town.
B: Yes, and not _____ expensive. Everything is _____ fresh.

A: I like jazz music.
B: Yes, if it isn't _____ modern.
A: A lot of modern jazz is _____ good.

A: How was your meeting with Kashamuro?
B: Good.
A: How good?
B: Good _____. We agreed to work together.

Transfer

Write six sentences about yourself and your work or studies. Include **very**, **too** and **enough**.

Already, Yet, Again and Still

See also
Unit 67   Adverbs

A Sample sentences

- **Have you got your medical insurance yet?**
- **We have already sold more than 300 units.**
- **When will you play it again?**
- **The company can still afford to advertise.**

B Form

Already, yet, **again** and **still** are adverbs of time. (See Unit 68.)

1. We put **already** at the end of a sentence or in the middle of a sentence:
   We have prepared the sales forecast already.
   We already use the latest software; we have already installed it on our PCs.

2. We usually put **yet** at the end of a sentence:
   A: Have you signed the contract yet?
   B: Yes, but I haven't sent it back yet.

3. We usually put **again** near the end of a sentence:
   A: I look forward to hearing from you again soon.
   B: Right. So, I'll contact you again next week.

4. Note the position of **still**:
   The building is still under construction. (after the verb **be**)
   They are still constructing the warehouse. (after the first modal or auxiliary)
   We still plan to open the new factory in September. (before the main verb)

C Uses

1. **Already** means 'by this/that time'; we use it in positive statements:
   This year we have already hired 50 people. (by this time, i.e. by now)

2. **Yet** means 'by this/that time'; we use it in negative statements and questions:

   A: Have you filled in your tax return yet? (by now)
   B: No, in fact I haven't got the form yet.

3. **Still** means 'up to this/that time':
   I am still working on the case. (up to this time) (I haven't finished it yet.)
   Mr Broadbridge was still finalising arrangements yesterday. (up to that time)
   (He hadn't finished making arrangements yet.)

4. **Again** means 'another time' or 'as before':
   Profits are increasing again. (as before)

Exercise 1

*Read the following text. Underline examples of **already**, **yet**, **again** and **still**. Then mark the statements that follow as true (T) or false (F).*

> John is still waiting for a new contract. The company have not agreed the terms yet. John may leave. In fact he's already had an interview with another company. Anyway, tomorrow he's going to talk to his boss again about the contract.

1. John has already agreed a new contract. ☐

2. He has still not agreed the terms of his contract. ☐

3. He has already left the company. ☐

4. He has already discussed the contract with his boss. ☐

5. He is going to see his boss again. ☐

Exercise 2

*Choose **already**, **yet**, **again** or **still** to complete the dialogue below.*

Lee: Are you _____ selling the Arco 26?
Klaus: Yes, it is _____ doing well.
Lee: Have you made a replacement _____?
Klaus: Yes, the Arco 28 is _____ available.
Lee: Are you going to stop making the 26?
Klaus: Yes, but not _____.
Lee: I thought you planned to stop making it.
Klaus: Last year we planned to stop, but we changed our mind. This year we also planned to stop, but _____ we have continued. The 26 is _____ very popular.

Exercise 3

Complete the text below with a word in each space.

Last year our sales overseas were down. This year exports are _____ poor. We expect low export profits _____, but the good news is that in our domestic market we have _____ reached our targets. Overall, things are not serious _____. The situation will be clearer at the end of the year.

Transfer

*Write six sentences about your actions or your plans. Include **already**, **yet**, **again** and **still**.*

UNIT

71

Articles

See also
Units 61, 62   Nouns

A Sample sentences

- They signed a contract to purchase two planes.
- He's an agent for an insurance company.
- The address of the company is on the policy.
- At present sales are increasing.

B Form

There are three forms of the article:

1. a(n) – the indefinite article:
Can I make a phone call?

2. the – the definite article:
The phone is on the left.

3. 0 – the zero article:
There are phones in all offices.

C Uses

1. A(n) – the indefinite article
We use **a(n)** with singular countable nouns (see Unit 61) when we use a word
for the first time:
A computer usually has a keyboard.

2. 0 – the zero article
We use the zero article with:
  a. uncountable nouns:
   Hardware and software are getting cheaper.
  b. plural countable nouns, when we are speaking generally:
   Computers are very useful machines.
  c. proper names and places:
   Mr Brown arrived at Charles de Gaulle airport at 9.30.

3. The – the definite article
We use the definite article when:
  a. we mention a word for the second time:
   A computer usually has a hard disk. The hard disk stores data.
   (**a** for the first mention; **the** for the second)
  b. it is clear what the speaker means:
   The PC on the desk is new. (There is only one PC on the desk.)
   You'll find your new PC on the desk. (There is only one desk.)
  c. we talk about institutions:
   The Minister of Education made a speech at the University of Ontario.
   Did you see it on the TV?

Exercise 1

A travel agent telephones Henry Fish with details of his trip to Münster in Germany. Underline all definite and indefinite articles. Indicate zero articles before uncountable nouns and before plural countable nouns with a zero (Ø).

'Mr Fish? I have, got details for your trip to Münster today. First, the flight. There's a British Airways flight from London Heathrow to Düsseldorf at 16.05 from Terminal 1. It arrives at I7.35. Then you can take a train to Münster from the central station at 18.45. The train arrives in Münster at 20.15. Coming back there's a flight to Manchester at 16.30, arriving at Manchester Airport at 17.50. There are trains every hour from Manchester to Leeds. You also asked about money and the ticket. You can change money at Heathrow and pick up the flight ticket from the B.A. desk in Terminal 1.'

Exercise 2

Read the dialogue about a problem in a chemical plant. Put in articles where necessary.

Arne: We've got _____ important safety problem on _____ production line in _____ West Building. _____ machine is not working properly.

Steve: Have you taken any action?

Arne: Yes, one of _____ engineers has switched it off. _____ valve is losing _____ oil.

Steve: What did _____ maintenance say?

Arne: _____ technician said he thinks _____ valve needs to be replaced.

Steve: So, are we losing _____ production?

Arne: Yes. As _____ result, _____ production is down by 15%.

Exercise 3

Below is an advertisement flyer from Beelo OE Ltd, office furniture designers. Complete the text with definite or indefinite articles in the spaces if necessary.

Beelo Comodo 20

On _____ left is _____ new office chair, _____ *Comodo 20*. Like all _____ Beelo chairs, it is made from _____ materials that are totally _____ fire resistant, but last _____ very long time. _____ tests allow us to give you _____ 5 year warranty on this superb chair. Great _____ value at only to $149.95.

OFFICE COMFORT!
OFFICE STYLE!

For rapid service telephone **FREEPHONE** 800800 **now!!**

Transfer

Look at any short text from an advertisement, a newspaper or a magazine in English. Circle the use of ten definite, indefinite, or zero articles.

A Sample sentences

- **We are going to meet them tomorrow.**
- **I'll send them full details.**

B Form

We use a pronoun in place of a noun:

The company is based in Bolton. **It** **employs 200 people.**
                                    (= the company)
This is the Marketing Director. **She** **joined the organisation three years ago.**
                          (= the female Marketing Director)

Personal pronouns have two forms: subject and object.

Personal pronouns		Subject	Object
1st person singular		I	me
plural		we	us
2nd person singular		you	you
plural		you	you
3rd person singular masculine		he	him
feminine		she	her
non-personal		it	it
plural		they	them

I'll **call** **you** **next week.**
subject   +   object
We **showed all the samples to** **them.**
subject   +   object

Notes
1. We use **he/him** for men and boys; we use **she/her** for women and girls;
   we use **it** for all non-personal forms.

2. We use the object form after prepositions:
   The information will be with them next week.

C Uses

A: **I'd like to introduce you to Karen Pusey.**
B: **I met her last week. She is the new publisher.**
A: **Yes, you are right. I forgot you were with us here last week.**

Note
I am sending you our latest catalogue. (I = the person)
We are sending you our latest catalogue. (We = the company)

Exercise 1

Underline 13 personal pronouns in the dialogue below.

Alice: Good morning. Ascis Ltd. How can I help you?
Don: Hello, Alice. Don Peters here. I'm calling from Bangkok.
Alice: Mr Peters, nice to hear you again. How are things?
Don: Oh fine. We're doing very well. Now, I'd like to talk to Lena. Is she in?
Alice: No, she had to go to Luxembourg to talk to our agents. They're having a meeting today. But Paul's here. Do you want to speak to him?
Don: OK, I'll do that. Thank you.

Exercise 2

Wim van der Jonk visits Educo, an Irish producer of educational materials. Here is part of a conversation with Joe Keeley, a Sales Manager. Write personal pronouns in the spaces.

Joe: So, what can _____ do for _____?
Wim: Well, _____ wonder if you can help _____ ? My company imports DVDs for schools and colleges. _____ would like a catalogue and a price list. Can _____ let _____ have these?
Joe: Of course. Tell _____, where are _____ from?
Wim: My company is A-Tech nv. _____ are based in Rotterdam, in the Netherlands.
Joe: Really? _____ have two agents in Amsterdam. _____ usually handle our Dutch business. Would _____ like to contact _____?
Wim: Oh yes. That would be fine.
Joe: One is Willy Leer. _____'s Dutch. The other is Susan Griffin. _____'s English. _____'ll give _____ all the details.

Exercise 3

Rewrite the email below. Replace the words in brackets with personal pronouns.

Date:	15/03/2011
To:	john.krupp@bwdpress.co.uk
From:	sam.beeley@bwdpress.co.uk
Subject:	Andrew Heysink

Dear John

I have sent (John) by email a report on the above employee. (Andrew Heysink) has been unwell for some weeks. (Andrew Heysink) is unable to do his work. (The Personnel Department) have suggested a transfer to the kitchen. Unfortunately the kitchen staff are not happy. (The kitchen staff) have referred to Susan Jenkins. (Susan Jenkins) was made redundant 4 weeks ago to reduce costs. (John and Sam) should meet to discuss a solution. Please contact (Sam) as soon as possible.

Best regards
Sam

Date:	15/03/2011
To:	john.krupp@bwdpress.co.uk
From:	sam.beeley@bwdpress.co.uk
Subject:	Andrew Heysink

Transfer

Write one or two paragraphs about some of your colleagues. Include as many personal pronouns as you can. Underline the personal pronouns.

Example:
Two colleagues work with <u>me</u>. <u>They</u> are ...

UNIT 73 Possessive and Reflexive Pronouns

See also
Unit 72   Personal pronouns

A Sample sentences

- **We scheduled our meeting for the next morning.**
- **She sailed the Atlantic Ocean by herself.**
- **We discussed my ideas to reorganize the company.**
- **Their products are not as good as ours.**

B Form

We use a pronoun in place of a noun.

1. We use a possessive pronoun in place of a possessive (genitive) noun:
   A: My name is Robert Wagner.
   B: Pleased to meet you. Mine's Sandra Fratelli.

2. We use a reflexive pronoun when the object is the same as the subject:
   I   would like to introduce   myself.
   subject   =   object

| | Possessive | | Reflexive |
	Determiner	Pronoun	
1st person singular	my	mine	myself
plural	our	ours	ourselves
2nd person singular	your	yours	yourself
plural	your	yours	yourselves
3rd person singular masculine	his	his	himself
feminine	her	hers	herself
non-personal	its	its	itself
plural	their	theirs	themselves

Notes
1. We use the possessive determiner in front of a noun:
   We would like to reduce   our   overheads.
                    possessive determiner   +   noun

2. We use the possessive pronoun in place of a possessive determiner + noun:
   A: Our company employs 300 people. What about yours? (your company)
   B: Ours is much smaller. (our company)

C Uses

1. Possessive pronouns:
   A: My company develops software products. (I am the owner of the company.)
   B: Are you the owner?
   A: Yes, the company is mine. (mine = my company)

   A: More than 600 people work at our factory in Chippewa Falls.
   (I am an employee of the company.)
   B: So many?
   A: Yes, ours is the biggest factory in the group. (ours = our factory)

2. Reflexive pronouns:
   Welcome to our first meeting. First, I'd like to introduce myself. I'm Janet Aspinall.
   Now could you say a few words about yourselves?

TASKS

Exercise 1

Underline examples of possessive and reflexive pronouns in the extract below. Label them
R *(reflexive),* ***PD*** *(possessive determiners) or* ***PP*** *(possessive pronouns).*

As you know we did the market research ourselves. I am sending our report to all managers. Their comments can be sent to me before our next meeting. Michael and Maria will study the comments. Their job will be to produce a new version of the report. The final conclusion will also be theirs. Alex Jenner may also add something himself. Everyone should feel that his or her views have been fully considered. Naturally, all opinions are important, including yours, so do contact me if you need to.

Exercise 2

Correct the following sentences.

1. Mary works by himself.
2. She keeps a record of all ourselves accounts.
3. Fred and Alex made this prototype. It's his design and they made it himselves.
4. Anna works here. This is hers office.
5. Can you tell me about you?
6. I work for me. I'm self employed.
7. I own the company. It's of me.

Exercise 3

Complete the sentences below each picture. Include a possessive or reflexive pronoun.

1. Fred hurt _____.
   He hit _____ finger.

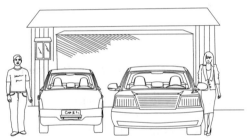

3. Marta and Jack have cars. _____
   is big, _____ is small.

2. Sally types all _____
   letters _____.

4. We do all _____ designs _____.
   Even the packaging is _____.

Transfer

Write five sentences about you and your family, or about colleagues at work. Use possessive and reflexive pronouns.

Demonstratives

A Sample sentences

- **A: Hello, is that the Marketing Department?**
  B: No, this is Customer Services.

- **A: I don't think these results are correct.**
  B: Well, I've checked those results very carefully. I think they are right.

B Form

Demonstratives point to something near or something far away:
I don't understand this analysis. (the analysis here)
I didn't attend that presentation. (the presentation there or then)

Demonstratives can be pronouns (see Unit 72) or determiners:
Could you spell   that,   please. (= that word or name)
                      pronoun
Those   points are very important.
determiner

	Singular	Plural
Near reference	this	these
Far reference	that	those

C Uses

1. Near reference can be:
  a. near in space:
    His secretary left these documents for you to look at. (the documents here)
  b. near in time:
    Can I come and stay with you this week? (the week now)
  c. near in the text:
    Payment should reach us by 1st July. This guarantees your rights. (payment by 1st July)

2. Far reference can be:
  a. far in space:
    Look at those two men. (the two men there)
  b. far in time:
    A: Can we meet on Tuesday?
    B: I'm afraid I will be in Auckland that day. (the day then)
  c. far in the text:
    In your report you recommended early payment. I don't think that is a good idea.
    (early payment)

Exercise 1

Cathy is showing a visitor around her company. Look at the demonstratives in the sentences below. Label them near (N) or far (F) + singular (S) or plural (P). The first has been done for you.

1. 'This (**NS**) is Peter, our Warehouse Manager.'
2. 'That's (   ) our Finance Department.'
3. 'Those (   ) vans are local deliveries.'
4. 'This (   ) is where we take telephone orders.'
5. 'These (   ) goods are ready for despatch.'
6. 'That (   ) order is for a customer in Dubai.'

Exercise 2

Carla and Petra are spending an evening together in a hotel. Complete the following exchanges with appropriate demonstratives.

1. *(In the hotel lobby.)*

   Carla: What are all _____ people doing here?

   Petra: I think there is a conference here tomorrow.

2. *(Entering the bar.)*

   Carla: _____ is a nice bar!

   Petra: Yes, very nice!

3. *(Later, in the restaurant.)*

   Waiter: Good evening. _____ is your table by the window.

4. *(Looking at the menu.)*

   Carla: _____ is a difficult decision. There are so many good things to eat.

5. *(After the meal.)*

   Petra: _____ meal was really good.

   Carla: Yes, I really liked the fish.

   Petra: Yes, _____ langoustines were superb.

6. *(At the end of the evening.)*

   Carla: _____ was a very pleasant evening. Thank you very much.
   I'll see you tomorrow at about 9 o'clock.

Exercise 3

Alex works for a drinks manufacturer. He is making a presentation. Complete the spaces with a demonstrative.

1. _____ picture shows our best seller, ZIGGO. _____ is very popular with children. A few minutes ago I mentioned PIPPO. _____ is also mainly for children.

2. Last year we agreed new prices. Now we know _____ prices were too low.

3. In terms of market share, there are five very small players. At least two of _____ will disappear, either _____ year or next.

Transfer

*Look around you. Write four sentences about things you can see using **this**, **these**, **that** and **those**.*

UNIT 75   Some and Any

See also	
Units 61, 62	Nouns
Unit 76	**Some, any** and related words

A Sample sentences

- We are waiting for the delivery of some new equipment.
- I didn't buy any tickets.
- Have you received any information about the event?
- If you have any further questions, please call me.

B Form

Some and **any** can be pronouns (see Unit 72) and determiners.

1. We use a pronoun in place of a noun:
   A: We need more toner for our printer. I'd like to order some. (some toner)
   B: And what about paper?
   A: No, we don't need any at present. (any paper)

2. We use a determiner in front of a noun:
   A: Do you have any questions?
   B: Yes, I have some questions about your figures.

	Positive statements	Negative statements	Questions
	some	any	any
Determiner	I need some information.	I don't need any information.	Do you need any information?
Pronoun	I'd like some, please.	I don't need any.	Do you need any?

C Uses

We use **some** and **any** with plural nouns, e.g. **managers**, and with uncountable nouns, e.g. **information**.

1. Some
   a. in positive statements:

   A: We are interested in buying some computer keyboards. (**some** + plural noun)
   B: I see. We have some in stock at present. I can show you some now. (pronoun)
   A: Good. I'd like to see some different equipment. (**some** + uncountable noun)

   b. in polite offers:

   B: Would you like to see some now? (pronoun)

2. Any
   a. in questions:

   A: Do you sell any American products? (**any** + plural noun)
   B: Yes, we sell this keyboard, but have you read any information about it?
      (**any** + uncountable noun)

   b. in negative statements:

   A: No, I haven't seen any. (pronoun)
      I haven't read any reports about this model. (**any** + plural noun)

Exercise 1

*Steve Marshall and Ben Long work for an engineering company. Steve has just returned from a week in Kuala Lumpur, at a trade fair. Underline examples of **some** and **any**. Label the sentence with **some** or **any** as positive statement (PS), negative statement (NS) or question (Q).*

Ben: How was Kuala Lumpur? Any contracts?
Steve: Excellent. We made some good contacts.
Ben: Contacts? I said did you get any contracts?
Steve: No, we didn't get any contracts. But I'm sure we'll get some soon.
Ben: I hope so. We've had some good news this week.
Steve: What was that?
Ben: Our American agent wants some more PX100s.
Steve: Good. Have they sold any more PX50s?
Ben: Some, but not many.

Exercise 2

Identify six mistakes in the following. Correct them.

Paula: We haven't launched any new products this year. Last year we had any. Four, in fact. We need some for next year.
Mohammad: I would like to show you designs.

Paula: Have you some pictures of the new designs?
Mohammad: No, we haven't some yet, but some will be ready next week.

Presenter: Some questions?
Participant: Yes, I've got some. Do you have some plans to build a new production centre?

Exercise 3

*Two colleagues are talking about a printing job. Put **some** or **any** in the spaces.*

A: Have we got _____ paper for the printer?
B: _____, but not much. We've got _____ more on order.

A: Good. I've got to print _____ reports.
B: If they are urgent, take them to the Sales Office. They usually have paper if we haven't _____ left.

A: The printer wasn't working yesterday!
B: It was fine. There just wasn't _____ toner left. I put _____ in. It's fine now.

Transfer

*Write a short dialogue about buying something in a shop or from a company Sales Office. Include **some** and **any**.*

UNIT 76 Some, Any and Related Words

See also
Unit 75   **Some** and **any**

A Sample sentences

- Someone must install the equipment before it can be used.
- Do you want to add anything to what I've said?
- Nobody in the company received an appraisal last month.
- Our pricing strategy is similar to any other business.

B Form

Below are the main forms of **some**, **any** and **no** words:

	Some words	Any words	No words
People	someone, somebody	anyone, anybody	no-one, nobody
Things	something	anything	nothing
Place	somewhere	anywhere	nowhere

C Uses

1. **Some** words
   We use these in positive statements:
   I spoke to someone from the marketing department.
   He told me something about the charity's work.
   I met him somewhere near Rennes.

2. **Any** words
   We use these in negative statements and questions:
   A: Does anyone have any questions? (*not*: any question)
   B: You didn't say anything about the location of the new equipment.
   A: You can install it near the main area.
   B: But can we place it anywhere?

3. **No** words
   We use these in negative statements and questions:
   No-one has accepted the offer.
   Is there nothing else that we can do?
   The car is now produced in Mexico and nowhere else.

Exercise 1

*Underline examples of **some**, **any** and related words in the text below. Label them positive statement (PS), negative statement (NS) or question (Q).*

A: Is anything wrong?

B: Yes, there's something wrong with one of our production machines. No-one knows what the problem is. We've looked in the User's Manual but we can't find the solution anywhere.

A: Have you contacted the manufacturers?

B: Yes, they think it's nothing very complicated. They're sending someone to visit us. He'll be here soon. He was already somewhere near here.

Exercise 2

Choose the best meaning a, b, or c for the sentences 1–5.

1. Some people prefer small hotels.
  a. All people prefer small hotels.
  b. Most people prefer small hotels.
  c. A number of people prefer small hotels.

2. I knew no-one at the meeting.
  a. I knew everyone at the meeting.
  b. There was not one person I knew at the meeting.
  c. I knew only one person at the meeting.

3. We sell anything you want.
  a. We have everything you want.
  b. We have most things you want.
  c. Sorry, we can't help you.

4. We can send orders anywhere.
  a. You have to collect your orders.
  b. We can deliver to most places.
  c. We can deliver to any place you choose.

5. There's something wrong with the figures.
  a. The figures are all wrong.
  b. The figures are partly wrong.
  c. There is one mistake in one figure.

Exercise 3

Ella and Pat are staying in a hotel. They are talking about problems. Complete the spaces in the conversation. Use words from the box.

anyone nothing somewhere something anywhere someone no-one anything

Pat: I hear you lost _____ yesterday.

Ella: Yes, my mobile phone. I wanted to phone _____ but I couldn't find the phone _____.

Pat: You must have put it down _____.

Ella: Yes, I asked at reception. They knew _____ about it.

Pat: So _____ found it?

Ella: No. I asked reception to call me if _____ found _____.

Transfer

Is there anyone working with you who speaks French? Have you been anywhere interesting recently? Does no-one help you with your work? Say something about your job.
Describe somewhere you have been recently.

Quantifiers (1)

See also	
Units 61, 62	Nouns
Unit 75	**Some** and **any**
Units 78, 79	Quantifiers

A Sample sentences

- Our website lists all the products that are available.
- We have upgraded most of our hotels.
- Do you have a lot of important meetings to attend?
- They had some problems with their suppliers.
- The hotel is full. There are no rooms available.

B Form

Countable	Verb singular or plural	Uncountable	Verb singular or plural
all	plural	all	singular
most	plural	most	singular
many	plural	much (see Unit 78)	singular
a lot of	plural	a lot of	singular
some	plural	some	singular
a few	plural	a little (see Unit 78)	singular
few	plural	little (see Unit 78)	singular
no	plural	no	singular

We use countable quantifiers with plural countable nouns; we use uncountable quantifiers with uncountable nouns. (See Unit 62.)

We have reduced   all   our   prices.
                 quantifier   +   countable noun

They are going to install   all   the   equipment.
                     quantifier   +   uncountable noun

C Uses

A: Do you know all the people here?
B: I know most of them. (*not*: the most of them)
A: Where did you meet them?
B: I met some of them at the last sales conference.
A: I see. So, let's start the meeting. We have a lot of points to cover. There is no time to lose.

A: We are returning all the goods from our last order.
B: Why is that?
A: Because most of our customers have complained. (*not*: the most of our customers)
B: What have they complained about?
A: Some clients said they were the wrong size.
B: But why are you returning all the goods?
A: Because no customers want to buy them.

Exercise 1

Place the following in order from 1 (maximum) to 6 (minimum).

None of our products are very successful. ☐

All our products are very successful. ☐

Most of our products are very successful. ☐

A few of our products are very successful. ☐

Many of our products are very successful. ☐

Some of our products are very successful. ☐

Exercise 2

The table gives the results of a quality test on electrical components at APKAL Ltd.

	Standard pass (no faults)	Sub-standard fail (1 or 2 faults)	Non-standard fail (3 or more faults)
Product A	76%	12%	12%
Product B	100%	0%	0%
Product C	88%	10%	2%

Mark the following sentences true (T) or false (F).

1. All product As passed the test as standard. ☐

2. A few product Cs failed the test as non-standard. ☐

3. Some product Bs failed the test. ☐

4. Many product As failed the test. ☐

5. Most product Cs passed the test. ☐

6. No product As failed the test. ☐

7. Most products failed the test. ☐

Exercise 3

Replace the underlined words with a word or phrase from the box. Change the verb if necessary.

| many   a little   no   little   few   all |

1. Not too much but some training helps all managers.
2. Not one of our customers was unhappy.
3. Every one of our products is guaranteed.
4. A large number of people came to the exhibition.
5. Not many exhibitors liked the exhibition space.
6. The organisers offered not much help.

Transfer

Write sentences about a company you know. Use quantifiers.

Quantifiers (2)

A Sample sentences

- **They didn't spend much money.**
- **How many employees do they have?**
- **Here are a few of my suggestions.**
- **Let me give you a little advice.**

B Form

Countable	Verb singular or plural	Uncountable	Verb singular or plural
all	plural	all (see Unit 77)	singular
most	plural	most (see Unit 77)	singular
many	plural	much	singular
a lot of	plural	a lot of (see Unit 77)	singular
some	plural	some (see Unit 77)	singular
a few	plural	a little	singular
few	plural	little	singular
no	plural	no (see Unit 77)	singular

We use countable quantifiers with plural countable nouns; we use uncountable quantifiers with uncountable nouns. (See Unit 62.)

They only made   a few   recommendations.
        quantifier   +   countable noun
They only gave us   a little   advice.
            quantifier   +   uncountable noun

C Uses

1. **Much, many** and **a lot of**
   a. in statements:
   There aren't many tourists around in the winter. (**many** + countable noun)
   People didn't earn much money in the 1940s. (**much** + uncountable noun)
   We normally use **much** and **many** in negative statements; in positive statements, we often use **a lot of** with both countable and uncountable nouns:
   We were given a lot of equipment.
   b. in questions:
   How much do I owe you? (how much money)
   How many companies increased their earnings last year? (**many** + countable noun)
   How much work are you prepared to do? (**much** + uncountable noun)

2. **A few, a little, few** and **little**
   There was time to write down a few details.
   (**a few** + countable noun = not many, but enough)
   I wanted a little information about the subject.
   (**a little** + uncountable noun = not much, but enough)
   There are few jobs for people without qualifications.
   (**few** + countable noun = not many, and not enough)
   There is little work in the shipyards.
   (**little** + uncountable noun = not much, and not enough)

Exercise 1

Amy wants to hire a car. Identify seven quantifiers in the following dialogue. Mark them countable (C) or uncountable (U).

A: Hello. I'd like some help, please.
B: Certainly.
A: How much does this car cost to hire?
B: That one is £120 a day.
A: That's quite a lot of money.
B: Well, we have a lot of other cars that cost a little less. How many days do you need a car?
A: Only a few. Three or four.

Exercise 2

Boris runs a mobile phone rental company. Here he talks about his business. Choose the correct quantifiers from the alternatives.

'We hire mobile phones. We have *much/all* types of phones. We keep *a lot of/no* phones in stock. *Most/a lot of* are hired for just one day. *A little/a few of* our customers keep them for a month or two. Not *all/few/many* people hire phones for longer than *many/a few* weeks.'

CITY MOBILE

Mobile & Cellular phone rental from $ 20 daily
Contact Boris on
FREEPHONE 200200.

Exercise 3

Replace the underlined phrases with quantifiers. Do not change the meaning.

1. <u>Not many and not enough</u> people understand how to program computers.
2. There is <u>not much and not enough</u> demand for our products.
3. We made <u>not many but enough</u> contacts at the Singapore Trade Fair.
4. There was <u>some, but not much</u> criticism in the report.
5. <u>A large number of</u> people answered our advertisement.
6. <u>Not even one</u> applicant was good enough for the job.

Transfer

Write five sentences about jobs, job advertisements, applications and people looking for work in your home town. Use quantifiers.

Quantifiers (3)

See also	
Units 61, 62	Nouns
Units 77, 78	Quantifiers

A Sample sentences

- **Hotel staff check each room before guests arrive.**
- **They meet every morning at 7.15.**
- **All employees must be given a written contract.**

B Form

Singular	Plural	Uncountable
each	all (see also Unit 77)	all (see also Unit 77)
every		

We use **each** and **every** with singular countable nouns.
We use **all** with plural countable nouns and uncountable nouns. (See Unit 62.)

We ask   each   candidate   to send a full curriculum vitae.
      quantifier + singular countable noun

We hold interviews   every   month.
          quantifier + singular countable noun

All   interviewees   spend a full day with us.
quantifier + plural countable noun

During their visit we show them   all   the machinery   in the factory.
       quantifier + uncountable noun

C Uses

Each and **every** have very similar meanings.

1. **Each**
   Police were checking each car. (many cars, one by one)
   The fee for each session is £50. (each individual session)
   (*not*: each sessions)

2. **Every**
   Every department faces cuts. (all departments, without exception)
   There is a staff meeting every Monday morning. (each Monday morning, without exception)

3. **All**
   We send all our clients a weekly update on airfares. (every/each client)
   They paid all the money last week.

Note
every + singular noun = **all** + plural noun:
Every manager/all managers must plan, lead, organise and control.

Exercise 1

*Underline examples of **each**, **every** and **all** in the following text.*

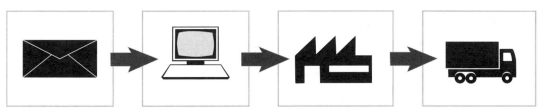

'Each day we process hundreds of orders. Every order comes by email.
All orders are entered into our database. Each request is checked with our
current stock. Every order is immediately transferred to the warehouse. All
orders are despatched within one hour.'

Exercise 2

*How many combinations with **every**, **each** and **all** can you make with these words or phrases?
Try to write full sentences.*

| person | money | customer | products |
| information | of us | week | department |

Examples:
In a team, each person has an important role to play.
Every person in this room is wearing shoes.
All the money in the world wouldn't change me.

Exercise 3

*Complete the sentences below using **each**, **every** or **all** + a word or phrase from the box.
The first has been done for you.*

| restaurant | ~~time~~ | accommodation | of them | cities | one |

1. *I always need a map. **Every time** I go to Rome, I get lost.*

2. *I have never had a bad meal in Paris. _____ I've been in has been excellent.*

3. *We have a lot of good customers in Malaysia. We need to look after _____ very carefully.*

4. *Last time I went to Dublin I visited several museums. _____ was free.*

5. *Quality hotels in Hong Kong are expensive. In fact, _____ is expensive.*

6. *The best thing in London is the parks. _____ British _____ have good parks.*

Transfer

*Write five sentences about your home town. Include **each**, **all**, **every**.*

UNIT
80

Numerals

See also

Business File 5   Numbers, dates and times

A Sample sentences

- Ten new plants will be built in the next five years.
- This is the third time the company has been sold.
- Department managers must spend half their time on the sales floor.
- The committee meets once a month.

B Form

1. Cardinal numbers

Written number	Spoken number	Written number	Spoken number
0	nought, zero, 'oh'	1,000	a/one thousand
10	ten	1,101	one thousand, one hundred and one
100	a/one hundred	3,000	three thousand
101	a/one hundred and one	1,000,000	a/one million

2. Ordinal numbers

Written number	Spoken number	Written number	Spoken number
1st	first	21st	twenty-first
2nd	second	100th	one (a) hundredth
3rd	third	1,000th	one (a) thousandth
4th	fourth	1,000,000th	one (a) millionth

3. Fractions and decimals

Written number	Spoken number	Written number	Spoken number
½	(a) half	1 ½	one and a half
¼	(a) quarter	2.5	two point five
⅓	a/one third	3.75	three point seven five
¾	three quarters	26.012 / 26,012	twenty six point zero one two / twenty six thousand and twelve

4. Frequency expressions

once	twice	three times	four times	etc.

C Uses

A: How many people does ITCorp employ?

B: We have about 5000 people at 28 plants worldwide.

A: And how long have you worked for the company?

B: I joined them in 2008.

A: And where were you before that?

B: Before ITCorp I worked for GloboSys for 5 years.

A: So is ITCorp your second job?

B: Yes. And how often do you come here?

A: I visit the country three times a year. At present we are thinking of building a second factory here.

B: Yes. The economic situation is very healthy at the moment.

A: Inflation is only 2.5%. So it's an attractive place to invest.

Exercise 1

Match the sentences 1–5 with the correct picture a–e.

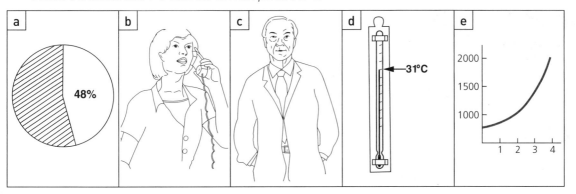

1. The temperature is thirty-one degrees Celsius.
2. We have a forty-eight per cent market share.
3. Our sales have reached two thousand units by the end of the third quarter.
4. Mr Robson has been Chairman for fifty-one years.
5. My telephone number is oh one three four seven, eight seven eight double seven nine.

Exercise 2

Read the following details about Abacus plc, a UK-based manufacturing company. Write all the numbers as you would say them.

Abacus plc. 2010

Annual turnover	£326.5m	Factories worldwide	12
Profit on sales	£18.32m	Employees	6,750
Share price	£4.18p	Company founded	1974
% increase on last year	15%	Details correct on	15 April 2009
Total capital assets	£407m		

Exercise 3

Use the table to give information to a colleague. Write exactly what you say in the spaces.

Annual Sales 2010

Quarter	Units	Turnover(£)	Profit (£)
1st quarter	336	7,302.52	3,450.00
2nd quarter	417	8,911.30	3,891.15
3rd quarter	410	8,820.77	3,700.50
4th quarter	215	4,391.02	1,943.21

I have some figures for sales in _____. In the _____ quarter we sold _____ units and had a turnover of _____. This produced a profit of _____. The _____ and _____ quarter performance was better with profit between _____ and _____ . In the _____ quarter, the number of units sold was _____, or about _____ the previous two quarters. Profit was also down, to _____.

Transfer

Find a newspaper or another document with a lot of numbers in it. Practise reading them aloud.

UNIT 81   Time

See also
Unit 17   The present perfect with **for**, **since**, **ever** and **never**

A Sample sentences

- **We agreed a deal in 2005.**
- **The meeting will start at 8.30 and finish at 10.30.**
- **The course will be held for six weeks from November 6th.**
- **I expect to be back in Britain on December 18th.**

B Form

A preposition is a grammatical unit. It comes in front of a noun,
e.g.   **in   the morning.**
   preposition +   noun
The most important prepositions of time are:

at	in	on	by	during	before	after
from … to …	up to	until/till	for		since	between

The next meeting will take place on Monday at 12 o'clock.
I would like to read your report before the meeting.

C Uses

1. At, in, on and by

at + clock time
at 6 o'clock
in + parts of the day
in the morning/afternoon/evening (*but*: **at** night)
on + days of the week
on Monday
on Thursday afternoon
on + dates
on 3rd May (spoken: **on the third of May**)
in + months and years
in May
in 1997 (spoken: **in nineteen ninety-seven**)
by + a deadline
You must finish the report by 4 o'clock. (at the latest)

2. By and until/till

We use **by** for an action which happens at or before a deadline:
The order must be ready by 3rd September. (at the latest)
We use **until/till** for an action which continues up to a deadline:
The parties will work until/till May 17th to convince voters to vote for them.

3. No preposition

In some time phrases, we do not use a preposition of time.
a. before **this**, **last** and **next**:
   The store will open next April. (*not*: in next April)
b. with speed and frequency expressions:
   The car was travelling at eighty miles an hour. (*not*: in an hour)
   The director visits each factory twice a year. (*not*: in a year)

Exercise 1

Underline all time prepositions in the following.

A: When's he coming?
B: In the morning.
A: Before 10 o'clock?
B: Probably. We'll show him the factory for an hour or two, then when Julie arrives at 12 o'clock we'll have our meeting.
A: So, during lunchtime?
B: Yes, from about 12 till around 2.30.
A: We must be finished by 3 because we've an appointment with Axis in the afternoon.
B: That's no problem.

Exercise 2

The time line below shows the product development of the XR20, a mini television made by Camicam. Complete the text with prepositions from the box.

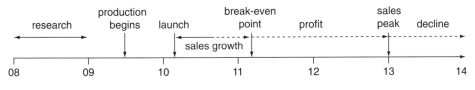

| for (2) | in | on | until | during | since | after | by |

We researched the XR20 _____ 12 months, then _____ 2009 it went into production. _____ 15th January 2010 the product was launched. _____ then we have had good sales and we will break even _____ March 2011. We expect increasing sales _____ about two years, _____ sales peak _____ the year 2013. _____ that, the sales will decline.

Exercise 3

Complete the sentences for the time lines below.

1. John left the company _____ 2006.

2. I'm going on holiday _____ two weeks.

3. _____ our research, we made three discoveries.

4. _____ 2004 we have made a profit.

Transfer

Write ten sentences about your activities. Include different time prepositions.

UNIT 82

Place (1)

See also
Unit 83   Place (2)

A Sample sentences

- **I paid in some money at the bank.**
- **Glover came into the office at 8am.**
- **He left his car in the car park.**
- **There's someone from People magazine on the phone.**

B Form

A preposition is a grammatical unit. It comes in front of a noun,
e.g.   **in**   **the factory.**
    preposition   +   noun
The most important prepositions of place are:

at	to	from	in	into	out of	on

Walk into the main building; the reception desk is on the left.
We import our components from Rotaronga.

C Uses

1. at
We use **at** to describe a place without any specific dimensions:
I'll see Lloyd tomorrow at the meeting.
A problem had arisen at work.

2. to
We use **to** to describe movement to a place without any specific dimensions:
He drove to work every day.
We deliver the goods to our customers within 72 hours.

3. from
We use **from** to describe movement away from a place without any specific dimensions:
He drove from the shipyard to Antwerp.
Retailers buy goods from the manufacturer.

4. in and into
We use **in** to describe a place:
I'll meet you in the restaurant.
We use **into** to describe movement to a place:
They packed the goods into the lorry.
A: We deliver the materials in cases.
B: And where do you deliver them?
A: We take them into the warehouse.

5. into and out of
Into and **out of** describe movement; they describe opposite movements:
First we put the components into the warehouse.
Later we take them out of the warehouse and take them into the assembly area.

6. on
We use **on** with objects which have a surface:
He looked at the notebook on his desk.
There are some lovely salads on the menu.

Exercise 1

Label the following with prepositions of place.

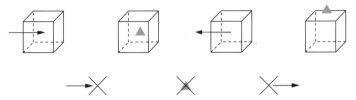

Exercise 2

Correct the following, where necessary. Two sentences are correct.

1. I went in Egypt last week.
2. Our company has built a factory at Argentina.
3. They want to meet us from the trade fair.
4. I sent the price list to Axis Ltd.
5. There's nothing about the company on the newspaper.
6. We decided to take some money out of our emergency bank account.
7. They put a lot of money onto research.
8. They have taken business at us.
9. The computer is in the desk.

Exercise 3

Complete the description of the process shown in the diagram. Use words from the box.

> from (2)   to (3)   in   into   on

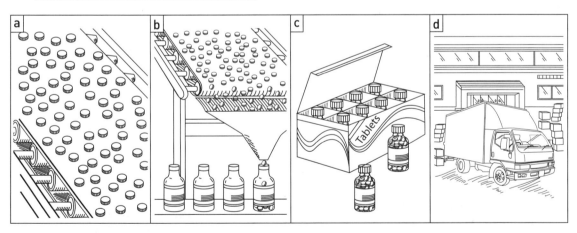

The finished tablets are sent _____ the production area _____ this machine which puts them _____ small bottles. Labels are put _____ the bottles which are then packed _____ boxes. The boxes are transferred _____ the warehouse. They are taken _____ the warehouse _____ the shops.

Transfer

*Write seven sentences about yourself or about a place you know well. Include place prepositions **at, to, from, in, into, out of, on**.*

165

UNIT
83

Place (2)

See also
Unit 82   Place (1)

A Sample sentences

- **We walked through the building to the main entrance.**
- **Graham pushed the report across the desk to me.**
- **The club is located above a restaurant.**
- **The water is stored in a tank below ground level.**

B Form

We use prepositions to describe:
- — place (see also Unit 82)
- — position
- — movement (see also Unit 82).

Sometimes, the same preposition can have different uses.

1. The main prepositions to describe position are:

above	below	over	under	in front of	
behind	beside	between	next to	on top of	opposite

The warehouse is next to the production area.
The meeting room is behind the MD's office.

2. The main prepositions to describe movement are:

into	out of	behind	in front of	along	across
over	onto	up	down	around	outside

Put the goods behind this table.
I have divided my presentation into four parts.
(See also Unit 82.)

C Uses

1. Describing position:
The computer room is above the reception area. We are planning to have a demonstration room next to the reception area.

This is our new logo. Over the company name are three small crowns. And under the name we have placed two lines.

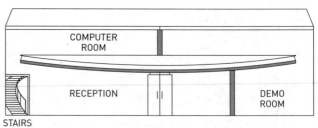

2. Describing movement:
You can move Mr Johnson out of the executive suite. Then you can put Mrs Deberis into it. I'm sure she will be comfortable there.

You can go up the stairs to the MD's office or you can take the lift.

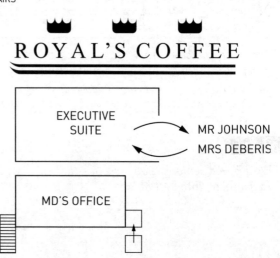

Exercise 1

Underline the prepositions in the following. Mark them position (P) or movement (M).

> When you arrive, go out of the airport and along the road to the taxis waiting outside. Ask to go to Jasons, on High Street. Our offices are between the Post Office and the Magnus foodstore. We're opposite Credit Bank International. Go through the main entrance and into the lift. Go up to the fourth floor. We're just next to the fire exit.

Exercise 2

Replace each preposition in the following sentences with another one which means the same. Match each sentence 1–5 with the correct diagram a–f. There is one more diagram than you need.

a.

1. The factory is *beside* the river.

2. There is a restaurant *opposite* our main office.

d.

b.

3. The hotel is *along* the road from the station.

e.

4. You can drive *across* the city in 20 minutes.

c.

5. The safe is in a cellar *under* the Managing Director's office.

f.

Exercise 3

Look at this picture of a factory.

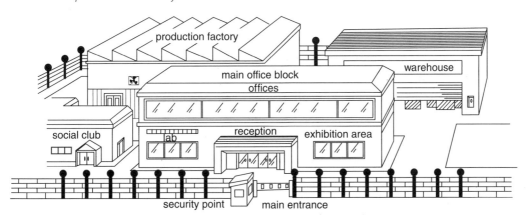

Answer the questions. Choose words or phrases from the box. You may use a word or phrase more than once.

behind	between	next to	beside	above	under	in front of

1. Where is the security point?
2. Where is the social club?
3. Where are the offices?
4. Where is the laboratory?

5. Where are the production facilities?
6. Where is the warehouse?
7. Where is the exhibition area?
8. Where is the reception area?

Transfer

Describe the position of various places where you work.

UNIT 84   Like, As, The Same As and Different From

A Sample sentences

- Supermarkets now sell things like clothes and homeware as well as food.
- I work as a waiter in a hotel.
- Prices this year are the same as last year.
- The Japanese market is different from the US market.

B Form

Like, **as** and **from** are prepositions.
We put a noun phrase after a preposition:

His briefcase is	**like**	a mobile office.
	preposition +	noun phrase
She works	**as**	**a financial adviser.**
	preposition +	noun phrase

C Uses

1. Both **like** and **as** mean 'the same as' or 'similar to':

  a. like
    Even in countries like Germany and Switzerland, banks have been running into trouble. (similar to)
    We make personal computers, like ITCorp. (the same as)

  b. as
    She works as a customer service manager. (it is her job)
    As you can see, the published accounts show little detail. (*not*: like you can see)

  c. the same as
    Flexitime is the same as flexible working hours. (not: the same like)
    The airline faces the same problems as other airlines.

2. **Different from** is the opposite of **the same as**:
  A certified public accountant is different from a licensed public accountant. (*not*: different to)
  This product is very different from existing products.

Exercise 1

Tick (✓) sentences 1–8 if you agree with them. If you do not agree, write a cross (✗).

1. Like Argentina, Chile has a lot of mountains. ☐

2. German cars have an image which is very different from the image of Japanese cars. ☐

3. As everyone knows, America is the world's leading economy. ☐

4. Food in Japan is the same as food in China. ☐

5. People who work as personal assistants have an easy life. ☐

6. One fast food store is often the same as any other fast food store. ☐

7. Life now is no different from 25 years ago. ☐

8. Italy is very like California. ☐

Exercise 2

Taruba is a car manufacturer. Here are details of two Taruba cars. Complete the advertisement below.

Taruba GX40. Engine: 1800cc   Taruba GX50. Engine: 2000cc

The GX40 looks _____ the GX50. But the engine of the GX50 is _____ _____ the engine in the GX40. It is bigger. _____ all Taruba cars, the GX models have a seven-year warranty. _____ you can see, we build for quality. _____ you, we don't want any trouble.

Exercise 3

Here is part of the Chairman's annual address to the shareholders of BBL plc. Five sentences have been jumbled up. Rewrite them, beginning with the word(s) given.

1. have   we   previous   done   in   well   ~~as~~   years.

As _____ .

2. the   the   ~~people~~   are   other   same   all   as   say   each   producers.

People say _____ .

3. are   we   ~~fact~~   ~~in~~   competitors   different   our   from.

In fact, _____ .

4. ~~like~~   business   we   are   them   in.

Like _____ .

5. quality   ~~always~~   commitment   special   a   ~~as~~   we   have   to.

As always, _____ .

Transfer

*Write five sentences about yourself, or about a company you know. Include **like**, **as**, **the same as** and **different from**.*

BUSINESS FILE

1

Industries and Jobs

INDUSTRIES

Manufacturing

Aerospace
Agriculture & food
    production
Apparel & fashion
Automotive
Chemical
Construction
Cosmetics & personal
    care
Dyes & pigments

Electrical
Energy
Engineering
Food & drink
Furniture
Gas
Metal
Mining
Petroleum
Pharmaceutical

Plastics
Power generation
Pulp & paper
Rail
Road
Rubber
Telecommunications
Textiles
Water

Services

Accounting
Advertising
Architecture
Banking & financial
    services
Charities
Civil service
Consultancy
Environment
Health & healthcare
Hotel & hospitality
Insurance

International relations
International trade
IT (Information Technology) &
    telecoms
Journalism
Law
Media
Military
Music
Politics & government
Printing
Public relations

Real estate
Retail
Security & protection
Tax
Tourism
Training (incl. education)
Transportation (incl. shipping)
Travel
Utilities
Volunteering

JOBS

Departments/Divisions

Administration
Design
Engineering
Environment
Finance & accounting
General management
Health & safety
Information technology
Journalism

Legal
Logistics (incl. distribution)
Marketing & PR (Public
    relations)
Materials management
HR (Human Resources) &
    training
Production
Project management

Purchasing
Quality assurance
Recruitment
Research & development
Sales
Security
Training

BUSINESS FILE

2

Countries and Currencies

Country	Currency
Algeria	Algerian Dinar
Argentina	Peso
Australia	Australian Dollar
Austria	Euro
Belgium	Euro
Bolivia	Peso Boliviano
Brazil	Real
Bulgaria	Lev
Canada	Canadian Dollar
Chile	Peso
China	Yuan
Colombia	Peso
Cuba	Peso
Cyprus	Euro
Czech Republic	Czech Koruna
Denmark	Krone
Ecuador	US Dollar
Egypt	Egyptian Pound
Finland	Euro
France	Euro
Germany	Euro
Ghana	Cedi
Greece	Euro
Hong Kong	Hong Kong Dollar
Hungary	Forint
Iceland	Króna
India	Rupee
Iran	Rial
Iraq	Iraqi Dinar
Irish Republic	Euro
Israel	New Shekel

Country	Currency
Italy	Euro
Jamaica	Jamaican Dollar
Japan	Yen
Jordan	Jordanian Dinar
Kenya	Kenyan Shilling
Kuwait	Kuwait Dinar
Laos	Kip
Lebanon	Lebanese Pound
Libya	Libyan Dinar
Liechtenstein	Swiss Franc
Luxembourg	Euro
Malawi	Malawi Kwacha
Malaysia	Ringgit
Malta	Euro
Mexico	Peso
Monaco	Euro
Mongolia	Tugrik
Morocco	Dirham
Mozambique	Metical
Myanmar	Kyat
Namibia	Dollar
Nepal	Rupee
The Netherlands	Euro
New Zealand	New Zealand Dollar
Nicaragua	Cordoba
Nigeria	Naira
Norway	Krone
Oman	Omani Rial
Pakistan	Rupee
Panama	Balboa
Paraguay	Guarani

Country	Currency
Peru	Sol
Philippines	Philippine Peso
Poland	Zloty
Portugal	Euro
Romania	Leu
Russia	Rouble
Rwanda	Rwanda Franc
Saudi Arabia	Riyal
Senegal	CFA Franc
Singapore	Singapore Dollar
Slovakia	Euro
Somalia	Somalia Shilling
South Africa	Rand
Spain	Euro
Sri Lanka	Sri Lankan Rupee
Sudan	Sudanese Pound
Sweden	Krona
Switzerland	Swiss Franc
Syria	Syrian Pound
Taiwan	New Taiwan Dollar
Tanzania	Tanzanian Shilling
Thailand	Baht
Turkey	Turkish Lira
United Kingdom	Pound Sterling
United States of America	Dollar
Uruguay	Peso
Venezuela	Bolivar
Vietnam	Dong
Zambia	Kwacha

Business Abbreviations and Short Forms

AAA	triple A – company rating		HQ	headquarters
abbr	abbreviation		HR	Human Resources
a/c or acct	account		HTML	Hypertext Mark-up Language
admin	administration		HTTP	Hypertext Transfer Protocol
ADSL	Advanced Digital Subscriber Line		i.e.	*id est* = that is
AGM	Annual General Meeting		ILO	International Labour Organization
a.m.	*ante meridiem* = before noon		IM	Instant Messaging
ANSI	American National Standards Institute		IMF	International Monetary Fund
AOB	Any Other Business		Inc.	Incorporated
approx	approximately		inc/incl	including
arr	arrival		ISDN	Integrated Services Digital Network
asap	as soon as possible		ISO	International Standardization Organization
ASCII	American Standard Code for Information Exchange		ISP	Internet Service Provider
asst	assistant		LAN	Local Area Network
att	attention (see also **FAO**)		Ltd	Limited company
B2B	Business to Business		MBA	Master of Business Administration
B2C	Business to Consumer		MD	Managing Director
BCC	Blind Carbon Copy		mfr	manufacturer
B/F	brought forward		MPEG	Motion Picture Exports Group
BTW	By the way		mth/mo.	month
c or ca	*circa* = about		n/a	not applicable or not available
c&f	cost and freight		NB	*nota bene* = pay attention to this
Cc	carbon copy; cubic centimetres		No	number
CCTV	closed circuit television		PA	Personal Assistant
CEO	Chief Executive Officer		p.a.	*per annum* = each year
c/f	carried forward		p&p	postage and packing
CGT	Capital Gains Tax		pd	paid
c/o	care of		PDA	Personal Digital Assistant
COD	cash on delivery		PDF	Portable Document Format
CPI	Consumer Price Index		PIN	Personal Identification Number
CPU	central processing unit		plc	public limited company
CRM	customer relationship management		pls	please
dd	dated		p.m.	*post meridiem* = after noon
dept/dpt	department		PR	Public Relations
DIY	Do It Yourself		PT	part-time
d.o.b.	date of birth		PTO	Please Turn Over
DP	data processing		p.w.	per week
EC	European Community		qty	quantity
e.g.	*exampli gratia* = for example		R&D	Research and Development
enc/encl	enclosed/enclosure		re	about
ETA	estimated time of arrival		ref	reference
et al	*et alii* = and others		ROI	return on investment
etc	*etcetera* = and so on		RSVP	please reply
EU	European Union		SWOT	Strengths, Weaknesses, Opportunities and Threats
FAO	For the attention of		USP	Unique Selling Point
FAQ	Frequently Asked Questions		VAT	Value Added Tax
FT	full-time		VP	Vice President
fwd	forward		WAP	Wireless Application Protocol
FYI	for your information		WTO	World Trade Organization
GDP	Gross Domestic Product		www	world wide web
GM	General Manager			

BUSINESS FILE

4

British English vs. American English

You can find difference between British English (BrE) and American English (AmE) at four main levels:

- grammar
- vocabulary
- pronunciation
- spelling

1. Grammar

Present perfect and past simple

Have you done it yet? (BrE) **Did you do it yet?** (AmE)
I have already done it. (BrE) **I already did it.** (AmE)
I haven't done it yet. (BrE) **I didn't do it yet.** (AmE)

Got and gotten

They have got a new Managing Director. (BrE)
They have gotten a new Managing Director. (AmE)

Verb Phrases

to meet someone (BrE) **to meet with someone** (AmE)
to agree to a proposal (BrE) **to agree a proposal** (AmE)
to appeal against a decision (BrE) **to appeal a decision** (AmE)

2. Vocabulary

BrE	AmE
Corporate Language	
Chairman	President
Managing Director	Chief Executive Officer/ Senior Vice-President
Finance Director	Vice-President – Finance
General Language	
flat	apartment
autumn	fall
biscuit	cookie
bill (for payment)	check
boot (car)	trunk
centre (of town/city)	downtown
chemist's shop/chemist	pharmacy/drugstore
chips	(French) fries
crisps	(potato) chips

BrE	AmE
Sales Manager	Sales Director
Board of Directors	Executive Board
fortnight	two weeks
holiday	vacation
motorway	freeway/highway
petrol	gas
post	mail
queue	line
rubbish	garbage/trash
solicitor	lawyer/attorney
tap	faucet

3. Pronunciation

BrE	AmE
detail	de**tail**
re**search**	**re**search

BrE	AmE
interested	in(t)erested
hos**tile** /taɪl/	hos**tile** /t(ə)l/

4. Spelling

BrE	AmE
-*our*: colour	-*or*: color
-*ize* or -*ise*: organize or organise	-*ize*: organize

BrE	AmE
-*eller*: traveller	-*eler*: traveller
-*re*: centre	-*er*: center

BUSINESS FILE

5

Numbers, Dates and Times

A Numbers

We can divide numbers into:
* cardinals
* ordinals
* fractions and decimals
* frequency expressions

1. Cardinals

0 – nought, zero (especially for mathematics and for temperatures),
oh (in British English for telephone numbers), nil (in sports)
100 – a/one hundred. **We offer a/one hundred different products.**
101 – a/one hundred and one
1,000 – a/one thousand. **At present we employ a/one thousand employees.** (*not*: one thousand of)
1,000,000 – a/one million

2. Ordinals

1st – first. **The first of April** (spoken)
2nd – second. **This is the second time we have visited the Paris fashion show.**
3rd – third. **Our third attempt to find an agent was successful.**
4th – fourth. **This is the fourth job I have applied for.**
21st – twenty-first. **We're living in the twenty-first century.**
100th – (one) hundredth. **This is our (one) hundredth trade fair.**
101st – one hundred and first
1000th – (one) thousandth

3. Fractions and decimals

½ – (a) half. **Over (a) half (of) our products are made in France.**
⅓ – a/one third. **We can usually offer a discount of one third.**
⅔ – two-thirds. **Over two-thirds of our workers live in the village.**
¼ – (a) quarter. **I start work at (a) quarter past seven.**
¾ – three-quarters. **It takes me three-quarters of an hour to walk to work.**
¹⁄₁₀ – a/one tenth
1½ – one and a half. **The whole process takes one and a half hours.**
2.5 – two point five
3.75 – three point seven five (*not*: seventy five)
26.012 – twenty six point zero (*or* oh) one two

4. Frequency expressions

once   twice   three times   etc
We meet our major customers twice a year.

B Dates

Notice the difference between the written and spoken forms and between
British and American English:
We opened our new office on 5 April 2010. BrE (written)
We opened our new office on the fifth of April, two thousand and ten*. BrE (spoken)
or **We opened our new office on April the fifth, two thousand and ten*.** BrE (spoken)
We opened our new office on April 5th 2010. AmE (written)
We opened our new office on April fifth, two thousand ten*. AmE (spoken)
*We also say *twenty ten* BrE/AmE (spoken)
5/4/2010 – BrE (written) for 5 April 2010, i.e. date/month/year
4/5/2010 – AmE (written) for 5 April 2010, i.e. month/date/year

C Times

Notice the written and spoken forms:
The meeting will start at 9.00/9.00am/9 o'clock. (written)
The meeting will start at nine a.m./nine o'clock. (spoken)
The meeting will finish at 4.30 p.m./16.30. (written)
The meeting will finish at four thirty p.m./(a) half past four/sixteen thirty. (spoken)

Irregular Verb Table

Infinitive	Past Simple	Past participle
be	was/were	been
beat	beat	beaten
become	became	become
begin	began	begun
break	broke	broken
bring	brought	brought
build	built	built
buy	bought	bought
catch	caught	caught
choose	chose	chosen
come	came	come
cost	cost	cost
cut	cut	cut
do	did	done
draw	drew	drawn
drink	drank	drunk
drive	drove	driven
eat	ate	eaten
fall	fell	fallen
feel	felt	felt
fight	fought	fought
find	found	found
fly	flew	flown
forget	forgot	forgotten
get	got	got (BrE)
get	got	gotten (AmE)
give	gave	given
go	went	gone
grow	grew	grown
have	had	had
hear	heard	heard
hide	hid	hidden
hit	hit	hit
hold	held	held
keep	kept	kept
know	knew	known
lay	laid	laid
lead	led	led
leave	left	left
lend	lent	lent
let	let	let

Infinitive	Past Simple	Past participle
lie	lay	lain
lose	lost	lost
make	made	made
mean	meant	meant
meet	met	met
pay	paid	paid
put	put	put
read	read	read
ride	rode	ridden
rise	rose	risen
run	ran	run
say	said	said
see	saw	seen
sell	sold	sold
send	sent	sent
set	set	set
shine	shone	shone
shoot	shot	shot
show	showed	shown
shut	shut	shut
sing	sang	sung
sink	sank	sunk
sit	sat	sat
sleep	slept	slept
speak	spoke	spoken
spend	spent	spent
split	split	split
stand	stood	stood
steal	stole	stolen
strike	struck	struck
swim	swam	swum
take	took	taken
teach	taught	taught
tell	told	told
think	thought	thought
throw	threw	thrown
understand	understood	understood
wake	woke	woken
wear	wore	worn
win	won	won
write	wrote	written

Answer Key

(M) = Model/suggested answers

TASKS 1

BE (1)

Exercise 1

Present positive	Present negative	Present question
1 3 5 7 8 10 11 14	6 13	2 4 9 12

Exercise 2

2. My name's Pierre Lapin. **I'm** a Sales Manager.
3. Mary and Hans are from my department. **They're** computer programmers.
4. This is Naomi Cox. **She's** a research scientist.
5. Hello. My name**'s** Franz Johann and this **is** Tomas Doll. **We're** from Salzburg.
6. Ah, Franz and Tomas! **You're** very welcome!
7. This is our office. It **isn't** very big.

Exercise 3

Axdal Electronics **is** a world leader in control systems. We **are** suppliers to the car industry. Car manufacturers **are not** our only customers. We **are** also suppliers to other industries. AE **is** an international company. Our customers **are** in the USA, Japan and Europe. Our Chief Executive **is** Paul Axdal. 'We **are** a family company and business **is** very good', says Paul.

TASKS 2

BE (2)

Exercise 1

Past positive	Past negative	Past question
3, 7, 10	5	4
Present perfect positive	**Present perfect negative**	**Present perfect question**
2, 9	6	1, 8

Exercise 2

Delco Ltd.
16–20 East Mount Road, Lincoln LN3 5RT

6 November.....

Dear Mary,

Last week Tom and Paula **were** here for a meeting. It **was** very useful. They **were** here for two days. We **have been** to Oslo in the last few days. We **were** there for a meeting with our Norwegian colleagues. Arne Sillessen **was** very interested in our ideas. Until now, I **have not been** happy with the project. Now I am very optimistic. See you next week.

Best wishes

Sandy Peel

Sandy Peel

Exercise 3

From: ipcs3@cc.uat.es
Sent: Mon 28 November 15:40
Subject: Short Bros

Dear Frances,

I am sorry I **was not** at the meeting yesterday. I **have not been** in the office this week. Tom and I **have been** in London. We **were** at a Sales Conference. I **have been** very busy recently. **Were** Short Brothers happy with the contract? **Have** they **been** in contact today?

Please contact me by email tomorrow.

Thanks
Juanito

TASKS 3

The Present Continuous Positive

Exercise 1

Date:	12 march 20…
To:	all staff
From:	Jenny Palmer
Subject:	John Bramwell leaving

Dear All,

John Bramwell is leaving the company after 30 years. We are organising a collection to buy John a present. Please see Janet in Room 40. Janet is planning a leaving party for John. At present, John is recovering in hospital after an accident. He is hoping to return to work next month, but only until the summer.

Best Regards
Jenny Palmer

Exercise 2

PT: Okay, I**'m looking** at it right now. What's the problem?

DL: It says we**'re investing** $250,000 in research. That's wrong. It's $25,000, not $250,000.

PT: Okay. I'll change that.

DL: Right. Remember, you**'re meeting** Mr Lally and his colleagues today.

PT: Yes, I know. They**'re coming** here at 2.30.

DL: Fine. Good luck. See you tomorrow, then.

Exercise 3

1. Total sales are going up.
2. Sales for Product A are increasing.
3. Sales for Product B are falling.
4. The company is stopping production of Product B.

TASKS 4

The Present Continuous Negative

Exercise 1

We are not increasing our prices this year. The market is not strong enough. We are launching new products for the domestic market. Most of our products are selling well at home. At present, we are not planning any new products for export. Sales are not increasing in our export markets. The company is not expecting improved sales this year.

Exercise 2

2. We're not/ We aren't spending much time in Milan.
3. The company isn't looking at new markets in southern Europe.
4. At the moment many companies aren't investing in new products.
5. Our marketing experts aren't changing our present sales strategy.
6. You're not/You aren't staying in a hotel.

Exercise 3

1. This year the company is not doing well in the USA.
2. At the moment we are building a new production plant.
3. At present we are not presenting a good image.
4. Mr Jackson is not working hard these days.

TASKS 5

The Present Continuous Question

Exercise 1

2. At the moment they working with Poland?
   ... are they working ...
3. Is Leo and Sam planning the conference together?
   Are Leo and Sam ...
4. What you think about? *What do you ...*
5. Is raining in Bangkok? *Is it raining ...*

Exercise 2

2. Why is she calling him?
3. Why are we having a meeting?
4. Are you working on the report now?
5. Is anyone helping you?
6. Are Kim and James coming to the meeting?

Exercise 3

1. Why is the computer not working?
2. Why is the fire alarm ringing?
3. Why are the birds dying?
4. Why is the oil leaking?

TASKS 6

The Present Simple Positive

Exercise 1

You work for a multinational company.
He/She studies foreign languages.
We/You/They travel a lot for work.
The company makes better products.
Our Research Department develops new solutions.

Exercise 2

1. d **2.** e **3.** c **4.** a **5.** b

Exercise 3

Atsuko Kyoto **lives** in Tokyo. She **is** a freelance journalist. She **often travels** to other countries. In London and Paris she **likes** to visit friends. She **usually writes** for newspapers and magazines and she **sometimes makes** television programmes. She **usually stays** in four star hotels and **often eats** in top class restaurants. She **never drinks** wine, beer or any alcohol.

TASKS 7

The Present Simple Negative

Exercise 1

The management doesn't want to invest in a new factory.
The company doesn't employ many people.
I don't work for a drug company.
They don't like working in the oil industry.
My friend doesn't work in research.
You don't understand what I am saying.

Exercise 2

2. We do not advertise on television.
3. The company does not sponsor sport.
4. I don't like fish.
5. Nakko S.A. does not process written orders for goods.
6. Cable PLC does not despatch products by train.
7. We do not deal with Latin America.
8. You don't live in an apartment.

Exercise 3

Dear Sir,
I want to tell your readers some facts about Teal Ltd. The company **does not use** chemical dyes in its products or bleach to make our materials white. The management **does not encourage** the use of company cars. We **do not allow** staff to park private cars on company premises. We do not burn our rubbish and we **do not throw away** glass or paper.
Yours faithfully,
PJ Teal
PJ Teal
Managing Director (Teal Ltd)

TASKS 8

The Present Simple Question

Exercise 1

1. Does your country make cars?
2. Do the largest companies in your area export products to many different countries?
3. How many people do you work or study with?
4. Do you know any internationally famous products from your country?
5. Does your hometown have a university?

Exercise 2

1. Do you come from Spain?   d
2. What time does the bar close?   h
3. Do you have an umbrella?   e
4. Do you have a meeting tomorrow?   b
5. Do you know a good restaurant?   c
6. Does the hotel have a swimming pool?   f
7. Do you often come to Paris?   a
8. Where do you usually go on holiday?   g

Exercise 3

2. Where do you work?
3. What does Papeleras Valles make?
4. How many people does your company employ?
5. Do you have/Does the company have just one plant?

TASKS 9

The Present Continuous vs. The Present Simple

Exercise 1

Present continuous	Statement	Negative	Question
Present continuous	3	5	4
Present simple	2	7	1, 6

Exercise 2

M: We **deal** mainly with Germany, France and Sweden.
C: And **are you negotiating** with Japanese customers at the moment?
M: No, not at the moment.
C: **Are you planning** to enter any new markets?
M: Yes, Italy. We **are launching** a range of products there later this year.
C: And Sweden? **Do you sell** much there?
M: Yes, we often **get** big orders from Swedish manufacturers.

Exercise 3

A: What**'s happening**?
B: We**'re opening** ten new branches in Argentina and Chile.
A: **Does** the bank currently **have** branches only in Buenos Aires and Santiago?

B: Yes.
A: But not Brasilia?
B: No, we **don't operate** in Brazil yet.
A: **Is** Pablo Hernandez **coming** here this week?
B: Yes, he **likes** these meetings.

TASKS 10

Positive and Negative Imperatives

Exercise 1

Please arrive at 10 o'clock prompt. Present your identity papers to the security officer at the gate. Do not park your car in the staff car park. Please go where the security officer tells you. He will give you an official pass. Walk to the reception. Present your official pass to the receptionist. Do not enter the office block. A guide will come to meet you. Please wait in reception. Do not smoke. Do not take photographs.

Exercise 2

1. Please use an ashtray.
2. Do not enter.
3. Do not take photographs.
4. You must wear a hard hat.
5. Do not eat this.
6. Do not consume food or drink.
7. Don't walk your dog here.
8. Please don't put paper in here.
9. Please call Freephone 0800.

Exercise 3

1. You must **arrive** at 9 o'clock.
2. Military airport: **Do not take photographs**.
3. This material is copyright. **Do not photocopy**.
5. Please **do not park** here. Garage in use.
6. Welcome! Please **knock** and **enter**.

TASKS 11

The Past Simple Positive

Exercise 1

increased   gave   helped   ran   supplied   received
delivered   met   ordered   lost   broke   climbed
came   read   wrote   spoke

Exercise 2

*On 25 April this year we stop (**stopped**) production of Arpol, a treatment for migraine. Arpol production begin (**began**) in 2004 and early sales was (**were**) very impressive. However, Belpharm Ltd did launch (**launched**) the Calpem range three years ago. This product was taking (**took**) a 30% market share in the first two years. At first we agree (**agreed**) to continue with Arpol. Now the situation is different.*

Exercise 3 (M)

Two years later Metfan launched the Stella range. Seven years ago Stella reached a 15% market share. In 20.. Metfan turnover rose 20% and two years later Metfan bought Lanco S.A. Last year Metfan had a 23% market share.

TASKS 12

The Past Simple Negative

Exercise 1

I joined this company five years ago. It was a difficult time. The company was not in a very good state. We didn't have a clear management structure. Our local markets were not very good. Our marketing didn't include America or the Pacific regions. We didn't have any clear marketing strategy. Now, things are very different.

Exercise 2

New products **were not** cheap to develop. We **didn't spend** a lot of money on research. Our market share **didn't increase** in the early 2000s. The company **didn't make** many good products.
Chemco **bought** the company. There **was** a big change in the organisation. The new management **wanted** to change everything. Most of the old management **left**. Things **improved**. Now, we are very optimistic.

Exercise 3

2. On the next day they **didn't send** the goods to Rotterdam by train.
3. On January 17 they **didn't load** the goods onto a ship in Bilbao.
4. On the next day the goods **didn't arrive** in Bilbao.
5. Carretera Trasportes **didn't take** the goods to Vitoria.
6. So Espofrigo **didn't confirm** the arrival.

TASKS 13

The Past Simple Question

Exercise 1

1. c   **2.** d   **3.** e   **4.** b   **5.** a

Exercise 2

Joelle: **Did you have** an interesting visit?
Bill: Yes, I made some useful contacts.
Joelle: **Did you see** Mr Keitel?
Bill: No, he was in New York.
Joelle: And **did you visit** our colleagues in Sabah?
Bill: No, I telephoned, but I didn't have time to visit.
Joelle: **Did you have time** for any tourism?
Bill: Tourism! No ... only work and more work!

Joelle: Don't you like work?
Bill: Of course I do. I love work!

Exercise 3

1. Did the maintenance engineer repair the copier?
2. Did John read the Caracas report?
3. Did you write to the Kongo Club?
4. Did Mr Fish phone?
5. Did you send the VISA application?
6. Did Larish Ltd collect their order?
   Did they pay?

TASKS 14

The Past Continuous

Exercise 1

'What was happening (Q) a few years ago? Well, the company wasn't doing (N) very well. During the 1990s we were competing (P) with many suppliers. We had (P) a small turnover. Then everyone was thinking about (P) mergers and takeovers. In the early 2000s we were operating (P) in a very different market. There were only four large companies. All four were making (P) big profits. We were all doing well (P) ...'

Exercise 2

T: From 8 o'clock until 9 o'clock **I was checking** the production system. From 9 o'clock until 10 o'clock **I was repairing** a computer. Then when the fire started **I wasn't working. I was having coffee**.
S.F: **Were your colleagues drinking coffee** too?
T: No, **they were installing** a new printer.
S.F: **Was the factory working normally**?
T: Yes, **everything was running perfectly**.
S.F: Okay. Thanks for your help.

Exercise 3

2. At 11.00 Sally was in the duty free shop. She was buying clothes.
3. At 11.30 Sally was at the Gate. She was waiting to get on the plane.
4. At 12.00 she was on the plane. She was reading.
5. At 2.00 she was (still) on the plane. She was having lunch.
6. At 5.00 she was at a meeting. She was giving a presentation.

TASKS 15

The Present Perfect Simple

Exercise 1 (M)

I have been to Belgium.
You haven't visited Saudi Arabia.
He's/She's studied economics.

She's/He's produced a report.
Our department has made a profit.
The company has developed new products.
The government has increased taxes.

Exercise 2

Product B has been profitable since 2008.
Product C has done well since 2006.
Product D has made a profit since 2007.

Exercise 3 (M)

2. I've known him/her since I was 16. Since I was 16.
3. No, it hasn't made any links. No, it hasn't.
4. Yes, it has owned a printing business since 1965. Yes, it has.
5. I've lived in·my present house for five years. For five years.
6. No, I haven't worked for an American company. No, I haven't.
7. Yes, I have (I've) studied for an MBA. Yes, I have.

TASKS 16

The Present Simple Continuous

Exercise 1

You've been looking for a new job.

Our exports have been doing well for the last ten years.

The Marketing Department has been studying the performance of our PX range.

I've been thinking about changing my job.

Michael has been working for us since 1995.

We've been analysing last year's sales figures.

Exercise 2

Since 2006 we've been using automated production.
Since 2008 we've been running training courses.
Since January we've been processing orders with electronic systems.
We've been building a new warehouse since February.

Exercise 3

> **EuroTV, 170 –174 Rue des Capucins, 2270 Lesigny, FRANCE**
>
> *Dear Hisashi,*
> *Thank you for your letter. EuroTV **has been developing** links with companies in other countries. In particular we **have been discussing** programme making with networks in Belgium and Germany. We **have been talking to** small, private companies. So far we have not tried to set up links with companies outside Europe. Many American TV stations **have been examining** ways to work in Europe.*
>
> *I look forward to meeting you in Paris. We can discuss these developments.*
>
> *Yours sincerely,*
> **Tom Kitsch**
> *Tom Kitsch*

TASKS 17

The Present Perfect with For, Since, Ever and Never

Exercise 1

1. c   2. d   3. b   4. a

Exercise 2

MC: Have you **ever** had a big fall in sales before?
PM: No, sales have **never** fallen so suddenly.
MC: How **long** have you **been** marketing this product?
PM: **Since** the beginning of last year.
MC: So, it's been on the market **for** less than two years?
PM: Yes, it **has**.
MC: **Have** you compared *Shine Plus* with competitors' sales results?
PM: Yes, our drop in sales **has** happened **since** January. The market has improved. The graph shows how our three main competitors **have** all benefited: they've all been selling better.

Exercise 3

Kate: How long have you worked for Abacus?
Matt: **For** about four years.
Kate: I see. Have you **ever** done business in China?
Matt: No, we've **never** tried the Chinese market.
Kate: Well, our business in China has been rising **since** the beginning of the 2000s.
Matt: And you've been making a profit since then?
Kate: Well, not always. **For** three years, yes.
Matt: Have you **ever** visited China?
Kate: Oh yes. Many times. In fact, my husband is Chinese.

TASKS 18

The Past Simple vs. The Present Perfect Simple

Exercise 1

1. The company has sold its London offices.
2. The Managing Director resigned three years ago.
3. I have not read the newspaper today.
4. A rival manufacturer has bought the company.
5. The top-selling product made over £3m last year.
6. Many shareholders have sold their shares.
7. Market analysts have estimated company turnover at over £40m.
8. Axam Ltd did not improve its sales.

Exercise 2

This shows the turnover for Lander. **It declined** between 2004 and 2006 but it **has risen** since 2006. The company **has spent** more on R&D.

This shows that the value of Lander shares **increased** between 2004 and 2005. It **has maintained** the same level since 2005. Competitors' share values **have increased**. The increase **has not been** very large.

Exercise 3

Dear Mike,

We **have decided** to close down the Beta plant for three weeks. On Tuesday maintenance inspectors **noticed** problems with the machines. **I have not read** the inspectors' report. Yesterday we **began** a detailed study. A few weeks ago we **repaired** the pump. It is possible that the pump **has broken** again. We **have transferred** production to our other plant. Fortunately, we **have not lost** much production. I will telephone you next week with more information.

Best Regards

TASKS 19

The Past Perfect

Exercise 1

1. After I <u>had shut</u> the door I realised my key was inside.
2. I <u>had finished</u> my sandwich when the phone rang.
3. When I returned I saw that someone <u>had left</u> a package on my desk.
4. Mrs Maw <u>had not finished</u> opening her post when John came in.
5. The work <u>had not been completed</u> before the Vice President arrived.

Exercise 2

2. The engineers had visited the plant before the accident happened.
   The engineers hadn't visited the plant before the accident happened.
   Had the engineers visited the plant before the accident happened?
3. The company had published the sales results before the share price fell.
   The company hadn't published the sales results before the share price fell.
   Had the company published the sales results before the share price fell?
4. The research team had completed the report before the management cut the investment.
   The research team hadn't completed the report before the management cut the investment.
   Had the research team completed the report before the management cut the investment?
5. When the deadline came she had finished the report.
   When the deadline came she hadn't finished the report.
   When the deadline came, had she finished the report?

Exercise 3

Tom: What happened?
Fred: Before the machine broke down, **I had made** 100 copies.
Tom: Then what?
Fred: When I **had done** 100, the paper jammed.

Tom: What did you do?
Fred: When I **had cleared** the paper, I pressed the start button.
Tom: Then?
Fred: I thought I **had solved** the problem. But I **hadn't noticed** another problem. Smoke was coming out of the back.
Tom: So then what happened?
Fred: After I**'d seen** the smoke, I telephoned you.

TASKS 20

The Present Tenses and The Past Tenses

Exercise 1

The world economy is slowing down (PresC). The World Bank has published (PPS) a report. It says (PresS) that the global economy is growing (PresC) at 2% per year. Last year growth was (PastS) 2.8%. The report contrasts (PresS) with a study by the OECD last year. This had suggested (PastP) that prospects were improving (PastC) for developing countries. According to Credit Bank International, the world economy has been slowing down (PPC) for a year.

Exercise 2

A: Peter, where **do you work?**
B: I **work for** Frobo Ltd.
A: How long **have you worked there**?
B: **I've worked there for** two years.
A: Where **did you work** before Frobo?
B: Allen Brothers.
A: Why **did you change?**
B: Because the markets **were** falling, and the company **was** going bankrupt.
A: Why **did you choose** Frobo?
B: **I had worked** there before I joined Allen Bros.

Exercise 3

1. From January until June last year we were building a new office block.
2. How much did it cost?
3. It cost $250,000.
4. In December we bought new lorries.
5. Unfortunately one has broken down.
6. This delivery is going to Spain.

TASKS 21

The Future with Will and Shall

Exercise 1

1. c   **2.** d   **3.** a   **4.** e   **5.** b

Exercise 2

g. So, now I'll explain the programme for the day.
c. After this introduction, we'll have a short tour of the plant.
e. Then before coffee we'll show you a film about our distribution system.

f. We'll have coffee at 11 then <u>we'll have</u> a meeting with Ken Levins, our Product Manager.

a. <u>We'll have</u> lunch in a local restaurant at about 1 o'clock.

h. After lunch <u>we'll discuss</u> future plans.

b. <u>We'll finish</u> at about 4 o'clock.

d. So, <u>shall we begin</u> the tour?

Exercise 3

2. John: I'll be in my office tomorrow.
   Marie: **I'll call you.**
3. Jacob: I need to see the report.
   Hisashi: **I'll get it.**
4. Pierre: Who'll tell us the answer?
   Imogen: **Erik won't.**
5. Juan: What about lunch?
   Amy: **Shall we go to** *Gigi's Restaurant*?

TASKS 22

The Future with Going To vs. Present Continuous

Exercise 1

Q: What <u>are you working on</u> for the next few weeks?

A: <u>We're setting up</u> a new distribution network in Asia. <u>We're not using</u> our own staff. <u>We're going to use</u> local agents. <u>We're going to recruit</u> top quality experts. <u>We're examining</u> some possible applicants next week. <u>We're going to run</u> psychometric tests as part of the recruitment procedure. <u>I'm meeting</u> colleagues later today to finalise plans.

Exercise 2

PhoneCo: Fine. How many people **are coming/are going to come?**

Caller: Well, **I'm sending out** 50 invitations this week.

PhoneCo: That's fine. **Are you going to hire** phones for everyone?

Caller: No, just about half, I think.

PhoneCo: And **are you going to need** anything else, faxes or modems?

Caller: No, **we're not planning** anything complicated.

Exercise 3

> **Memo**
>
> To: HJ
>
> From: KP
>
> Re: KJE/Weisskopf Joint Venture
>
> As you know, we **are going to manufacture** a new engine with Weisskopf GmbH. We **are having** a Department meeting next week and I **am travelling** to Bremen on the 16th. We **are going to sign** contract then. **Are you coming** to the meeting? That's all. Good luck.
>
> P.S. Helen **is not joining** the design team. She is too busy.

TASKS 23

The Future with Will vs. Going To vs. Present Continuous

Exercise 1

A: What are we going to do (1) about the promotional material for the exhibition?

B: I'm taking (2) it to the printer's this afternoon. They told me it'll be done (3) by Monday.

A: Okay. Tell them I'll pick it up (4) at 10 o'clock.

B: It's not necessary. They're coming (5) here about something else.

A: Okay. I'm going to find out (6) who can do some translations for us ...

Fixed plans/ *present continuous*	Intentions/ *going to*	Facts/specific times/*will*
2, 5	1, 6	3, 4

Exercise 2 (M)

Byant: Of course we **aren't going to close** the factory. 800 people work here. We're **installing** a new purification system next summer.

Journalist: People think your new system **won't be** enough.

Byant: I'm sure it **will be**.

Journalist: **Are you going to invest** more in environmental protection?

Byant: **We're increasing** spending on this by 25% this year and next year.

Journalist: Is that too little, too late?

Byant: No, certainly not. We're **spending** a lot of money. And now, we can promise you something else. The river **will be** clean again by the end of this week.

Exercise 3

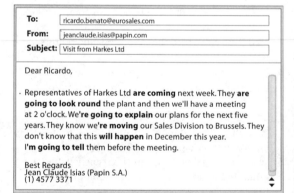

> **To:** ricardo.benato@eurosales.com
> **From:** jeanclaude.isias@papin.com
> **Subject:** Visit from Harkes Ltd
>
> Dear Ricardo,
>
> Representatives of Harkes Ltd **are coming** next week. They **are going to look round** the plant and then we'll have a meeting at 2 o'clock. We're **going to explain** our plans for the next five years. They know we're **moving** our Sales Division to Brussels. They don't know that this **will happen** in December this year. **I'm going to tell** them before the meeting.
>
> Best Regards
> Jean Claude Isias (Papin S.A.)
> (1) 4577 3371

TASKS 24

Conditional I

Exercise 1

2. <u>If we are successful</u> (IC) <u>our share price will go up</u> (MC).

3. If the market declines (IC) we won't buy Axam (MC).
4. One of our competitors will buy Axam (MC) if we don't (IC).
5. We can take our time (MC), unless Chemco makes a sudden offer for Axam (IC).

Exercise 2

2. If the computer crashes, we'll lose the data.
3. If our market share increases, we'll give (staff) a pay rise.
4. If they send the goods today, they will arrive tomorrow.
5. Sales will fall if we raise prices.
6. Unless we have good weather we won't make a profit.

Exercise 3

Date:	29/03/11
To:	jay.taylor@modaplc.com
From:	g.sartori@modaplc.com
Subject:	Next season's forecast

Dear Jay,

If we have another year like last year **we will produce** excellent results. The Marketing Department thinks that if the new summer collection sells well, **we will do better** than last year. However, **unless the economy recovers,** we won't do as well. We also need good weather. If it rains a lot, **our products won't sell.**

TASKS 25

Conditional II

Exercise 1

If we sell Mago in Asia it will help to establish our brand name. But if we set up our own distribution network (IC) it would cost too much (MC). Unless we spent millions (IC), we wouldn't make any money (MC). If we use local people it will be much cheaper. If Mago does well in Asia, then we'll expand there in the future. If it failed of course (IC), we'd be in trouble (MC).

Exercise 2

2. If someone stole the plans, it would be a total disaster.
3. If sales collapsed, people would lose their jobs.
4. If the plane crashed, we would miss the meeting.
5. Mary would be happy if Fred resigned.
6. If we increased the R&D budget to $500m we would be the market leader.

Exercise 3

2. **If we spent less on hotels** the company would pay more tax.
3. Travelling would be harder work **if we didn't go first class.**
4. **I would like travelling** if I didn't have to wait for hours in airports.
5. If I didn't like the travelling **I would get a different job.**
6. **My company wouldn't use this hotel** unless it was really good.

TASKS 26

Tense Review 1

Exercise 1

2. Where are you staying at the moment?
d. (I'm staying with a colleague) in London.
3. What are you working on these days?
f. (I'm preparing) a customer survey.
4. Where do you work?
c. (I work for) Ford (UK).
5. When did you start your present job?
j. (I began) in January this year.
6. How long have you been doing that?
h. (I've been doing it) for about two weeks.
7. What are you doing this evening?
i. I'm meeting a friend in a bar.
8. What are you going to do next summer?
e. I'm going to Australia with my sister.
9. If you had a completely free choice, where would you work?
b. I'd go to the USA.
10. If you learn English perfectly, how will it help you most?
a. Understanding in meetings will be easier.

Exercise 2

1. What**'s your name?**
2. Where **do you come from?**
3. When **were you born?**
4. Where **do you work?**
5. How long **have you worked (there)?**
6. Before that, **what did you do?**
7. At the moment **what are you working on?**
8. In future, what **are you going to do?**

TASKS 27

Tense Review 2

Exercise 1

	Positive	Negative	Question
Present	3, 8, 9	12	1
Past	5	7	4, 6
Future	2, 10	13	11

Exercise 2 (M)

The two companies **had been** competitors.
In 1965 Ardanza Pascual **had 45 shops in Spain.**
Between 1965 and 1980 the company **was growing by 5% every year.**
Since 1980 the company **has been exporting all over Europe.**
Now the company **is planning 20 new products.**
The company **is going to buy into** the US market.
In 2020 it **is opening a new factory in Poland.**

TASKS 28

Infinitive + To

Exercise 1

I was pleased <u>to talk</u> to you on the telephone last night. We will be glad <u>to see</u> you in Washington next month, but I am sorry <u>to hear</u> that Sam is not coming. Tell him, of course, we'd like <u>to meet</u> him another time...

Exercise 2

1. I was sorry to hear that John was not well.
2. It will be good to see you again.
3. We plan to spend more on advertising next year.
4. We always want to give a good service.
5. We expect to do well next year.

Exercise 3

"Friends, I am pleased **to have** the opportunity to speak again at our Annual General Meeting. I am glad **to see** so many old friends. It is difficult **to know** what to say after 20 years as Chairman of the Group. I will be sad **to leave** the company after so long. The good news is that I plan **to play** more golf next year! But also, I hope **to come** to the AGM next year. I expect it will be difficult not **to follow** the news about the company. Now, of course, I would like **to thank** the many people who have helped me in 20 years ..."

TASKS 29

Verb ...ing

Exercise 1

Dear George

We are planning a meeting next week. We are interested <u>in hearing</u> colleagues' views on the sales campaign for the Shello range. <u>Before attending</u> the meeting, please read the interim report, Shello Advertising SA/JD 3421JD. I <u>suggest inviting</u> the marketing group to attend the meeting, but we should <u>avoid having</u> long discussions about individual markets.

Regards
Sophie Allen

Exercise 2

1. Before <u>coming</u> to the meeting, please read the attached report.

2. Thank you for <u>buying</u> the Oakham 50 Printer. On <u>opening</u> the box, please make sure all the contents are complete.

3. If you are interested in <u>knowing</u> more, please contact us on 0800 600600.

4. We hope you enjoyed <u>visiting</u> us. Please come again!

5. Don't stop <u>thinking</u> about quality!

Exercise 3

Ben: Claude, listen. Before **taking** a decision on the Combo advertising, I would appreciate **knowing** your views on the agency we are working with, Kinetics.

Claude: Well, avoid **signing** the contract this week. Tell them we're interested in **learning** more about their plans.

Ben: Good. Thanks. I'll tell them we're looking forward to **meeting** them again soon to discuss things in more detail.

Claude: Yes. And ask them to stop **talking** about television advertising. We said it was too expensive.

TASKS 30

Infinitive + To or Verb ...ing

Exercise 1

1. We continue **to promote** the use of recycled materials in our factory.
2. Would you like **to see** our latest products?
3. I tried **to phone/phoning** you yesterday.
4. Our Overseas Director intends **to visit/visiting** all our subsidiaries this year.
5. I remember **meeting** you in Madrid last year.

Exercise 2

1. I like drinking coffee
b. Coffee is what I like to drink.
2. I forgot to telephone Mr James.
b. I did not call him.
3. Try calling him in the evening.
a. If you call in the evening, it is possible that you will reach him.

Exercise 3

I'm on a tour of our European suppliers as I'm responsible for **checking** quality control. I had intended **to see/seeing** all our suppliers but it's impossible **to do** that in only one week. I'm in Rome at the moment. I remember **arriving** in Rome last year. I had forgotten **to bring** the address of our supplier. I found the number in the telephone book. I love **coming** here. I enjoy **hearing** the language. Tomorrow I'm in Spain. I like **going** there too. We have an excellent supplier in Tarragona.

TASKS 31

Do

Exercise 1

1. **Does he** come here often?
2. **Does he** **work** here?
3. **Does she** **work** for your company?
4. Did they **come** from Osaka yesterday?
5. He **doesn't** like flying so he **came** by train.
6. We **didn't** sign the contract yesterday.
7. Please **don't speak** so fast.

Exercise 2

1. **a.** He **doesn't like** his job.
   b. We **don't** sell computer software.
   c. He **doesn't work** for RYG.
2. **a.** **Does he live** in the city centre?
   b. **Does she speak** Arabic?
   c. **Did you like** California?
3. **a.** Jo **went** to Oslo every week.
   b. He **didn't** like the hotel.
   c. I **didn't** understand.

Exercise 3

1. **Q: Did you** fly here yesterday?
   A: No, **I didn't**. I came by train.
2. **Q: Do** you export to the USA?
   A: No, we **don't**.
3. **Q: Does** your company make computers?
   A: Yes, **it does**.
4. **Q: Do you** spend a lot on R & D?
   A: Yes, we **do**.

TASKS 32

Will and Would

Exercise 1

1. Will you send me more details? (R)
2. If I'm interested I'll call tomorrow. (C)
3. I'll post you our price list. (O)
4. John'll visit you early next week. (F)
5. The contract will be ready in March. (F)
6. I'll meet you at the airport. (O)
7. Would you reduce the price if I ordered 20? (C)
8. Will you help with these figures, please? (R)

Exercise 2

Tom: I'd like to discuss our situation.
Bill: If I can, I'**ll** help you. If it's a small problem, we'**ll agree**.
Tom: **Will** you give me a bigger discount?
Bill: Sorry, Tom, I **won't** drop the price any more. We'**d** lose money.
Tom: No, you **wouldn't**. If you sell more, you'**ll** make a bigger profit.

Exercise 3

AX: Hello, After Sales Department.
PC: Hello. Peter Cord from Leeds, here. I'd like some help with an AX20. The power isn't working.
AX: Okay. If you use the emergency switch on the back, the light will come on. (d)
PC: No, it won't. There's no power.
AX: Right, I'll ask an engineer to visit you. (c)
PC: Will you send someone today?
AX: I'm not sure if that will be possible. Will you hold on please? (a)
PC: Certainly.
AX: Hello again. Someone'll be there at 2 p.m. tomorrow. (e)
PC: Okay, thank you.
AX: Will you give me your address, please? (f)
PC: Yes, it's Beta Foods Ltd, 350 Otley Road, Leeds.

AX: Okay. We'll sort it out. (b)
PC: Thank you. Goodbye.

TASKS 33

May and Might

Exercise 1

A: May I ask you something?
B: Of course you **may**.
A: May I deliver the report next week?
B: You **may not**. The meeting is tomorrow.
A: Well, I might ~~to~~ arrive late.

Exercise 2

1. might not/may not
2. may
3. may not
4. may
5. may not/might not
6. may/might

Exercise 3

2. No, you **may not**.
3. I'll probably finish it by Friday but it **might be** ready by Thursday.
4. Yes, of course **you may**.

TASKS 34

Can and Could

Exercise 1

1. **A: Can you** come at 3 o'clock?
   B: I could, but 4 would be better.
2. **A:** Her appointment is today.
   B: Yes, but she phoned yesterday to say **she couldn't** come.
3. **A:** When you saw the figures, **could you** understand them?
   B: No, **I couldn't**.
4. **A: Can you** speak German?
   B: No, **I can't**.

Exercise 2

1. **c**   2. **a**   3. **b**   4. **a**

Exercise 3

1. **Can I** help you? Yes, I need some advice.
2. **Can I** come in? Of course.
3. Sorry, **I can't** understand.
4. The plane **couldn't** take off. It was too foggy.
5. My car has broken down. I **could** be very late.

TASKS 35

Must, Have To and Have Got To

Exercise 1

1. F   3. F   5. F
2. T   4. F   6. F

1. We **have** got to pay more tax this year.
2. We **must not** spend too much on special promotions.
3. Last year we **had** to advertise a lot on television.
4. Our competitors are in trouble. They **have** got to reduce their prices.
5. We must ~~to~~ plan our marketing carefully.

Exercise 3

1. 'We **must** buy some more trucks.'
2. 'I've no money. I'll **have to** borrow some from the bank.'
3. 'You **have to** present a business plan.'
4. 'There's only one problem. We**'ve got to/will have to/'ll have to** pay the money back.'

TASKS 36

Mustn't, Needn't, Don't Have To and Haven't Got To

Exercise 1

2. Companies do not have to pay a minimum wage.
3. We do not need to meet health and safety regulations.
4. Our competitors did not have to reduce their prices.
5. We haven't got to advertise in national newspapers.

Exercise 2

2. **You do not need** a visa to go to Poland from Germany.
3. **You haven't got to** pay by cash.
4. **We didn't need to** increase production.
5. **He doesn't have to** learn a new software program.

Exercise 3

Dear Sir,

You reported last week that Larssen S.A. had a strong market position. Then you said that the company **does not have to** think about its competitors. This is not true. We **must not** believe that our market share is permanent. We **do not need to** worry about our jobs today, but we certainly cannot forget about our competitors. A year is a short time in business.

Yours faithfully,

Bo Johannessen
Chairman Larssen S.A.

TASKS 37

Should and Ought To

Exercise 1

A: **Ought we** to have a meeting?
B: We **shouldn't** have one today.
 We **ought** to wait a few days.
A: **Should** we?

Exercise 2

Jim: Should we discuss the problem with the bank? (S)
Alice: I don't know. You ought to talk to Jeremy first. (A)
Jim: Well, the bank charges ought to come down next year. (P)
Alice: Maybe we should close the account. (S)
Jim: First, I think I ought to write to the bank. (S)

Exercise 3

1. You **ought to/should** see a doctor.
2. The truck **ought to/should** arrive tomorrow.
3. We **ought to/should** cut our prices.
4. Inflation **ought to/should** fall soon.

TASKS 38

Question Tags

Exercise 1

1. Business is important, isn't it?
2. Businesses have to make a profit, don't they?
3. Profit creates jobs, doesn't it?
4. People will always have new ideas, won't they?
5. Most companies have improved working conditions, haven't they?
6. Companies haven't always spent much on training, have they?
7. Businesses cannot forget their customers, can they?
8. Government must help businesses, mustn't it?

Exercise 2

2. You can't tell us the price of BKD, **can you**? No, I **can't**.
3. You're going to London now, **aren't you**? Yes, I **am**.
4. There will be another meeting in the morning, **won't there**? Yes, there **will**.
5. So discussions are still continuing, **aren't they**? Yes, **they are**.
6. But you haven't agreed a price, **have you**? Not yet. Goodbye.

Exercise 3

A: This **is** a good hotel, **isn't it**?
B: Yes, it's fine. You **haven't** stayed here before, **have you**?
A: No, this is my first time.
B: It's 8 o'clock. We **should** have dinner, **shouldn't we**?
A: Yes, I'm hungry. Oh dear! I didn't book a table.
B: We **don't** need to, **do we**?
A: I don't know. We'll find out, **won't we**?

TASKS 39

Active

Exercise 1

2. He flew to Miami last night.
3. He took his laptop with him.
4. He wanted to finish writing the report on the plane.
5. He will give it to Head Office in Miami.

Exercise 2

rent a car
accept an offer
appoint a secretary
design a new product
investigate a problem
write a letter
borrow money
pay an invoice
quote a price

Exercise 3

1. Our prices have **risen** this year.
2. Last year our sales **fell**.
3. We **reduced** our prices.
4. We have also **improved** our products.
5. Our sales have **recovered**.

TASKS 40

Passive

Exercise 1

New products (are/were/will be) tested in our laboratories.
Customers (are/were/will be) sent a company newsletter.
Company policy (is/was/will be) based on quality.
Profits (are/were/will be) invested in new projects.

Exercise 2

1. Orders are taken by telephone.
2. The information is sent to the warehouse.
3. The goods are loaded into vans.
4. They are delivered to the shops.

Exercise 3

'There are many important activities before take off. The fuel tanks **are filled** and the aircraft systems **are checked**. Food **is brought** on board. All the baggage **is loaded** in the hold. The captain and the co-pilot **are informed** of runway conditions and other details about take off. When everything is almost ready, passengers **are invited** to board the plane.'

TASKS 41

Active vs. Passive

Exercise 1

Users <u>should change</u> **(A)** their password every week. All confidential information <u>should be stored</u> **(P)** on computer hard disk. Users <u>should copy</u> **(A)** confidential information on to floppy disks. Disks <u>should be placed</u> **(P)** in the safe in the Finance Office. Confidential information <u>should not be removed</u> **(P)** from Chemco PLC without the permission of a Department Manager. <u>Report</u> **(A)** all security incidents to an appropriate manager.

Exercise 2

1. Paper should **be recycled**.
2. Please **switch off the lights**.
3. Visitors should **leave coats and bags, etc.** here.
4. Eye protection must **be worn**.

Exercise 3

First, we'**ll** see a film about Eastern Water. Then the Managing Director **will give** a talk on the history and future for EW. Then we'**ll go on** a tour of the factory. We'**ll see** demonstrations of how water **is distributed** and how water **is treated**, Finally, we'**ll have** dinner.

TASKS 42

It Is/They Are vs. There Is/ There Are

Exercise 1 (M)

Are they French?
There are many tourists here.
They aren't French.
Are there a lot of museums?
Are they expensive?
There is a good restaurant here.
Is it French?
It is expensive.

Exercise 2

A: **There are** many good hotels in Tokyo. I like the Tokyo Hilton. **It is** in the centre of the city.
B: **Are there** many small family hotels?
A: No, **there aren't**.
B: I imagine **they are** very expensive.
A: In Tokyo? Yes, **it is** an expensive city.

Exercise 3

Clerk: Yes, **there are** many trains. Now **it's** 11.25. **There was** a train at 11.21. The next one is at 11.41.
Maria: **Is it** direct?
Clerk: No, **it isn't**. It goes via Essen. **There is** a train to Münster via Essen every 20 minutes.
Maria: **Are there** direct trains to Münster?
Clerk: Yes, **there is** a direct train at 11.50. **It's** direct to Münster.

TASKS 43

Have and Have Got

Exercise 1

I didn't have **(V)** a very good job last year. Now I've got **(HG)** a new position in the company. I've **(AUX)** taken control of export sales. We've **(V)** many new clients in America and Asia. Have **(AUX)** you seen our product brochure? We've **(AUX)** had a new one printed this week. Mary, have you got **(HG)** a copy?

Exercise 2

1. d		**4.** c	
2. e		**5.** f	
3. a		**6.** b	

Exercise 3

Fumi: How many employees **do you have**?/**have you got**?

Mike: **We've/we've got** about 2,000.

Fumi: **Do you have/have you got/have you** many sales reps?

Mike: About 300. **We've/We've got** 30 in the Far East.

Fumi: **Have you** worked in Malaysia?

Mike: Yes, I **have**. And we**'ve got/**we **have** three big customers there.

Fumi: What about Indonesia?

Mike: No, we **haven't/haven't got** any customers there.

TASKS 44

Get and Have Got

Exercise 1

A: <u>Did</u> you <u>get</u> **(G)** my letter yesterday?

B: I <u>didn't get</u> **(G)** it yesterday. It came today. I've got **(HG)** it here on my desk.

A: The problem <u>is getting</u> **(G)** serious, but I <u>haven't got</u> **(HG)** time to discuss it now. I'll call later.

B: Well, I've got **(HG)** a meeting this afternoon.

A: Okay. I'll call you before lunch.

Exercise 2

1. f		**4.** b	
2. d		**5.** c	
3. a		**6.** e	

Exercise 3

1. Beth: **Getting better**.

2. Mike: What **have** you **got**?

3. Peter: We **didn't get** the contract.

4. Amy: **Did** you **get** the money?

5. Syd: Yes. I **got it** yesterday. Thank you very much.

6. Alice: I've got a new job and it's really difficult.

7. Billy: It'll **get easier**, I'm sure.

TASKS 45

Say vs Tell

Exercise 1

1. What did you say?

e. I said I would like fish.

2. Tell me which you prefer.

f. I prefer white wine with fish.

3. Tell me about the work in India.

d. Have I told you about Mr Singh?

4. Say anything you like.

c. What shall I say?

5. Tell the waiter you want another knife.

a. I've told him already.

6. Let me pay.

b. No, I said I would this time.

Exercise 2

Delta: Tell ~~to~~ me again, how much do you want?

Langer: I said $20,000.

Delta: But tell me a lower price.

Langer: I am telling **you** our lowest price.

Delta: What did you say ~~me~~ last week about terms of payment?

Langer: I **told** you 60 days' payment.

Exercise 3

To:	k.brand@abcsolutions.com
From:	r.patel@abcsolutions.com
Subject:	Your meeting with Dennie Flowers (Axis Ltd) Tuesday 20 March

Dear Karen,

What did Ms Flowers **say** about the delivery last week? I saw her on Monday. She didn't **say** anything about it. Did she **tell** you anything about the invoice? On the telephone I **told** her we would give a 10% discount. In fact I forgot. Please phone her. **Tell** her I made a mistake. **Say** we can send a new invoice. Note: I have **told** all our sales reps to offer a 10% discount.

Best Regards
Rajiv

TASKS 46

Make vs Do

Exercise 1

1. made		**5.** did	
2. do		**6.** making	
3. making		**7.** make	
4. made		**8.** Do	

Exercise 2

Amy: Was it a good meeting?

Leo: Yes, we **made** a decision. We are going to increase production of *BIGGO*.

Amy: What about the costs?

Leo: We **made** a new budget. We think we will **do** more business next year. We'll **make** a profit of £200,000.

Amy: Good. Do you know that Rospa Ltd. have **made** a complaint about our BIGGO promotion?

Leo: Yes, they are **making** a big mistake. We have **done** nothing wrong. We have **done** our research. Rospa know that *BIGGO* is going to **make** money. With good marketing we will **make** sure that we **do** better than Rospa next year.

Exercise 3

1. We **do** business in France.

2. You are **making** a mistake.

3. They **did** a good job.

4. We have **made** progress.

5. They **made** an offer, but it was too low.

6. We had to **make** a choice.

7. They **have done** the research.

TASKS 47

Used To

Exercise 1

Peter: Do you travel a lot?

Janis: Yes, but I <u>am used to</u> **(GH)** working away. I am away more than I am at home.

Peter: That is hard. What about your husband?

Janis: He<u>'s used to</u> **(GH)** it. He looks after our children.

Peter: Have you always worked?

Janis: I <u>used to</u> **(PH)** stay at home when the children were very young. Now they are at school, I am always travelling. The children <u>are used to</u> **(GH)** a 'weekends only' mum.

Peter: I hope you like flying.

Janis: I <u>used to</u> **(PH)** hate it, but it's okay now. My husband hates flying. He <u>used to</u> **(PH)** be a pilot.

Exercise 2

1. He has lived abroad. He **used to live** in Italy.
2. He **is used to making** presentations.
3. He likes going for walks. When he was young he **used to go** for walks with his father.
4. He works long hours. He **is used to working** late.
5. He likes going out with friends. He **is used to eating** in restaurants.
6. Michael has a new car. He **used to have** a motorbike.

Exercise 3

Ann: I don't mind. I**'m used to** it.

Peter: Have you always driven to work?

Ann: No, I **used to** go by train.

Peter: Is this your first job?

Ann: No, I **used to** work for RYG. You ask so many questions!

Peter: I**'m used to** it. I'm a journalist!

TASKS 48

Rise vs. Raise

Exercise 1

In the first half of the year prices <u>rose</u> **(I)** by 10%. Wages <u>rose</u> **(I)** at the same time. The government raised **(T)** taxes and the banks <u>raised</u> **(T)** interest rates. Inflation continued to <u>rise</u> **(I)**.

Exercise 2

1. **c.** Sales rose by 10%.
2. **b.** The advertising budget has risen.
3. **c.** Costs will probably rise.
4. **a.** The number of unemployed workers rose this year.
5. **b.** Electricity companies have raised their charges.
6. **c.** Bank charges will rise next year.

Exercise 3

1. The National Telephone Company **has raised** the price of making a call.

2. The R + D budget **will rise** next year.
3. In summer prices rise.
4. Inflation **rose** in 2008.
5. The Company will **raise** agents' commissions.

TASKS 49

Verb + Preposition

Exercise 1

succeed in
ask for
hear about
depend on
consist of
look forward to
agree with

Exercise 2

Dear James,

Thank you for **agreeing to** attend our meeting on 28 October. We will **talk about** our marketing strategy for next year. The agenda will **consist of** just three points: recruitment, training, advertising and promotion. I think we will **succeed in** reaching our target of a 10% increase. For our Sales Staff, obviously we need to **invest in** training. We cannot **depend on** our present reputation.

I am **looking forward to** seeing you on 28 October.

Yours sincerely
P Jones, Chairman

Exercise 3

Sam: The meeting was really good. We got almost all we were **asking for**.

Paula: Yes, in fact, I was surprised we **managed to** obtain a very low price.

Sam: Also, we got good terms. We don't have to **pay for** the goods until January.

Paula: That's true. I think they have lost some business recently. They were **relying on** getting the contract from us. We got a good deal because they knew we have other suppliers. We were not **depending on** them. Also, we weren't in a hurry. We can **wait for** smaller companies to supply us.

Sam: But obviously, we were **hoping for** a quick deal.

TASKS 50

Verb + Adverb (Phrasal Verb)

Exercise 1

return (goods) = send back
reduce (production) = cut back
abandon (plans) = call off
buy (a company) = take over
go out of business = close down
start (a machine) = switch on

Exercise 2

1. The meeting has been <u>put back</u> two months. **d**
2. AD Industries <u>closed</u> the plant down ten years ago. **a**
3. We've <u>called in</u> the suppliers to fix the machine. **c**
4. AGCO has <u>turned down</u> an offer of $800,000 for the company. **b**

Exercise 3

Boris: If we cannot sell all the goods we have, we must **cut back** production.

Susan: Yes. Our agents want to **send back** goods they cannot sell. But I also think we should **set up** an agency network in Asia.

Boris: But we **turned down** that idea last year.

Susan: I think the Board should find ways to **build up** our reputation for quality service.

Boris: Certainly. That would be better than **putting up** prices again.

TASKS 51
Positive Statements

Exercise 1

<u>Sales</u> **(S)** <u>have been very disappointing</u> **(VP)** this year. <u>Our costs</u> **(S)** <u>are rising</u> **(VP)** every day. Clearly, <u>our marketing team</u> **(S)** <u>need to market</u> **(VP)** our products better. But <u>our R & D Department</u> **(S)** <u>are confident</u> **(VP)**. <u>They</u> **(S)** <u>are developing</u> **(VP)** a brilliant new product. <u>It</u> **(S)** <u>will need</u> **(VP)** support from the bank. <u>A new business plan</u> **(S)** <u>is being prepared</u> **(VP)** at the moment.

Exercise 2

a. Now United Electric exports all over the world. **7**
b. In 2000 Keele Brothers was taken over by United Electric Inc. **4**
c. In those days Keele Brothers made bicycles. **2**
d. Between 1980 and 2000 the main products were pumps and small engines. **3**
e. The name of the company was changed to United Electric (UK) Ltd. **5**
f. Keele Brothers Ltd was started in 1970. **1**
g. Since then the company has developed an international market. **6**

Exercise 3

1. In 2009 Hebden **joined** an international consortium to develop a new aircraft.
2. Since 2004 the company **has realised** continual growth.
3. Our products **have been exported** all over the world for many years.
4. Our production **uses** highly automated systems.
5. Our market share in our home market **is** now 12%.
6. 7,000 people **are employed** by the Hebden group.
7. The annual report **contains** details for our 21 different product areas.

TASKS 52
Negative Statements

Exercise 1

To:	nick_fox@jdloughman.com
From:	maria_aubert@jdloughman.com
Subject:	Ibros S.A. negotiation

Dear Nick,

<u>We</u> **(S)** <u>did not have</u> **(NV)** a meeting with Ibros S.A. because we rejected their offer. <u>The offer</u> **(S)** <u>did not come</u> **(NV)** by email. We received a fax on Thursday. We understand that the <u>Managing Director of Ibros, Mr Kalkos,</u> **(S)** <u>will not sign</u> **(NV)** the contract. <u>We</u> **(S)** <u>have not accepted</u> **(NV)** the present proposals. At the moment <u>we</u> **(S)** <u>are not planning to continue</u> **(NV)** production of the Alisia range. Last year <u>we</u> **(S)** <u>didn't reach</u> **(NV)** agreement immediately. Now, I think it **(S)** <u>will not be easy</u> **(NV)** to find a solution.

Exercise 2

1. We **won't finish** our business tomorrow afternoon.
2. The meeting **wasn't planned** to last three days.
3. We **can't go** home tomorrow.
4. We **shouldn't go** to the Castle restaurant tonight.
5. It **doesn't open** every night.
6. Friday **isn't** a good night to go.
7. They **don't cook** fish on Fridays.
8. I **haven't eaten** a lot of fish recently.
9. The Castle restaurant **hasn't been** recommended to us.
10. We **didn't go** there last time.

Exercise 3

2. Inflation won't rise in the near future.
3. Sol's market share has not increased in ten years.
4. The sales volume did not improve between 2004 and 2006.
5. Actual sales did not reach forecast sales in 2009.
6. Hammond Ltd will not be taken over next year.

TASKS 53
Questions: Yes/No

Exercise 1

A: <u>Do you live near your company?</u>
B: No, it's about 25 km to the office.
A: So how do you travel to work?
B: I go by train or sometimes by car.
A: <u>Is it quicker by train?</u>
B: Yes – and I can work on the train.
A: <u>Isn't it crowded?</u>
B: No, not usually. It's okay.

Exercise 2

1. e	3. d	5. a
2. f	4. c	6. b

Exercise 3

2. Will Mandy meet/Is Mandy going to meet Joanne next weekend?
3. Will Alex be back from Nairobi tomorrow?
4. Does Tom usually rent a car for trips abroad?
5. Are you prepared for your presentation next week?
6. Did Rolf go to New York in June last year?

TASKS 54

Questions: Wh-

Exercise 1

1. <u>When</u> did you get here?
d. I came on Monday.
2. <u>Where</u> are you staying?
e. In the Crescent Hotel.
3. Do you plan to stay long?
h. Just two days.
4. <u>What</u> kind of business are you in?
f. I work for a bank as a financial advisor.
5. <u>Which</u> bank?
g. Credit Bank International.
6. <u>Why</u> are you in New York?
a. For a meeting with our partners.
7. <u>Who</u> is the senior Vice-President of CBI?
b. Roland K. Saxman.
8. Have you been here before?
c. No, this is my first visit.

Exercise 2

Which lorry is going to Belgium?
Where is the other one going?
What are they carrying?
Which one is carrying meat?
Who is our client in Greece?
Where are they based?
Who is the driver?

Exercise 3

2. What did he decide to increase?
3. Where do we need to advertise?
4. What did you write?
5. Who did they give the report to?
6. Who said the report was excellent?
7. What are the reasons for supporting the idea?
8. When could the project start?
9. Which office will control the project?

TASKS 55

Questions: How

Exercise 1

1. How many people came to the exhibition?
2. How often do you attend exhibitions?
3. How do you organise the promotion of your company?
4. How long did the exhibition last?
5. How much does a stand cost at a fair?
6. How big is the Paris trade fair?

Exercise 2

Date:	18/10/2010
To:	k.r.nijran@amtel.com
From:	marketing@amtel.com
Subject:	RE: AMTEL MARKET SURVEY

Dear Kevin,

How much are we going to spend? *US $450,000*
How many people will get questionnaires? *3,000*
How long will the research take? *two months*
How often do we need to repeat this survey? *every two years*
How far will the survey extend? *all over Japan*
How big is the consultancy which is carrying out the research? *the 4th biggest in Japan*
How will they analyse the result? *by computer and personal interview*

Answers by Monday please! Thanks.

Exercise 3

Willy: **How much** does employee insurance cost?
Ben: Employee insurance costs about 10% of the salaries.
Willy: **How many** employees do you have?
Ben: Around 850.
Willy: **How long** do they stay with Aranco?
Ben: Normally, if they stay, they stay for a long time.
Willy: **How often** does the company make a detailed study of employee insurance?
Ben: We make a detailed study very often. Every year. It's very important.
Willy: **How big** is Aranco's turnover?
Ben: Our turnover is £30m. This is increasing by between 3% and 6% every year.

TASKS 56

Commands – Positive and Negative

Exercise 1

<u>Please arrive</u> at about 8.30 and <u>register</u> with reception. You will be given a key. You may relax until 9.30. At 9.30, <u>please meet</u> at the Main Entrance. <u>Don't go</u> directly to the Seminar Room. <u>Wait for</u> your group leader. He/she will give you instructions. <u>Please don't telephone</u> the office except in an emergency. Further information can be obtained by email or letter.

Exercise 2

1. c		**5.** e	
2. g		**6.** h	
3. d		**7.** a	
4. b		**8.** f	

Exercise 3

Then **listen to** voicemail. **Don't fix appointments** for Friday or Monday. **Book tickets** to Munich. **Write to** Kelso and TBM, and finally **do not accept** Jade & Co's offer on Monday.

TASKS 57

Sentence Types: Simple vs. Complex

Exercise 1

The Amco 75 went into production in the Spring. Sales were very good **(MC)** <u>and</u> we quickly established a significant market share **(MC)**. We have begun exporting the Amco 75 **(MC)**, thought early sales are weak **(SC)**. We will have a satisfactory year **(MC)** if our exports improve **(SC)**. Profit has gone up this year **(MC)** because our domestic sales have increased **(SC)**. Our research has been very productive **(MC)** <u>but</u> costs have risen **(MC)**. Now we have many competitors **(MC)** who are seen as important dangers in some key markets **(SC)**.

Exercise 2

B: Yes, we have agreed to recruit another secretary, **though** we have not decided when.

A: But we need one now. There will be problems **if** we don't get one soon.

B: I think there will be resignations **because** everyone is working too hard.

A: I agree. People will resign **or** they will simply be less effective at work.

B: I'm going to speak to Patrick, **who** will accept that the situation is critical.

Exercise 3

9 sentences, all S (simple)
I work for Arkop GmbH **which** makes car components. The company is based in Kirchheim, **which** is in Southern Germany. This is a good location **because** many of our customers are very close. We sell our products all over Germany **and/though/but** we also export a lot, **but/though** our domestic market is the most important part of our business.

TASKS 58

Subordinate Clauses

Exercise 1

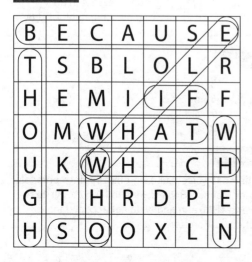

Exercise 2

We will know if there are any problems after the first six months' sales.
The product will be launched next week though at first only in the home market.
It's a new concept so it will need a lot of promotion.
We are going to promote it heavily because we need a major new success.
We will target young people who have always been our key market.

Exercise 3

'We need to increase our prices **because** our costs are rising. Many companies are in a similar position, **though** our costs are especially high. We have a strong export market **where** our sales are still good. We have identified some key problems **which** make the home market very difficult at present. We will have continued problems **if** we do not take some difficult decisions. There is no time to lose, **so** we have to do something quickly.'

TASKS 59

Relative Clauses with Who and Which

Exercise 1

ANTIBIOTICS TODAY

The conference, <u>which will discuss the action of antibiotics on diseases</u> **(ND)**. will be held at University College, <u>which is one of the oldest colleges in the city</u> **(ND)**. People <u>who wish to attend</u> **(D)** should send an application form to the President of the Society, <u>who is in charge of bookings</u> **(ND)**. Anyone <u>who is presenting a paper at the conference</u> **(D)** will automatically receive full details.

Exercise 2

2. The woman who said our collection was wonderful is the editor of *Style*.
3. We use the best agencies, who charge a lot of money, to show our collection.
4. We depend on magazine publicity, which increases our international reputation.
5. Many important magazine editors, who have massive influence, attend the fairs.
6. The design team which plans our participation is very experienced.

Exercise 3

2. The Director who came here yesterday is Italian.
3. Our main clients, who are in Europe, are sports clubs.
4. In 2008, which was a record year, we supplied floors for the Olympic Games.
5. Our R and D institute, which is based at Newtown University, is developing new floor materials.
6. The floors which we sent to Finland last year are specially for outdoor use.

TASKS 60

Clauses Of Cause or Reason with Because

Exercise 1

Our financial position changes during the year <u>because our sales are seasonal</u>. They are seasonal <u>because we have always been specialists in winter clothing</u>. This creates problems <u>because in summer we have a shortage of money</u>. We are planning to enter new markets <u>because if we do not, we will not survive</u>.

Exercise 2

2. We are going to build one next to the sea because our business needs sea transport.
3. This is also a good location because we are near the train station.
4. We need a large development site because we are building a big warehouse.
5. We do not need many staff because the company has an automated process.
6. We will keep costs down because we plan to employ few people.

Exercise 3

Benson Ltd won the National Prize for Industry because the company managed record exports. The company managed record exports because it makes excellent products. The company makes excellent products because Benson has a commitment to research. Benson has a commitment to research because the company has high quality management.

TASKS 61

Singular and Plural Nouns

Exercise 1

singular	plural	singular	plural
export	exports	fish	fish
information	✗	turnover	✗
research	✗	record	records
accountant	accountants	capital	✗
figure	figures	sale	sales

Exercise 2

Every **year** the company publishes its annual **accounts** in a report for the **shareholders**. The main **details** concern the financial report. This contains **information** about **sales**, **turnover**, **costs** and **profit**. It also reports the **assets** that are held by the company, and the **liabilities**. These are any **debts** or **cash** that the company owes. All this **data** is presented in the **profit and loss** account and the balance sheet.

Exercise 3

A: Where is your **factory**?
B: It's near Orleans, but our **headquarters/head office** is in Paris.
A: How many **employees** do you have?
B: About 2,000 including our **sales staff**.
A: What's the annual **turnover**?
B: This year it'll be about £85m.
A: And what will be the **profit** on that?
B: Around £5m.

TASKS 62

Countable and Uncountable Nouns

Exercise 1

CHANGES (CP) IN RETAILING (CP)

The rationalisation **(C)** of retailing **(UP)** has been a major characteristic **(C)** of recent years **(CP)** and many small shops **(CP)** have disappeared. Large chains **(CP)** and supermarkets **(CP)** now dominate the sector **(C)**. In the UK **(U)**, 70% of food **(U)** is sold by just four retailers **(CP)**. Many people **(UP)** have criticised this trend **(C)**. They say it leaves the consumer **(C)** with less choice **(U)**.

Exercise 2

1. Hello. I would like some <u>informations</u> (information) about your products.
2. How many <u>works</u> (jobs) have you had since you left school?
3. I asked my bank manager for <u>an advice</u> (advice). He told me to get a new <u>work</u> (job).
4. Please can I change this money? I need some <u>coin</u> (coins) for the telephone.
5. Please do not leave <u>baggages</u> (baggage) unattended.
6. We have spent a lot of money on new machines. All the <u>equipments</u> (equipment) in this room <u>are</u> (is) new.

Exercise 3

1. We don't have enough information. Ring them and ask for more **details**.
2. John works for a company that makes agricultural **machinery**.
3. We are a financial services company. We give **advice** on insurance, pensions and other aspects of money management.
4. I asked him for **advice**. He made two **suggestions**. First, do more advertising and secondly, find a new Sales Assistant.
5. Please can you help me with these **cases**? They are very heavy.
6. John has changed his **job**. He now works for a bank.
7. Many **people** work in insurance or banking, but most work in commerce.

TASKS 63

Noun Compounds

Exercise 1

weather forecast   market forces
credit card   satellite dish
hotel room   container ship
alarm clock   identity card

Exercise 2

> *Please send*   ***product information**
> ***price list**
> *and details of*   ***customer services**
> *and*   ***payment terms**
> *I would like a **product demonstration** and I want to arrange a meeting with a **sales representative**. Also, do you have any special **sales promotions** at present? Please send a **fax message** to the above number ASAP.*

Exercise 3

2. If you apply for a job, you complete and send a **job application**.
3. The result of the test is a **test result**.
4. When you need to change money to another currency, you ask for the **exchange rate**.
5. If a company wants to spend money on advertising, it prepares an **advertising budget**.
6. Before getting on a plane, you have to wait in the **departure lounge**.
7. People who travel a lot on business make many **business trips**.
8. We use a lot of computers. We live in an age of **information technology**.

TASKS 64

Genitive Forms

Exercise 1

'<u>Tambo's results</u> are very good. <u>Last year's figures</u> were also pleasing, but now our turnover has improved by 15%. <u>Our competitors' results</u> are not as good. <u>The work of all our staff</u> has been excellent. Our products have answered <u>the needs of our customers</u>. <u>The company's dedication to quality</u> has been total. <u>The decision of the Board</u> to enter new markets was also very important. The former Chief Executive, Bill Machin, made a very big contribution – <u>Bill's ideas</u> made Tambo the success it is today.'

Exercise 2

1. **b.** Fred's car
2. **b.** the Chief Executive's car
3. **b.** KLP's market share is 12%
4. **b.** yesterday's paper
5. **a.** the workers' canteen
6. **a.** the design of the computer

Exercise 3

The **Research Director's report** was very positive. We hope that all **Frodo's customers** will like the new product. We think it will meet **our customers' needs**. I agree with **John Tudor's opinion**. He thinks **Frodo's market share** will increase. With this new product, **next year's performance** will be very good. As always, we must focus on the **quality of our products and services**. The **Chairman's speech** at the AGM will say that quality and new products are most important.

TASKS 65

Adjectives vs. Adverbs

Exercise 1

Excellent (**adj**) results have helped MODO. In an unusually (**adv**) wet (**adj**) summer, the company did really (**adv**) well. The fashionable (**adj**) clothes were popular (**adj**) with young (**adj**) consumers. Now the company will definitely (**adv**) increase its production. Staff are busily (**adv**) planning an equally (**adv**) successful (**adj**) range for next (**adj**) year, but the market will be very (**adv**) competitive (**adj**).

Exercise 2

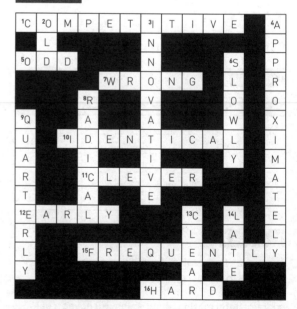

Exercise 3

Alan: The changes in the market are going to affect the company quite **seriously**.
Helga: We need to make some **quick** decisions.
Alan: We **urgently** need a new marketing strategy.
Helga: **Fortunately**, the products are **excellent**.
Alan: I agree **absolutely**, but we have to get people **interested**.
Helga: I'm **confident** that we will do that.
Alan: Good, because our sales have fallen **dramatically**.

TASKS 66
Comparison of Adjectives

Exercise 1

Positive	Comparative	Superlative
cheap	cheaper	cheapest
strong	stronger	strongest
modern	more modern	most modern
useful	more useful	most useful
bad	worse	worst
experienced	more experienced	most experienced
near	nearer	nearest
comfortable	more comfortable	most comfortable
weak	weaker	weakest
difficult	more difficult	most difficult
much	more	most
little ·	less	least

Exercise 2

1. Product B is the most successful.   F
2. Product A has sold more than product B.   T
3. Product C is the least expensive.   F
4. Product B is cheaper than product A.   F
5. Product A is the oldest.   T
6. Product B is newer than product C.   F

Exercise 3

It has a **smaller** market share than Rotobank Ltd. Gold Bank has **the most** capital reserves. It is **the strongest** bank. In terms of branches, Credit Bank International is **bigger** than the other two banks. It has many **more** branches. It also has **more** capital reserves than Rotobank Ltd.

TASKS 67
Adverbs

Exercise 1

fast (M)   abroad (P)   never (T)
quietly (M)   soon (T)   on time (T)
currently (T)   late (T)   outside (P)
tomorrow (T)   hard (M)   since Monday (T)

Exercise 2

1. **Yesterday** Mr Roach got up **early**.
2. He had a coffee, then **calmly** began to read the paper.
3. **Suddenly** he noticed the time.
4. **Immediately** he ran out of the house.
5. He looked **urgently** for a taxi.
6. The taxi went **very fast** to the airport.
7. He was **just in time** for the plane.
8. **Fortunately**, he was not **too late** for the meeting.

Exercise 3

A: When will she be **back**?
B: Perhaps she'll be back **later** today.
A: OK. I'll phone **tomorrow**.
B: Can I take a message?
A: Well, yes please. Tell her the meeting with Blanchard went very **well**. We have to prepare a contract **immediately**, but it must be done **carefully**. The details are very important.
B: OK. Thanks. Goodbye.
A: Bye.

TASKS 68
Expressions of Frequency

Exercise 1

often	rarely	occasionally	never	always	frequently	sometimes
3	6	5	7	1	2	4

Exercise 2

1. I go to London **twice a year**.
2. We have meetings **every day**.
3. Our share price changes **every hour/hourly**.
4. I write a sales report **every Friday/once a week**.
5. We report to Head Office **three times a week**.
6. Our Sales Report is published **annually/every year/in December**.
7. I **never** go to America on business.

Exercise 3

Wim: **How often** do you go to New York?
Maurice: **Frequently**. We have an office there, so I have to go about once or **twice** a month.
Wim: Do you **always** fly with KLM?
Maurice: Well, I **usually** use KLM because my partner works in Amsterdam. I **normally** visit him before I go to New York, but I **sometimes** fly with British Airways from London.
Wim: Are there a lot of flights to New York from London?
Maurice: Oh yes. There's one about six **times a day**.
Wim: Well, before the flight, I'll get some Duty Free. I **usually** get something.
Maurice: Really? I **never** do. I don't smoke and I **rarely** drink so I don't buy anything from Duty Free.

TASKS 69

Degree with Very, Too and Enough

enough time
very/too difficult
strong **enough**
very beautiful
very/too many people

very/too dangerous
not big **enough**
very/too important
very profitable

1. 'There's **too** much on the plate.'
2. 'I'm hungry! This isn't **enough**.'
3. 'The table's **too** small.'
4. 'I can't eat this! It's **too** hot!'
5. 'This looks **very** good.'
6. 'The meal was **very** expensive.'

A: There's a lot of traffic on the roads.
B: Yes, I agree. There's **too** much.

A: The Chien Andalou restaurant is one of the best in town.
B: Yes, and not **too** expensive. Everything is **very** fresh.

A: I like jazz music.
B: Yes, if it isn't **too** modern.
A: A lot of modern jazz is **very** good.

A: How was your meeting with Kashamuro?
B: Good.
A: How good?
B: Good **enough**. We agreed to work together.

TASKS 70

Already, Yet, Again and Still

John is <u>still</u> waiting for a new contract. The company have not agreed the terms <u>yet</u>. John may leave.
In fact he's <u>already</u> had an interview with another company. Anyway, tomorrow he's going to talk to his boss <u>again</u> about the contract.

1. John has alread y agreed a new contract. F
2. He has still not agreed the terms of his contract. T
3. He has already left the company. F
4. He has already discussed the contract with his boss. T
5. He is going to see his boss again. T

Lee: Are you **still** selling the Arco 26?
Klaus: Yes, it is **still** doing well.
Lee: Have you made a replacement **yet**?
Klaus: Yes, the Arco 28 is **already** available.
Lee: Are you going to stop making the 26?
Klaus: Yes, but not **yet**.

Lee: I thought you planned to stop making it.
Klaus: Last year we planned to stop, but we changed our mind. This year we also planned to stop, but **again** we have continued. The 26 is **still** very popular.

Last year our sales overseas were down. This year exports are **still** poor. We expect low export profits **again**, but the good news is that in our domestic market we have **already** reached our targets. Overall, things are not serious **yet**. The situation will be clearer at the end of the year.

TASKS 71

Articles

'Mr Fish? I have got Ø details for your trip to Münster today. First, <u>the</u> flight. There's <u>a</u> British Airways flight from London Heathrow to Düsseldorf at 16.05 from Ø Terminal 1. It arrives at 17.35. Then you can take <u>a</u> train to Münster from <u>the</u> central station at 18.45. <u>The</u> train arrives in Münster at 20.15. Coming back there's <u>a</u> flight to Manchester at 16.30, arriving at Manchester Airport at 17.50. There are Ø trains every hour from Manchester to Leeds. You also asked about Ø money and <u>the</u> ticket. You can change Ø money at Heathrow and pick up <u>the</u> flight ticket from <u>the</u> B.A. desk in Ø Terminal 1.'

Arne: We've got **an** important safety problem on **the** production line in **the** West Building. **A** machine is not working properly.
Steve: Have you taken any action?
Arne: Yes, one of **the** engineers has switched it off. **A** valve is losing (–) oil.
Steve: What did (–) maintenance say?
Arne: **The** technician said he thinks **the** valve needs to be replaced.
Steve: So, are we losing (–) production?
Arne: Yes. As **a** result, (–) production is down by 15%.

Beelo Comodo 20 On **the** left is **a** new office chair, **the** *Comodo 20*. Like all (-) Beelo chairs, it is made from (-) materials that are totally (-) fire resistant, but last **a** very long time. (-) tests allow us to give you **a** 5 year warranty on this superb chair. Great (-) value at only $149.95.

OFFICE COMFORT!
OFFICE STYLE!

For rapid service telephone **FREEPHONE** 800800 **now!!**

TASKS 72

Personal Pronouns

Exercise 1

Alice: Good morning. Ascis Ltd. How can <u>I</u> help <u>you</u>?

Don: Hello, Alice. Don Peters here. <u>I</u>'m calling from Bangkok.

Alice: Mr Peters, nice to hear <u>you</u> again. How are things?

Don: Oh fine. <u>We</u>'re doing very well. Now, <u>I</u>'d like to talk to Lena. Is <u>she</u> in?

Alice: No, <u>she</u> had to go to Luxembourg to talk to our agents. <u>They</u>'re having a meeting today. But Paul's here. Do <u>you</u> want to speak to <u>him</u>?

Don: OK, <u>I</u>'ll do that. Thank <u>you</u>.

Exercise 2

Joe: So, what can **I** do for **you**?

Wim: Well, **I** wonder if you can help **me**? My company imports DVDs for schools and colleges. **I/we** would like a catalogue and a price list. Can **you** let **me/us** have these?

Joe: Of course. Tell **me**, where are **you** from?

Wim: My company is A-Tech nv. **We** are based in Rotterdam, in the Netherlands.

Joe: Really? **We** have two agents in Amsterdam. **They** usually handle our Dutch business. Would **you** like to contact **them**?

Wim: Oh yes. That would be fine.

Joe: One is Willy Leer. **He**'s Dutch. The other is Susan Griffin. **She**'s English. **I**'ll give **you** all the details.

Exercise 3

> Dear John
>
> I have sent **you** by email a report on the above employee. **He** has been unwell for some weeks. **He** is unable to do his work. **We** have suggested a transfer to the kitchen. Unfortunately the kitchen staff are not happy. **They** have referred to Susan Jenkins. **She** was made redundant 4 weeks ago to reduce costs.
> **We** should meet to discuss a solution. Please contact **me** as soon as possible.
>
> Best regards
> Sam

TASKS 73

Possessive and Reflexive Pronouns

Exercise 1

As you know we did the market research <u>ourselves</u> (**R**). I am sending <u>our</u> (**PD**) report to all managers. <u>Their</u> (**PD**) comments can be sent to me before <u>our</u> (**PD**) next meeting. Michael and Maria will study the comments. <u>Their</u> (**PD**) job will be to produce a new version of the report. The final conclusion will also be <u>theirs</u> (**PP**). Alex Jenner may also add something <u>himself</u> (**R**). Everyone should feel that <u>his</u> (**PD**) or <u>her</u>

(**PD**) views have been fully considered. Naturally, all opinions are important, including <u>yours</u> (**PP**), so do contact me if you need to.

Exercise 2

1. Mary works by **herself**.
2. She keeps a record of all **our** accounts.
3. Fred and Alex made this prototype. It's **their** design and they made it **themselves**.
4. Anna works here. This is **her** office.
5. Can you tell me about **yourself**?
6. I work for **myself**. I'm self employed.
7. I own the company. It's **mine**.

Exercise 3

1. Fred hurt **himself**. He hit **his** finger.
2. Sally types all **her/our** letters **herself**.
3. Marta and Jack have cars. **Hers** is big, **his** is small.
4. We do all **our** designs **ourselves**. Even the packaging is **ours**.

TASKS 74

Demonstratives

Exercise 1

2. 'That's (**FS**) our Finance Department.'
3. 'Those (**FP**) vans are local deliveries.'
4. 'This (**NS**) is where we take telephone orders.'
5. 'These (**NP**) goods are ready for despatch.'
6. 'That (**FS**) order is for a customer in Dubai.'

Exercise 2

1. **Carla:** What are all **these** people doing here?
2. **Carla:** **This** is a nice bar!
3. **Waiter:** Good evening. **This** is your table by the window.
4. **Carla:** **This** is a difficult decision.
5. **Petra:** **That** meal was really good.
6. **Carla:** Yes, **those** langoustines were superb.
7. **Carla:** **That** was a very pleasant evening.

Exercise 3

1. **This** picture shows our best seller, *ZIGGO*. **This** is very popular with children. A few minutes ago I mentioned *PIPPO*. **That** is also mainly for children.
2. Last year we agreed new prices. Now we know **those** prices were too low.
3. In terms of market share, there are five very small players. At least two of **those** will disappear, either **this** year or next.

TASKS 75

Some and Any

Exercise 1

Ben: How was Kuala Lumpur? <u>Any</u> contracts? (**Q**)

Steve: Excellent. We made <u>some</u> good contacts. (**PS**)

Ben: Contacts? I said did you get <u>any</u> contracts? (**Q**)

Steve: No, we didn't get <u>any</u> contracts. (**NS**) But I'm sure we'll get <u>some</u> soon. (**PS**)

Ben: I hope so. We've had <u>some</u> good news this week. (**PS**)

Steve: What was that?

Ben: Our American agent wants <u>some</u> more PX100s. (**PS**)

Steve: Good. Have they sold any more PX50s? (**Q**)

Ben: <u>Some</u>, but not many. (**PS**)

Exercise 2

Paula: We haven't launched any new products this year. Last year we had **some**. Four, in fact. We need some for next year.

Mohammad: I would like to show you **some** designs.

Paula: Have you **any** pictures of the new designs?

Mohammad: No, we haven't **any** yet, but some will be ready next week.

Presenter: **Any** questions?

Participant: Yes, I've got some. Do you have **any** plans to build a new production centre?

Exercise 3

A: Have we got **any** paper for the printer?

B: **Some**, but not much. We've got **some** more on order.

A: Good. I've got to print **some** reports.

B: If they are urgent, take them to the Sales Office. They usually have paper if we haven't **any** left.

A: The printer wasn't working yesterday!

B: It was fine. There just wasn't **any** toner left. I put **some** in. It's fine now.

TASKS 76

Some, Any and Related Words

Exercise 1

A: Is <u>anything</u> wrong? (**Q**)

B: Yes, there's <u>something</u> wrong with one of our production machines. (**PS**) <u>No-one</u> knows what the problem is. (**NS**) We've looked in the User's Manual but we can't find the solution <u>anywhere</u>. (**NS**)

A: Have you contacted the manufacturers?

B: Yes, they think it's <u>nothing</u> very complicated. (**NS**) They're sending <u>someone</u> to visit us. (**PS**) He'll be here soon. He was already <u>somewhere</u> near here. (**PS**)

Exercise 2

1. Some people prefer small hotels.
c. A number of people prefer small hotels.
2. I knew no-one at the meeting.
b. There was not one person I knew at the meeting.
3. We sell anything you want.
a. We have everything you want.
4. We can send orders anywhere.
c. We can deliver to any place you choose.
5. There's something wrong with the figures.
b. The figures are partly wrong.

Exercise 3

Pat: I hear you lost **something** yesterday.

Ella: Yes, my mobile phone. I wanted to phone **someone** but I couldn't find the phone **anywhere**.

Pat: You must have put it down **somewhere**.

Ella: Yes, I asked at reception. They knew **nothing** about it.

Pat: So **no-one** found it?

Ella: No. I asked reception to call me if **anyone** found **anything**.

TASKS 77

Quantifiers (1)

Exercise 1

None of our products are very successful.	6
All our products are very successful.	1
Most of our products are very successful.	2
A few of our products are very successful.	5
Many of our products are very successful.	3
Some of our products are very successful.	4

Exercise 2

1. All product As passed the test as standard. F
2. A few Product Cs failed the test as non-standard. T
3. Some Product Bs failed the test. F
4. Many Product As failed the test. T
5. Most Product Cs passed the test. T
6. No product As failed the test. F
7. Most products failed the test. F

Exercise 3

1. **A little** training helps all managers.
2. **No** customers **were** unhappy.
3. **All** of our products are guaranteed.
4. **Many** people came to the exhibition.
5. **Few** exhibitors liked the exhibition space.
6. The organisers offered **little** help.

TASKS 78

Quantifiers (2)

Exercise 1

A: Hello. I'd like <u>some</u> (**U**) help please.

B: Certainly.

A: How <u>much</u> (**U**) does this car cost to hire?

B: That one is £120 a day.

A: That's quite <u>a lot of</u> (**U**) money.

B: Well, we have <u>a lot of</u> (**C**) other cars that cost a little (**U**) less. How <u>many</u> (**C**) days do you need a car?

A: Only <u>a few</u> (**C**). Three or four.

Exercise 2

'We hire mobile phones. We have **all** types of phones. We keep **a lot of** phones in stock. **Most** are hired for just one day. **A few of** our customers keep them for a month or two. Not **many** people hire phones for longer than **a few** weeks.'

1. **Few** people understand how to program computers.
2. There is **little** demand for our products.
3. We made **a few** contacts at the Singapore Trade Fair.
4. There was **little** criticism in the report.
5. **Many** people answered our advertisement.
6. **No** applicant was good enough for the job.

TASKS 79
Quantifiers (3)

Exercise 1

'Each day we process hundreds of orders. <u>Every</u> order comes by email. <u>All</u> orders are entered into our database. <u>Each</u> request is checked with our current stock. <u>Every</u> order is immediately transferred to the warehouse. <u>All</u> orders are despatched within one hour.'

Exercise 2

each customer	every customer
all products	all information
each of us	all of us
each week	every week
each department	every department

Exercise 3

2. I have never had a bad meal in Paris. **Every restaurant** I've been in has been excellent.
3. We have a lot of good customers in Malaysia. We need to look after **all of them** very carefully.
4. Last time I went to Dublin I visited several museums. **Every one** was free.
5. Quality hotels in Hong Kong are expensive. In fact, **all accommodation** is expensive.
6. The best thing in London is the parks. **All** British **cities** have good parks.

TASKS 80
Numerals

Exercise 1

1. d		**4.** c	
2. a		**5.** b	
3. e			

Exercise 2

two thousand (and) ten (*or* twenty ten)
three hundred and twenty-six point five million pounds
eighteen point three two million pounds
four pounds eighteen (pence)
fifteen per cent
four hundred and seven million pounds
twelve
six thousand seven hundred and fifty
nineteen seventy-four
the fifteenth of April two thousand (and) nine (*or* twenty oh nine)

Exercise 3

I have some figures for sales in **two thousand and ten**. In the **first** quarter we sold **three hundred and thirty-six** units and had a turnover of **seven thousand three hundred and two pounds fifty-two pence**. This produced a profit of **three thousand four hundred and fifty pounds**. The **second** and **third** quarter performance was better with profit between **three thousand eight hundred and ninety-one pounds fifteen**, and **three thousand seven hundred pounds fifty**. In the **fourth** quarter, the number of units sold was **two hundred and fifteen**, or about **half** the previous two quarters. Profit was also down, to **one thousand nine hundred and forty-three pounds twenty one pence**.

TASKS 81
Time

Exercise 1

A: When's he coming?
B: <u>In</u> the morning.
A: <u>Before</u> 10 o'clock?
B: Probably. We'll show him the factory <u>for</u> an hour or two, then when Julie arrives <u>at</u> 12 o'clock we'll have our meeting.
A: So, <u>during</u> lunchtime?
B: Yes, <u>from</u> about 12 <u>till</u> around 2.30.
A: We must be finished <u>by</u> 3 because we've an appointment with Axis <u>in</u> the afternoon.
B: That's no problem.

Exercise 2

We researched the XR20 **for** 12 months, then **during** 2009 it went into production. **On** 15th January 2010 the product was launched. **Since** then we have had good sales and we will break even **by** March 2011. We expect increasing sales **for** about two years, **until** sales peak **in** the year 2013. **After** that, the sales will decline.

Exercise 3

1. John left the company **in** 2006.
2. I'm going on holiday **in** two weeks.
3. **During** our research, we made three discoveries.
4. **Since** 2004 we have made a profit.

TASKS 82
Place (1)

Exercise 1

into, in, out of, on,
to, at, from

Exercise 2

1. I went **to** Egypt last week.
2. Our company has built a factory **in** Argentina.
3. They want to meet us **at** the trade fair.
4. I sent the price list to Axis Ltd. (✓)

5. There's nothing about the company **in** the newspaper.

6. We decided to take some money out of our emergency bank account. (✓)

7. They put a lot of money **into** research.

8. They have taken business **from** us.

9. The computer is **on** the desk.

Exercise 3

The finished tablets are sent **from** the production area **to** this machine which puts them **into** small bottles. Labels are put **on** the bottles which are then packed **in** boxes. The boxes are transferred **to** the warehouse. They are taken **from** the warehouse **to** the shops.

TASKS 83

Place (2)

Exercise 1

When you arrive, go <u>out of</u> (**M**) the airport and <u>along</u> (**M**) the road <u>to</u> (**M**) the taxis waiting outside. Ask to go <u>to</u> (**M**) Jasons, <u>on</u> (**P**) High street. Our offices are <u>between</u> (**P**) the Post Office and the Magnus foodstore. We're <u>opposite</u> (**P**) Credit Bank International. Go <u>through</u> (**M**) the main entrance and <u>into</u> (**M**) the lift. Go <u>up to</u> (**M**) the fourth floor. We're just <u>next to</u> (**P**) the fire exit.

Exercise 2

1. The factory is **next to** the river.   c
2. There is a restaurant **in front of** our main office. d
3. The hotel is **down/up** the road from the station. a
4. You can drive **through** the city in 20 minutes.   e
5. The safe is in a cellar **below** the Managing Director's office.   b

Exercise 3 (M)

1. Next to the main entrance/in front of the main office block.

2. Beside the offices and the main office block.

3. Above the reception area.

4. Next to the reception area.

5. Behind the main office block.

6. Beside the production facilities.

7. Next to the reception area.

8. Between the laboratories and the exhibition area/under the offices.

TASKS 84

Like, As, The Same As and Different From

Exercise 1 (M)

1. Like Argentina, Chile has a lot of mountains. (✓)

2. German cars have an image which is very different from the image of Japanese cars. (✓)

3. As everyone knows, America is the world's leading economy. (✓)

4. Food in Japan is the same as food in China. (✗)

5. People who work as Personal Assistants have an easy life. (✗)

6. One fast food store is often the same as any other fast food store. (✓)

7. Life now is no different from 25 years ago. (✗)

8. Italy is very like California. (✗)

Exercise 2

The GX40 looks **the same as** the GX50. But the engine of the GX50 is **different from** the engine in the GX40. It is bigger. **Like** all Taruba cars, the GX models have a seven-year warranty. **As** you can see, we build for quality. **Like** you, we don't want any trouble.

Exercise 3

1. As in previous years, we have done well.

2. People say the producers are all the same as each other.

3. In fact, we are different from our competitors.

4. Like them, we are in business.

5. As always, we have a special commitment to quality.

Index